WOMEN LOVE WRESTLING:

AN ANTHOLOGY ON PROFESSIONAL WRESTLING

EDITED BY JASON NORRIS

www.womenlovewrestling.net

ISBN: 9781654164942

Imprint: Independently published

First Printing in paperback, 2020

First Printing in hardback, 2022

Cover design by Liam Warr

Cover photography © 2020 Ami Moregore. All rights reserved.
https://twitter.com/happypeep

Curated, edited and published by Jason Norris.

The profits from the publication of this book are being donated to RAINN and Women's Aid.

www.womenlovewrestling.net

Dedication

For Emiko Kado, Mariko Umeda, Ashley Massaro, Elizabeth Hulette, Joanie Laurer, Gertrude Vachon, Sherri Russell and all the women of wrestling that died before their time.

Author's Note

When we originally published Women Love Wrestling in early 2020 the world was a different place. In the time since there have been several big developments in the world of wrestling, and in the world overall.

Covid caused major disruption to the world just two months after we published our book. It led to the cancellation of the hit Netflix series GLOW without a proper conclusion. It put on hold a lot of wrestling events, limiting the likes of Pro-Wrestling: EVE, Shimmer and Stardom from running regular shows. Even WWE was impacted with the 2020 WrestleMania event taking place on a closed set, rather than in a packed stadium, and no fans attending their live events for a year.

Many wrestlers featured in the book faded from the scene. #SpeakingOut led to wrestlers being outed for their awful behavior with many disappearing from the industry. This included Joey Ryan, who was a featured performer in intergender wrestling and is mentioned several times in this book. Velveteen Dream saw allegations of improper content with younger male fans, which he denied, that saw his push in NXT stall and eventually his release from the company after not being used regularly for a year. Tessa Blanchard did indeed win the Impact World Championship, just as accusations of bullying from several other wrestlers emerged and fan support for her eroded. Covid restrictions meant Tessa dropped the belt and was hardly seen until early 2022 when she returned to the relaunched Women of Wrestling. Rhonda Rousey also never returned to wrestling after the WrestleMania 35 event despite being the focus of the WWE storylines for over a year, quitting to instead start a family.

There was also good news. AEW built momentum and became a viable alternative to WWE, slowly building a diverse roster of women such as Nyla Rose, Jade Cargill, Brit Baker and Ruby Soho. The NWA ran its own all women pay-per-view that was put together by Mickie James to great acclaim. Stardom was able to have showcase matches on New Japan's Wrestle Kingdom event, previously a male only show. Even WWE gave us positives as two black women, Sasha Banks and Bianca Belair, headlined night one of WrestleMania 37 as live crowds returned.

We knew none of this in January 2020, and we have chosen to not amend the book, capturing the moment in time before so much changed.

Content Summary

The content of this book has been structured in order to help the reader learn as they progress, giving different context along the way and following certain themes. The chapters however can be picked up and read in any order, so if you wanted to drop in and out of the book you can start at any point that interests you. Below is a summary of each chapter so you can decide where to start.

Introduction
Jason Norris provides context on how this book was created and the ways in which it supports our chosen charities.

Women Have Always Been Wrestling Fans
Sarah Parkin on how the popularity of women's wrestling in 1980's Japan highlights that women are a market worth serving for any wrestling company.

Fantasy Wrestling Federation: The Role of the Fan in Modern Wrestling
Australia culture critic Scarlett Harris speaks to the women involved in custom wrestling, how it differs compared to apartment wrestling, and how elements have existed on WWE PPVs. The interest in customisation leads her to explore gender-bending art and cosplay, all related to wrestling fandom.

Passion for Wrestling
How wrestling has helped Harley Johnson though some tough mental health times and helped her become the person she is today.

Being a Woman Journalist in Wrestling Media
Kristen Ashly is the co-owner of the women's wrestling site Bell To Belles. She details her path in journalism to where she now resides, and the

issues she has encountered along the way as a woman in a male dominated space.

Meet The Ladies Of G.L.O.W., The 80s Female Wrestling League

LA based writer/comic Ilana Gordon looks into the history of the original GLOW and the acclaimed Netflix series based on the big hair and body slams of this landmark wrestling show.

Equals Fights Movement

ESPN writer Hallie Grossman explores how the optics of intergender wrestling can be shocking, but those who participate say pitting women against men in the ring is a step toward equality.

The Stare: Empowerment in Women's Wrestling

Manasi Nene brings an Indian perspective to women's safety and the empowerment aspect of women's wrestling.

Wrestling and The Gay Community

The gay wrestling fan community is growing and making their voice heard. Valerie Quartz explains how she discovered a way to share her love of wrestling and it leading to group projects to design and sell merchandise with members of the community.

The WrestleMania 35 Experience and the Fallout for the Women's Division of WWE

Book editor Jason Norris looks back on his time in New York for the biggest wrestling event of the year, from indy stars to the fallout of women finally main eventing the big show.

The Boss and The Bard: Reflections on Shakespeare and Pro Wrestling

Did you ever notice how much the works of the greatest playwright ever crop up in the squared circle? Writer and filmmaker Manasi Nene explores the parallels.

Breaking into the Indy scene: a US experience

Sarah the Rebel is also know her as Razor on the AXS TV show Women of Wrestling, the promotion owned by original GLOW founder David McLane. Sarah covers her start in professional wrestling, the training process, her time as a valet, how she became involved in WOW, and her views on the current representation of women in AEW, NXT and WWE.

Breaking into the Indy scene: a UK experience

Heather Bandenburg grew up wanting to be a writer, and then accidentally became a lucha libre wrestler. She covers her start in professional wrestling, appearing on big lucha events in the UK, the current representation of women in wrestling and what led to her publishing 'Unladylike: A Grrl's Guide to Wrestling.'

Why We Need to Talk About Stereotypes

An extract from Heather Bandenburg's book 'Unladylike: A Grrls Guide to wrestling' (London: Unbound 2019). Very few people within wrestling address the quite problematic aspect of harmful stereotypes, this extract focuses on why we need to talk about them more.

"Blinded by the Light that is Your Velveteen Dream": Queer Villainy in Professional Wrestling

The performance of queer villainy in the WWE has progressed over time, as societal norms have become marginally more accepting of queerness. Shannon Vanderstreaten shares her study on the topic, built around the previous (Goldust) and the current (Velveteen Dream).

The RiSE of SHIMMER and the Renaissance of Women's Professional Wrestling

Spenser Santos gives a detailed history of the all women wrestling company Shimmer, while also looking at the history of women's wrestling. The 40s and 50s in the US, 80s Japan, 90s WWF and the lows of the mid-2000s are covered as they lead to Shimmer and the recent boom.

Wrestling Never Sleeps: The Emergence of Indie Wrestling in New York City
Giselle Francisco and Reginia Walker, aka The DeadassGirls Podcast, take you on a tour of the New York scene that they get to enjoy. Its not just the home of WWE, its producing future stars.

Becoming a Ringside Photographer
Ami Moregore takes up close photos at CZW and WSU events. She describes how she ended up in this (sometimes dangerous) position in amongst the action, and includes a selection of her work.

Yelling Into the Void: The Invisibility of Marginalized Identities in Wrestling Fandom and Media
Chicago-based pop culture writer Allyssa Capri talks about how hard it can be for those with marginalized identities to love wrestling due to the insidious oppression that plagues the industry. Endeavouring to love wrestling when you are all but invisible on screen is part confusing, part frustrating, and part heart-breaking.

Luna-tic Girl
Sonya Ballantyne is a lifelong wrestling fan from Northern Manitoba in Canada. She shares a story from her childhood of meeting the giant wrestlers that passed the Indian reservation on their way to shows, and what wrestling meant to her growing up.

Separate but (Un)Equal: The Rhetorics of Representation in Gender-Segregated Professional Wrestling
Jacqui Pratt, Ph.D. takes aim at the term 'women's division' and how the rhetoric relegates to a secondary position, while intergender matches oppose this classification.

Wrestling and Me
Carole Strudwick gives the perspective of a UK woman that has adored wrestling since she was little, but explains how she fell out of love when

trying to conform to social norms, and how she has since returned as a bigger fan than ever.

How Skirts Are Changing Bolivian Wrestling

In ornate skirts and bowler hats, Indigenous female fighters claim their place in the ring. Nell Haynes looks at the growing interest in women's wrestling in Bolivia.

The Four Horsewomen of WWE

Kiana Parvizi has a passionate view on how the Four Horsewomen helped move women's wrestling from bra and panties matches to main eventing the Superbowl of wrestling.

The History of Pro Wrestling EVE

Emily and Dann Reed are the co-owners of Pro Wrestling EVE, the ground-breaking feminist-punk-rock wrestling promotion. They discuss EVE's history, how training women is different to men, and their role in the popularity and increased exposure of the female professional wrestling scene.

This Ain't No Bra and Panties Match, Little Boys: An Accomplished Novice Takes on Joshi

In a letter to the boys who watch wrestling, Joseph Telegen, Ph.D. Explains how you should appreciate Japanese women's wrestling.

Diversity in Wrestling Performers: a UK Perspective

Journalist and podcaster Sonal Lad on her path to enjoying the diverse UK independent scene, highlighting how the largest wrestling companies in the US are still getting it wrong.

The Current Stars of Intergender Wrestling

A selection of biographies on the wrestlers best known for intergender matches, collected by longtime fan Samuel Preston.

Grappling with History: The Search for Jack Wannop, champion wrestler of late-Victorian England
Wrestling trainee Sarah Elizabeth Cox has rediscovered Jack Wannop, champion wrestler of late-Victorian England, now a forgotten man. Sarah shares her research on this fascinating gent and his era.

Why wrestling crowds can be intimidating for women
Gemma Coombs explains what pulled her into the wrestling world and how women are trying to enjoy live shows.

Improvements in Gender Equality in WWE
WWE continues to face criticism for its treatment of its female talent, but Chloe Warner-Harris highlights the rapid and continued progress the company is making.

Introduction

Early March 2019. I'm having a drink with Heather Bandenburg in a hipster tap room in an East London back alley as we chat into a basic USB microphone, capturing our conversation, the ambient bar noise and the trains going past on the bridge overhead. We are recording an interview to air on the Holy Shoot Wrestling podcast that I work on with friends, discussing the upcoming release of Heather's book 'Unladylike'. I had learned about the book via a tweet from the Pro-Wrestling EVE Twitter account and had chipped in my money for the crowd funding efforts, with the book now set for release in a couple of months. I am talking to Heather about how her book came to exist and she makes a point; there are almost no books about wrestling that are written by women. Sure, a couple exist that cover the careers of big name WWE stars Chyna and Lita, written with male ghost writers, and a couple of women have self-published profile collections, but there are no books that give the point of view of female fans or show the world of wrestling outside of WWE for women in the industry.

I had been trying to work out how to write a book on women in wrestling (working title 'Hit Like A Girl'), and it was proving hard to find women to speak to. There are just not as many women working in prominent roles in the wrestling industry as you would hope, and women wrestlers were proving rightly skeptical to my approaches. Speaking to Heather to arrange our meeting she made it clear we had to meet in a public place (after I had suggested my office), not being a creep I had not thought about how women need to be much more aware of their encounters with men they do not know. I imagine some random guy off the internet asking you to meet to discuss a book is a red flag for most women.

Months later and I had kept thinking about how to develop a project that I could enjoy working on and that would add something new to the world of wrestling books, when I interviewed Jacqui Pratt, once again for the Holy Shoot podcast. We had recorded a really fun episode recently where I went into detail about music albums that were wrestling themed, with Cheap Pop's 'In Gorilla' being my favorite. The songs were punky slices of incredibly well written wrestling references, clearly by someone with talent as a writer, which it turned out was the band's lead singer Jacqui. After a few messages back and forth, I learned Jacqui was now completing her PhD and had somehow been able to include a chapter about a wrestling match to look at the art of storytelling. She shared with me a 50-page study of The Young Bucks vs The World's Cutest Tag Team, a violent intergender match that included Candice LeRae taking a thumbtack covered boot to the face as she saved her male partner, which resulted in her bleeding all over the ring. I had never seen writing about wrestling that broke down a match in such a way, looking at independent, hardcore, women's and intergender wrestling through the eyes of someone finally skilled enough to explain why wrestling fans loved the sport so much. Sure, not everyone could explain the rhetoric and composition of a match and how it stirs such passion like Jacqui did, but I figured there must be people with a similar level of passion that wanted a way to share their love of wrestling with others.

The book you hold in your hands, be it the sweet smell of ink on paper or the glowing light of your reading device, is the result of trying to answer that question. I asked people I knew, I researched people via social media (now conscious of context), I sent lots of messages, requested retweets and was able to eventually find this talented group of writers and creative people. What follows is a mix of wrestling history, personal stories and studies of professional wrestling, written by women and a handful of men that each gave their time for free because they cared about the topic. We focus on women's wrestling of course, but include stories from the wider world, including lost Victorian legends and reflections on how wrestling can be compared to the masterpieces by Shakespeare. We have tried to balance views, while a lot of advancement has been made in recent years in the wrestling industry there is still a long way to go before women are seen as equal to men when it comes to both being fans and players in the ring and behind the scenes. We've also tried to help those with limited wrestling knowledge still enjoy the book, keeping it simple and explaining key wrestling terminology. You will find each chapter varies in writing style with links to contact each writer if you want to give them feedback or ask about their work.

No one is being paid for their contributions to this book, each person is putting in time because they had something they wanted to share to help advance the role of women and how both fans and those in the industry are viewed. After publishing and promotion costs, all of the money from sales will be donated to charities focused on supporting women. You can keep up to date with the charities we support and donations made via www.womenlovewrestling.net. Your purchase of this book will help us support these charities.

Sarah Parkin - Women Have Always Been Wrestling Fans

How the popularity of women's wrestling in 1980's Japan highlights that women are a market worth serving for any wrestling company.

Sarah was 22 years old when she learned The Undertaker and Kane were not actually related. She now tells everyone who will listen that Bull Nakano should be in the Hall of Fame. Follow Sarah at twitter.com/SarahParkin1.

She refuses to win the title on an injury.

August 1988. Lioness Asuka is awarded the WWWA championship after Chigusa Nagayo injures her arm. She is the number one contender and the obvious choice to hold the title in Chigusa's absence. But she hasn't defeated her friend to earn it, so she simply turns the title down.

Nobody else could possibly lay claim to the championship, so it stays vacant for the next five months. No-one wants to see a tournament for the biggest prize in women's wrestling. The only title match the audience wants is a war between the Crush Gals.

January 1989. The bell rings. Each woman enters to a standing, screaming ovation. The air is thick with streamers – red first for Chigusa, then blue for her former tag partner. And thousands of wrestling fans roar in unison as the most popular wrestlers in Japan lock up.

You can hear it in the screams. The crowd is almost entirely young women.

In the 21st century, and especially in the US and the UK, we are used to a few standard lines when we tell other people that we like wrestling: "You're a girl who likes wrestling? Marry me!"

"You're just pretending to watch wrestling to find a man."

"Did your boyfriend get you into it?"

The idea of wrestling as masculine entertainment is firmly embedded in popular culture, creating the image of the female wrestling fan as a mythical, or at least exceptional, creature. The truth is we've always been around. We just haven't always been watching the same product as the men.

It's almost certain that women's wrestling emerged from the same tradition as other carnival acts. We know that Josie Wahlford, who performed as Minerva, combined wrestling with strongwoman shows and travelled across the US in the 1890s as one of the first women to hold a wrestling championship. The *National Police Gazette* sponsored the title – think of it alongside titles like *National Enquirer;* wrestling has never exactly been high culture – which passed from Wahlford through the hands of women like Laura Bennett and eventually to Cora Livingston.

Where Wahlford defended her title in the back rooms of pubs across America, Livingston would later frequent vaudeville theatres and music halls issuing open challenges, including cash prizes to any woman who could last ten minutes with her. Sometimes, those challenges would be open to men, although when the crowd realized Livingston's husband had been planted in the audience the reception would often turn cool.

It's impossible to judge what proportion of the viewers at these performances were women – and indeed, hard to assess what constituted a crowd. Such low culture was hardly appropriate for respectable society, and while men's wrestling was regulated and presented as an athletic contest, women's matches were outlawed by several state athletic commissions.

But in the burlesque halls of America, women kept standing up to challenge these champions, and some of them turned it into a job. We do know that as the Great Depression set in there was an uptick in private wrestling shows, and some markets with more relaxed approaches grew exponentially: in 1933, Clara Mortensen wrestled on a show in Honolulu in front of 31,000 people.

As economies recovered in the middle of the century, there was a consistent demand for women's wrestling, albeit not at the same level as the men's. The great Mildred Burke defended her title in front of 12,000 spectators in Mexico City in 1944 and there was a pipeline of new women being inspired to get into the business: June Byers, Mae Young, and an overlooked tradition of women of color including Babs Wingo and Ethel Johnson. There was certainly enough interest for agents including Burke's husband, Billy Wolfe, to spring up offering a pool of female talent.

But while there were clearly women turning up to wrestling shows and getting into the industry, women's wrestling had always been squarely aimed at the people with spending power: heterosexual men. Scandalous women performing feats of physical prowess had an erotic appeal that promoters – almost entirely male – never tried to resist. It took an upswing in the disposable income of new demographics to inspire a wrestling product that moved away from this approach, and it came first in Japan in the 1970s.

All Japan Women's Wrestling (AJW) developed a successful formula. Clean-cut, attractive young women would wrestle as the good girls (faces) against slightly older and larger women playing the bad girls (heels), starting with the company's first literal poster girls, Jackie Sato and Maki Ueda. As a team they were known as the Beauty Pair. Once they had parlayed their popularity into their first hit single, AJW had proven that wrestling had serious mainstream appeal, so the business model adapted to ensure that their talent could perform onstage as well as in-ring. Wrestlers-cum-pop-stars were the next big thing in entertainment, and they turned AJW's fanbase into something unprecedented: a fandom of young women, by young women.

Next big things didn't come bigger than the Crush Gals.

Chigusa Nagayo and Lioness Asuka invented new moves and wrestled with unusual intensity, pushing the boundaries of what women could do in the ring without losing the ordinary, girl-next-door relatability that earned the devotion of thousands of fans. Each had a plethora of incredible singles matches. In 1985 alone, a bloody hair vs hair match that ended with Chigusa shaved bald saw Dump Matsumoto's name cursed in a thousand Japanese bedrooms, while Asuka fought brutal battles against Devil Masami. However, it was as a tag team that their friendship inspired a level of emotional investment that could only be understood through the passionate screams of the crowd when they wrestled each other.

Asuka finally got a decisive win over Chigusa in 1989, adored all the more for having waited to win the title the right way. Huge, predominantly female crowds followed the journey for the rest of the women's careers – which at first appeared very short. AJW's policy of insisting that wrestlers retire aged 26 forced both women out of the ring by the end of the year. In *Sisterhood of the Squared Circle*, Pat Laprade and Dan Murphy write that Chigusa's retirement show in May 1989 – including a Crush Gals tag match, as well as Chigusa's last rematch against Asuka – was the first women's wrestling show to draw a $500,000 house.

Both women would eventually resurface and draw big houses for other companies, including GAEA, which Chigusa created. But once AJW parted with its two biggest stars, business slowed down. By the time AJW was producing the greatest wrestlers in history in the early-mid 1990s, all of whom were inspired by women like the Crush Gals, the company could still fill an arena, but wasn't quite what it used to be. The gender balance of the crowds had also shifted. Some women moved on as they got older and simply stopped following wrestling. Others brought their boyfriends and families, pushing male attendance upwards. It's difficult to pin down the reasons, but wrestling has rarely, if ever, reached the disproportionately female audience that AJW attracted in the era of the Crush Gals.

WWE now claims that 40% of its audience is female, but this claim still surprises the casual fan. Perhaps if the biggest wrestling company in the world hadn't spent so much of the last 25 years actively driving away female fans with bra and panties matches, live sex celebrations (yes, this actually happened in front of millions of people), and five-minute comedown spots after the men perform, that figure would be much higher today. But the discussions around the 'Divas Revolution' of the past few years show WWE is finally starting to understand that women will seek out and support a product that caters to what they want to see.

Massive growth in women's sports has played a huge part in this, creating the conditions for a wrestling product where women are presented as athletes on a par with men (though how well WWE does this is regularly up for debate). There is also a wealth of competition, as streaming has made it easier than ever before to find the kind of wrestling each fan wants, with independent companies able to offer variety that serves this audience, running local shows with worldwide distribution. However, it's a project that started with, and is being shaped by, Total Divas: the WWE's first real attempt to use mainstream entertainment to capitalize on the popularity of existing talent while attracting young women to wrestling. Vince McMahon is coming to understand what AJW saw four decades earlier.

The talent has always been there and so have the fans. However, with a historically all-male creative team, it's hardly surprising that nobody in WWE noticed and thought about building a product we would pay for. Now with male viewership reportedly in decline and young women accruing more spending power than ever, we are much, much harder to ignore.

Scarlett Harris - Fantasy Wrestling Federation: The Role of the Fan in Modern Wrestling

Scarlett Harris is an Australian culture critic. She is writing her own book about women's wrestling for Fayetteville Mafia Press, to be published in 2021. You can find her previously published work at her website, scarlettwoman.com.au/about, and on Twitter at twitter.com/ScarlettEHarris.

The day of a custom wrestling shoot for Lexie Fyfe, former professional wrestler and proprietor of SLAMminLadies, begins "super early," she tells me via email. "[I] make sure all the outlines are printed out and the schedule is ready to go. My husband checks the cameras and spare batteries. Wrestlers start showing up and it usually takes [between] thirty and forty-five minutes for everyone to catch up and start getting ready to shoot. Pot #1 of coffee is gone and I'm making more." A shoot day can be up to ten hours long, for which Fyfe will cater to her female wrestlers by cooking; the benefit of the SLAMminLadies ring being off her house, where there are multiple bathrooms and guest rooms for the wrestlers to get changed in. "We do chicken and sweet potatoes and if the shoot is long enough I will make a big pot of spaghetti for dinner," she says. "It can be a long day but we have fun with it and it's nice to catch up with everyone."

So what exactly is custom wrestling? "From a customer's aspect, it is the customer's way of 'booking' a match. They get to be the promoter and pick who wrestles against who[m] and what the outcome will be," Fyfe says. She provides me with a sample outline of a previous custom match SLAMminLadies has produced, wherein the customer will choose things such as outfits and movesets. Ultimately, though, custom wrestling is "really is just wrestling matches in an empty arena," Fyfe says. Furthermore, it's "a way for wrestlers to get paid good money for doing what they do," Fyfe tells me.

Fyfe, who began wrestling in 1995, saw herself edged out of a business that she had been relatively successful in when the Attitude Era of the late 1990s hit. "The popularity of women like Lita got a lot of other women interested in becoming wrestlers, [and] just wrestling shows wasn't an option [anymore]." So, in 2004, Fyfe started SLAMminladies, which "seemed like a good way to stay in wrestling and still make a living. "I wanted to have a company that put out material on a regular basis and would be able to augment mine and other wrestlers' income," she says.

There can be some confusion as to the difference between custom wrestling and apartment wrestling. Fyfe is quick to point out that "the custom wrestling that SLAMminladies promotes is done in a ring in a professional setting. No apartments or hotel rooms—a real ring and trained wrestlers. There are companies that can be a bit fetishy and might not be exactly pro style or might use people that aren't trained in professional wrestling. I always tell my wrestlers to make sure they know who they will be wrestling for and to be comfortable with what is being asked of them."

According to Brian Solomon, writing in the book Pro Wrestling FAQ: All That's Left to Know About the World's Most Entertaining Spectacle, apartment wrestling became popularized in the 1960s and took place in private apartments or hotel rooms wherein women—seldom professionally trained wrestlers as Fyfe implies—would stage "matches" in lingerie, bikinis or, sometimes, in the nude. The matches were photographed and published in wrestling magazines, up until the 1980s when mainstream wrestling became somewhat more family friendly and women such as Wendi Richter and the titular gorgeous ladies of the wrestling show GLOW got more airtime.

One of the actresses on GLOW, Jeanne Basone, who played Hollywood in the campy, all-women's wrestling league that ran from 1986 to 1990, even got into custom wrestling herself after the conclusion of the show.

"Wrestlers would go to [a] house, which had a professional-style ring in [the] backyard, and get paid $350 to wrestle fans that had booked an hour session. The fans would get charged an extra hundred to use the ring," Basone told Thrillist. "It was easy, fast money." Basone realized she could get a larger slice of the custom wrestling pie by, like Fyfe, starting her own company. "I got a photographer/video guy from one of the other girls and was working with other girls I had worked with before. I'd take custom photos for fans, or videos. Fans would script out the holds they wanted to see, the girls they wanted to wrestle each other, and how they wanted the match to end. I'd charge them to make the video, and once they got their copy, I'd sell it on my site to make more money," she said. "I have asked clients why they like hiring women to wrestle in hotel rooms," she says. "I think it all stems from something that turned them on during childhood."

Basone is quick to differentiate what she does from apartment wrestling, though, which has roots in sex work and the fetish community. "I make it clear from the start: no sex, no nudity. I have a whole thing on my website that clients can read about what I accept and don't."

In this way, custom wrestling highlights the intricacies of consent in wrestling, which can often get blurred to viewers in the thralls of simulated violence often criticized as fake fighting. But professional wrestling involves the explicit consent of all parties involved, with the action occurring in the ring having been agreed to prior or while it's happening, to ensure minimal physical harm. When fans are active participants in wrestling, whether through cheering from the audience or directly financing the kinds of moves and gear they want to see, it both strengthens and deconstructs the traditional relationship between performer and fan. Fyfe agrees, telling me, "the majority of our customers are very respectful and do their research on our wrestlers. They know their signature moves and are big fans of women's' wrestling and/or wrestling in general."

Though custom wrestling usually involves independent performers, the phenomenon has occurred in the largest wrestling company in the world, World Wrestling Entertainment. In 2004, WWE debuted the pay-per-view Taboo Tuesday, during which fans could vote for opponents and match types via texting. A second Taboo Tuesday followed in 2005, after which it would become known as Cyber Sunday until 2008, the last iteration of the event. While the male wrestlers had their weapons chosen for them, women wrestlers were at the mercy of (predominantly male) fans' fantasies which dictated that they wrestle in schoolgirl outfits and a lingerie match, harkening back to an apartment wrestling ideal. Taboo Tuesday's video game aesthetic calls to mind the gaming industry more broadly in that it puts the control back into the consumer's hands and allows them to create their own realities.

Justine Colla also works in the video game industry and was the community manager and a co-founder of Underworld Wrestling in Melbourne, Australia. Colla is well known in the internet wrestling community as Pasta Sauca, the artist behind such iconic pieces as Seth Rollins Crossfit Jesus and New Day as mermen that featured on Big E's ring gear. She frequently draws her favorite wrestlers—namely the WWE cruiserweight division—as gender-bent and in same-sex intimacies.

"I just believe there is not enough regular and genuine queer intimacy in our entertainment and want to insert it wherever possible," she says. Colla also tells me that things like gender-bending fan art and fan fiction have helped her understand her own sexuality, and she is sure to mention her growth and acknowledgement of non-binary genders. "I feel much more of a responsibility now to help bring good, genuine stories of women and queer people to the future of wrestling, rather than explore existing or past canon I have no control over."

Paul LaPorte is an independent wrestling promoter and the creator of Book It!, a wrestling card game that gender-bends some of the wrestlers depicted therein. "I think that the experience of gender-swapping the characters and the response to that outlines something that's obvious when you think about it but isn't immediately on the surface," LaPorte explains the ethos behind Book It! "Male wrestlers get a much more broad spectrum of characters they can play as opposed to women. Seeing women in roles that are normally expected to be filled by men is a refreshing concept and breathes life into the game and the characters we create.

"The artist for the game is a woman, I'm very heavily influenced by women's wrestling, and while we do use a variety of women's wrestlers to inspire the characters, we like to see what certain inspirations would look like if they were female instead of male," he continues. "We've found that far and away the female and gender-swapped characters tend to be the most popular," such as Mox Ambrosia, a play on WWE's Dean Ambrose, known now in AEW as Jon Moxley, and Bay Bae, inspired by Adam Cole's habit of adding "baybay" to the end of his name.

Shipping, too, allows fans to become even more emotionally invested in their favorite wrestlers. To ship—a shortened version of "relationship"—is to pine for your favorite characters to become romantically involved and is quite a popular pastime online amongst members of a fandom.

One such ship is that of Kota Ibushi and Kenny Omega, who make up the Golden Lovers tag team, formed in Japan in 2009, and whose in-ring chemistry is ripe for IRL fantasy. Wrestling fan and artist Hayley Weber is a hardcore shipper, fan artist and cosplayer of the two.

Weber tells me about how Ibushi is her favorite wrestler and how, through him, she came to know Omega and their "big, epic, gay love story".

"I learned that 'gay' was part of their gimmick and, as a gay person myself, [I] was immediately interested," she says. "Their story is one about soulmates, destiny—two people from completely different backgrounds who manage to share the same mind, the same soul."

26

It's clear from the way Weber talks about the Golden Lovers that she's deeply emotionally invested. "I don't have to pretend to be aloof or whatever," she says. "After being in fandoms where I've felt ridiculous for being too invested in pairings involving two men or two women, it feels very affirming."

While there is concern that shipping blurs the lines between wrestlers' personal lives and how much of it they want to keep private, especially a medium in which many of the characters are just heightened versions of the people who play them, Colla believes that, from what she's seen, "fanfic writers stay in their lane and respect the boundary between performer and fan and really that's the way it should be." Stephen Wentzell, a freelance journalist, ships Sasha Banks and Bayley, but it's their real-life friendship he gravitates towards, not fantasizing about a possible romantic relationship. "Their friendship both on and off-screen is one of pure love and trust," he tells me via email. "I'd be lucky to find my Mercedes or my Pam [Banks and Bayley's real names, respectively] someday.

Wentzell began watching wrestling around the beginning of the women's evolution in World Wrestling Entertainment, when the company began prioritizing women's wrestling as more than eye candy or a bathroom break. "As a young gay man, it was my first time seeing the kind of women in Sasha and Bayley I needed to look up to in my youth. They're role models, scrappy and tough, and unapologetic about it all," he says. "It fills my heart to know young children can watch these women and feel strong and capable, because these were the kind of role models I needed but lacked growing up."

The soft-spoken Kiera Vallone, a cosplayer I met at WWE SummerSlam in 2017, says cosplaying as her favorite characters, wrestling or no, has helped her be more outgoing, too. "I cosplay for fun, creativity and especially to increase my sewing skills and to meet new people," she tells me via phone from her home in Long Island. "Wrestlers are larger than life characters even though they're real people, they're just exaggerated personas. So I think it's fun to take that [persona] on and have that confidence."

Vallone, who navigates making her cosplay creations with the chronic illnesses Crohn's and coeliac, says there's a strong community of disabled and chronically ill cosplayers "so you know you're not alone in your struggles," she says. "It's nice to be able to have that connection with someone [who gets] it. They get it 100% because they've been there.

"I don't take when I have energy for granted. [When] I was out of commission [with a flare up] even the projects I did get done I got a lot of positive feedback [about]. I was able to feel productive while having this tough time."

Vallone's favorite cosplay that she's made is that of Alexa Bliss. "It was one of my more intense applique projects to date because of all the little, precise geometric shapes that I had to line up just right and that had to be spaced just right," she says. "I was on the floor with a ruler making sure—to the millimeter—that everything was right!"

The fact that Vallone got to meet Bliss that fateful SummerSlam weekend in 2017 while wearing the costume doesn't hurt! "She said she really liked my costume so that was a big deal for me. It's a different level of showing appreciation. You actually get that one-on-one, direct feedback from the source, from the person who is that character or that persona. It's really cool," says Vallone.

Weber, like Vallone, uses cosplaying and fan art to combat social anxiety and show appreciation for her favorite wrestlers. "Especially ones that I can't really talk to because of a language barrier," she says.

While Wentzell is yet to wear his Sasha Banks Legit Boss ring set in public, "I have The Legit Boss inscribed on my glasses, so every time I go to put them on, it's a reminder of a self-confidence I want to carry with me throughout my days."

Wentzell has also made wrestling t-shirts to support his favorite wrestlers. "My favorite homemade wrestling shirt is a 'It's Boss Time' shirt with a quote Sasha has on her Twitter on the back, that reads 'she remembered who she was and the game changed'," he says. "I feel empowered when I wear that shirt and feel as if finding powerful women to look up to has helped remind me of who I am and the self-concept I'm looking to create for myself."

*

All of these forms of wrestling fandom are ways for fans to indulge their own fantasies by taking their involvement one step further from consumer to controller. Hence, video gaming, fan art and fiction, cosplaying, shipping and customs are extensions of this. If someone doesn't have the disposable income to splurge on a video game or custom wrestling scene, they can create their own fan art or fictional versions of the kind of wrestling and representation they want to see in the world. Furthermore, these interactions allow fans to be more creative. And, as Vallone and Weber state, nothing beats the experience of being able to meet your favorite wrestler dressed as them.

But, like most fandoms, it's as much about fostering connections with fellow fans as it is getting to appropriate the likeness of and possibly meet your favorite wrestler.

"A lot of my love for wrestling does come from the community that surrounds it," Weber says. "I share this connection with others in a way that goes beyond just being a fan of the same thing [to] being part of a community, having a place where I fit in."

Harley Johnson - Passion for Wrestling

This piece is scheduled for 12 twelve minutes, hailing from 'whenever the hell her heart is,' weighing in at any opportunity, for your reading pleasure or not, this work is by Harley "The Hummingbird" Johnson! She posts at instagram.com/harleyq317

Trigger warning - this chapter refers to mental health and depression.

Throughout my many trials and adventures in life, the thing that causes the most shock to people is the fact that wrestling is one of my biggest passions. I can't explain their shock but I will try and explain my passion.

I first started watching wrestling when I was around 10. I had moved to London from somewhere 120 miles away and at school I was bullied daily because I spoke differently. I never told my parents and the teachers did nothing to help the situation but this was a different time and I'm not bitter. As the bullies taunted me, I remained silent, as any words I spoke would make them laugh harder. Soon silence was my main mood. Consequently, I didn't have many friends, but I became okay with this (kind of), as other characters kept me company and occupied my thoughts!

I was visiting my much-missed cousin in my much-missed hometown when he put some wrestling on his new cable TV. We sat in his front room and I watched awestruck as huge men beat the crap out of each other. They had finesse, showmanship, brutality and so much emotion - mostly anger which I instantly connected to! As I sat watching this spectacle of brightly coloured warriors, underhanded villains, pretty boys, fucking weirdos and little shit commentators, I felt these emotions vicariously - the first I'd felt for a long time: anger, joy, pain and sheer excitement. In my, usually, numb brain, these feelings were a warm rush, caressing my synapses, bringing color to my dark, grey world, raising the hair on the back of my neck, giving me goosebumps on my arms and filling me with feeling.

One of the characters I was loved most at this time was Jake 'the Snake' Roberts. He embodied the traits of a snake, sliding into the ring on his belly; cool, calm and tough as hell, he was everything and as he spoke clearly and decisively about how he was going to destroy his enemies, introverted little me felt as though I was not alone – grown men had enemies too. Well if Jake could deal, I could deal.

(Sidenote - I never developed the habit of referring to wrestlers by their surname and I still don't understand it. I've grown up with these characters and feel like I know them well and I'd never call someone I know well by their surname.)

I also loved 'Macho Man' Randy Savage – he had a level of intensity and 'Don't fuck with me' attitude that were tough to beat, and he wore the brightest colors. A grown man wearing sequins in purple, yellow, and bright green made my eyes happy. Just the opening bar of his entrance theme was enough to make me leap up and start jumping up and down!

On the drive back to London after my first exposure, I had move after move and hold after hold moving through my head. I never said a word when I got back to school – I had no friends to share this with and I became the worst (or best, depending on who you ask) child ever! I responded to taunts by punching kids, drop kicking them and putting on (trying to anyway) the occasional arm lock or sleeper hold! I was only young and they totally deserved it!

By the time I moved to secondary school – at age 11 here in the UK, I had reinvented my character. Now I was a cold, calculating, quiet bitch who, dare I say it, was also a bit of an extrovert! I would pass between being Jake when I needed to protect myself and being Macho when I wanted something.

A little later Bret Hart also became a hero of mine. I loved his straight talking cool but he also had honor and way too much pride for one man, but he did what he said he would and he could wrestle rings around anyone. He was also man enough to wear pink! I'm woman enough to wear blue, mostly shirts and trouser suits too and I don't care what anyone thinks of this. Bret gave me that and he also gave me the passion to always be the best at what I do. This has made me super competitive, a great employee and manager but also an amazing friend – if I say I will do something, it's done. This has gotten me into trouble more times than I care to remember but it takes a lot to stop me from keeping my word!

At age 14 I saw my first live show. I remember seeing the Beverley Brothers with The Genius, Virgil, the Steiner Brothers, Money Inc. and Mr Perfect among others. The last match of the night was Bam Bam Bigelow vs Bret Hart. Bam Bam was huge and he moved well for a big guy – quick and hard was the action and they kept us at the edge of our seats. A wrestling match is a story told between two bells and Bret is one of the greatest storytellers there is. After Bret finally beat Bam Bam, the crowd moved forward, I was in the seventh row and easily made it to the front where Bret gave me a high five! Gave ME a high five!!! I was so excited - I went home and didn't wash my hand for days. Seriously! After over a week my mum threatened to "put you in that bath and wash it myself!" That wasn't happening, so I had a bath, washed my hand and cried all night. True story!

I got my first job the summer after my GCSEs and between my mum's advice (Just do the best you can!) and Bret's mantra (The best there is...), all I did each day was my best and the job that was initially for two weeks ended up lasting four years around studying at college and university. This mindset laid the foundation for how I would approach all employment from that point on.

Lita emerged around this time and she was one of my first female role models! She was just like the me inside – cool, punky, edgy (pardon the pun), she did not give a fuck, she was the first Fearless one with her swanton dives, suicide dives and her own hurricanrana, she was always on the top rope and she did DDTs. DDTS! She could wrestle properly! She never did any of those bra and panty matches! She was the ultimate grown up tomboy and everything I wanted to be. I wore combat trousers low with my thong pulled high in homage to Lita. When Trish came along, I thought revolution was in the air but Trish often partook in very sexual storylines, which sucked because she was such as fierce wrestler. But along with Victoria, Jacqueline, Molly Holly and Chyna, Lita and Trish definitely set the table for those who would come later.

During my college years The Rock and Steve Austin became top guys and even though I was nowhere near rock bottom, the depression I'd always struggled with began to take a darker hold on me. As I burrowed deeper into my mental cocoon, I watched Steve Austin; not only was he the king of promos but he could wrestle and wrestle really well. He said what he felt, and he did not give a rat's ass what people thought. I felt like his kindred spirit, just trapped in a body that was resistant to stimuli, feeling and, on bad days, movement. But I watched and admired, I felt potential to grow and those synapses in my brain were firing again. I had no idea who I was but I knew I liked this attitude.

When The Rock held a mic, he had millions... and millions around the world in the palm of his hands. He truly was electrifying and when his music hit, I wanted to hear what he had to say, I'd chant along in my living room, bringing shouts of protest from whoever was home and I would feel energized, connected to millions who I'd never know. Then I'd go back into my shell, slightly warmer.

My depression reached new lows during my time at university not helped by the fact that in the halls where I lived I had minimum contact with the main characters in my life. I missed watching their lives develop, the goosebumps when entrance music hit, different costumes for different events, the promos and of course the matches. I was home for the big 4 (as they were then) WWE pay-per-views without fail.

In the following years, as I continued to struggled with my demons, I heard that Jake 'The Snake' was fighting similar demons and he was now living less than 20 miles away in England. Somehow that gave me strength, though I feared that Jake would end up on the ever-growing list of wrestlers who died too young. Every night, morning, and throughout most days I would plead with the universe to keep myself and Jake safe 'just for today. Please.'

When the Chris Benoit tragedy occurred years later in 2007, I'm sorry to say that I wasn't surprised. I had always seen a darkness within Chris, but it served as a reminder of how easy it is to hide every thought and feeling you have with silence or a smile. I had been doing that for nearly 20 years and I often wondered (I still do sometimes) how long Chris had been doing the same. My heart breaks for what happened in his last days and I'm so glad he achieved his dream of becoming the top guy in the company, but I also wonder if having achieved his dream he felt like he had nothing left to live for...

I was able to start watching live events regularly at venues including Wembley (now the SSE) arena, the Royal Albert Hall and more recently the O2. Every time I go away, I check to see if my team are playing in town. I've seen them in Florida and Chicago so far, and New Orleans – that visit was 10 years in the making!

Back to 2004 and I sat in my living room with my 3 flat mates watching WrestleMania 20 – what a show! Eddie Guerrero slowly loosening that boot against Kurt Angle to escape Kurt's famous submission hold the Angle Lock – Viva la Rasa! The clinic Jericho and Christian put on! The dressing room promo with Chris Benoit and Eddie where Eddie lit a fire under Chris who then beat Triple H and Shawn Michaels to become the Heavyweight Champ, the emotion on Chris's face when he won, the hug from his brother Eddie who then gave him the space to celebrate the goal he'd worked his whole life for. In the final seconds of that show I promised my depressed self that no matter where in the world WrestleMania 30 was (and I was sure it would be in New York) I would be there!

Over the next several years my depression slowly began to lift but that's another story. However, one night at about 1am, I'd finished another 18 hour shift and was looking through my emails in bed with a glass of ice-cold Sauvignon Blanc when I saw packages for WrestleMania 30. It was going to be in New Orleans, which wasn't New York, but it had always seemed like a cool city to me. As I looked through the offerings, I got goosebumps and the hair stood up on the back of my neck. With zero forethought or hesitation, I booked a WrestleMania package.

I ended up going alone to New Orleans but this turned out to be the best thing ever! My depression was on its way out, I was in a bustling city with 72,000 close friends (I just hadn't met them yet) and we were all there to have a good time while enjoying a shared passion. My package included a VIP meet and greet with Bret Hart, one with Shawn Michaels (I hate him – It should have been CM Punk!) and front (audience, not guest) row at the Hall of Fame ceremony, as well as some other components.

At the meet and greet with Bret we were able to have a decent conversation so I told him all about me not washing my hand for days many years ago and my mum getting stressed about it. He laughed and laughed - he loved that I was travelling alone for wrestling and that many years ago I pre-ordered his biography from Canadian Amazon so I didn't have to wait for it to be released in the UK. He gave me a big hug and drew a heart in his autograph in my copy of his biography. It was my first wrestling related day in New Orleans and if I had to go home at that point, I would not have been disappointed. I was floating. Two days later at the Hall of Fame ceremony, I was casually sitting in my full evening gown in the front audience row, high fiving and shaking hands with a bunch of wrestlers as they walked past when Bret approached – I leap out of my seat, waved my hands and shouted, "Bret! Bret! I washed my hands; I washed my hands!" He looked at me and my world slows down as my brain registers what a psycho I sound and look like. The security guard who was flirting with me earlier says, 'Mam. Take your seat, Mam!" and rests his hand. On. His. Gun. Bret looked at me before quick-walking away to his seat! I like to think that when he got there he thought, 'Ah, that was Harley from London' and smiled, but I'll never know.

Later that night, I stood on my feet (I was in with the security guard again) and cheered as Lita entered the Hall of Fame, then I almost cried as Jake entered it. I wondered what his darkest days had been like and whether he felt my pleas. I was so proud of both us in that moment for conquering our darker days and standing tall. I thanked the universe for blessing us with such an amazing weekend! Then Warrior came out and during his speech I shed a tear. I don't cry much at all but that night watching Warrior and Vince leave it all in the past and mend those fences was magical. Warrior was bursting with pride and emotion and I was dreaming of seeing him back in my life again every week in some capacity. You couldn't write a more tragically beautiful story.

A year later, I'm in bed reading through my Twitter and I watch in awe as AJ Lee drops a pipe bomb bigger than her husband's when she calls out Stephanie McMahon for her philanthropic hypocrisy. I had a front row seat to the beginning of the long overdue evolution of women's wrestling and I sat back with sheer excitement. Over the years many women – Beth Phoenix, Michelle McCool, Layla, Melinda, Natalya and even Nikki Bella had tried to step up to the plate but they didn't have the backing of their sexist overlord. But one day a new King was born and in his NXT kingdom, the rules were different. Wrestler Triple H had married into the family and Vince was giving him more and more power, including ownership of the developmental wrestler division, which he used to create the NXT program for the WWE network. Women had the same training as men, they had similar screen time and in this kingdom four queens began their reign: Charlotte, Becky, Bayley and Sasha. Even though I'd had wrestling queens in my life before, we'd never had a platform where they could wrestle equally and wrestle equally well. It was exciting to watch and like ten-year-old me, I watched in awe, with goosebumps on my arms. The woman I was had triumph and possibility running through her veins. She was emboldened and righteous and it was beautiful.

Many people have asked me why I didn't become a wrestler when growing up, but I never once thought that it was a career for me – for one thing breast implants have never appealed to me and that seemed a requirement back then. But I can honestly say that if I was growing up watching these new queens in today's more accessible, varied product, featuring women of different shapes, sizes, colors, backgrounds and talents, I could have been a wrestler. Even though Bayley versus Sasha at TakeOver Brooklyn and Charlotte versus Asuka at WrestleMania 34 made my heart swell, my head explode and my eyes water, I'm still excited for what comes next for our women and who they inspire.

I could go on and on about why I love wrestling, I haven't mentioned Edge or The Miz. I haven't explained why I love the business model that is WWE, how it takes risks and does (rightly or wrongly) whatever the CEO wants to do, who even though he is the emperor of a publicly traded billion-dollar company, still does not give the fuck he should! I enjoy watching this business grow and evolve and respond to the challenges of the day. Even though I can't agree with some of their decisions, I have to respect the guts it takes to make them.

I haven't mentioned entrance themes, but I listen to them a few times a week and I have themes that I listen to when I need to evoke certain feelings and remember my awesomeness. I could talk about being young, and still to this day, recognizing entrance themes from the first millisecond, about being triggered by them and feeling instantly excited, pissed off, curious, happy or annoyed, but whatever I felt, I had to watch and see what happened next.

I could mention the biographies I read, giving me a further insight into the challenges these people face. From being laughed at and discouraged when they shared their dreams, to working harder than they ever thought possible to achieve them anyway. From adventures all around the world, to dodgy dealings, excesses, exhaustion, ribs and road trips. These are full lives and I love my front row seat to them all. The podcasts I listen to weekly share further insights into lives and personalities. I have listened to Steve Austin's podcast for over five years, I was gutted when he sold the Broken Skull Ranch, the stories of him up there each Christmas helped me get through Christmas! When he decided to take a break from podcasting – I was devastated, it literally felt like a friend had gone missing, even though I knew he was safe, he was gone from my life and I really missed him.

If you are wondering why I've only mentioned WWE, that's because I mostly watch WWE. Don't get me wrong I keep up to date with other promotions and wrestlers, but between my addictive personality and the other passions in my life, I physically cannot give any more time to wrestling, not without quitting my job anyway! I love small, but clearly deep, instead!

I'm very aware that this passion makes me sound somewhat unhinged. I'm very okay with that as I love who I am. Examining this passion of mine, in a way I never had before has shown me how much of an influence my wrestling role models have had on my life. They say your personality is a mixture of the five people you are closest to, well my depression has completely gone (thank you universe) and although I can be cold when needed (Jake), I usually aim to exceed expectations and smash stereotypes, while breaking molds and rules (The Rock). I'm definitely an introvert (and totally fine with this) but I have many close friends that I would do anything for (every tag team ever {at first}). I will say what needs to be said with no sugar coating, I'm honest in every situation (Steve) and I work hard at whatever I put my mind to (Bret). Lita taught me that when I'm the only woman in the room, my abilities and knowledge are on the same level as everyone else in there.

Steve Austin says to be a believable character, you should be yourself dialed up to 11... sometimes I hit 12 and like this crazy sport/entertainment, I am fucking awesome, proud, fearless and independent. I look at the person I am today and I love her so, so (too) much (every character ever).

I am woman! Born of woman, man and wrestling!

Kristen Ashly - Being a Woman Journalist in Wrestling Media

Kristen Ashly is the co-owner of the women's wrestling site Bell To Belles. You can find her work at Fightful, Pro Wrestling Sheet, and many other sites. When she's not watching women kick ass, she's watching the Packers, horror movies, and working for a sustainable food non-profit. She tweets at twitter.com/KristenAshly

Ever since I've been able to hold a pencil, I've wanted to be a writer. Writing to me felt like more than just telling a story, it was like finding the missing puzzle piece you've been searching for all these years.

But, I also knew from a young age, that writing was not a sure-fire way to make a living. There were no guarantees, and so being a prudent young lady, I turned my attention elsewhere: psychology, theology, even biochemistry. But, I kept turning back to my true love. One day, I decided to give it a go.

I tried every type of writing I could muster semi-successfully: creative, poetry, screenwriting, fiction, non-fiction, research, scientific, copywriting, journaling. When I finally got a job in journalism, however, I knew I was home. The thrill of chasing down a lead, the combination of creativity and facts, the tight deadlines and feeling of a hurried turnaround. The feeling of breaking a piece of news, or grabbing a scoop from a source, is unlike anything I had ever felt before. It was almost transcendent.

I tried my hand at so many different fields within journalism, because truthfully, I never seem to find a completely comfortable fit. I never found the place where I felt completely at ease, creatively.

I started off by reporting local news, specifically, news as it relates to the local education board. I would attend board meetings and report things live as they happen. It was awful. Not just dry and listless, but extremely boring and political in nature, something I was not interested in.

I turned to the internet to see what I could find for freelance work. Mind you, this was 2011, and it was hard to find anything solid or paid well. A geek culture website titled "Find Your Geek" was hiring for a movie and television reviewer. I was a self-proclaimed movie nerd, and so the work seemed to fit well within my life and interests. The site seemed to be haemorrhaging, though, and the owner offered to give it to me. I overtook the site as an owner, but it was too much for me to handle, and the site finally died.

That was the basic story for each and every site I worked for after that. I worked within the fields of horror, entertainment, and sports, and each time, the site went down, or the owner had to completely rework the system, and it made for a hard working relationship. This was all happening leading up to the end of 2016.

At the end of 2016, I "accidentally" became a wrestling fan. I was the type of person who scoffed at wrestling and how "fake" it was. My brother and dad watched wrestling religiously, at the time, and I would be scolded out of the room because I couldn't take it seriously. One day, they convinced me to watch it, and the rest was history. I was immediately hooked.

A few months later, I was recruited to write for a wrestling site for an editor I worked with at an NFL site. I joined their site roster, and soon was writing for several different wrestling websites. I fell in love. I got to be creative and sporty. I used stats and figures to drive my point home, but was writing on a creative art I never knew existed.

One thing in my new field of journalism stood out to me, though: women, much like in other sports fields, were being mistreated and undervalued.

I saw how marginalized women wrestlers still were. I saw the mistreatment they were forced to deal with just to follow their passion, and I could relate. When writing for sports, I was constantly undervalued and underestimated simply because I was a woman. The pain women wrestlers dealt with in a daily fashion was something I could connect with, and I wanted to tell their stories. I needed to shine a light on their struggles. I had to push forward their goals any way I could.

I had no idea what that mission would do to me personally, but it consumed my story. Shortly after struggling with women wrestlers, I was hired as the Editor-in-Chief for a women's wrestling site but found myself working for someone who went against all ideals I held as a woman, and so I left. The sudden change from the editor of a huge site to holding absolutely no title and working for no site really traumatized me in a way I did not expect. I had always tied my identity to writing. If I wasn't writing for the cause, who was I even?

I decided to take things into my own hands, because if I couldn't find a site that I believed did women wrestlers justice, then I would make one. And so, Bell To Belles was born. I was able to hire my own staff, ensure it was as diverse as the pool of wrestling fans was, and control what content would be pushed out to the masses.

I'm the co-owner of a women's wrestling site, and I wouldn't have it any other way, but sometimes, the work is completely thankless.

Why? The fans. The harassment. The impossibility of advancement or a decent living pay. The deep-rooted sexism that seems to be the undercurrent for wrestling fans and journalism. The job made me hate watching wrestling. The job made it hard to be a fan. Male fans who sent me tweets daily spewing sexism and hate created panic every time I opened Twitter. I couldn't stand wrestling. I would turn off my phone, turn off my television, and hole up in my apartment, convinced the world didn't want me to succeed.

But eventually, the sun would shine, and I would dust myself off. I knew that if women weren't strong and stood up to those who had held them back, the world would never be better for anyone. I choose to support women wrestlers and women in this field, because I had a handful of strong women and reasonable men who pushed me a long an extraordinary path. If we aren't here to help each other, no one will.

I may step away from wrestling one day, and focus on another aspect of my life and interests, but one thing is for certain: I will never give up on equality and women's rights. When the world is able to treat each other equally and fairly, my job will be done.

Ilana Gordon - Meet The Ladies Of G.L.O.W., The 80s Female Wrestling League

Jenji Kohan's Netflix show boasts big hair and body slams.

Ilana Gordon is a writer and comic based in Los Angeles. You can keep up to date with her work at Ilanagordon.com, twitter.com/IlanaAbby and instagram.com/IlanaAbby.

The writer and producer Jenji Kohan is known for creating smart, multi-dimensional female characters who inhabit seldom-explored worlds. "Orange is the New Black," "Gilmore Girls" and "Weeds" offered insights into the areas of female prisons, single parenting and the drug trade. In the Netflix series "G.L.O.W." Kohan sheds light on a different subculture: female wrestling.

G.L.O.W., which was released in June of 2017, is based on the "Gorgeous Ladies of Wrestling," an hour-long TV show that aired weekly from 1986-1990. The all-female wrestling league started as a wrestling promotion, but soon became a cultural phenomenon, influencing the future of the sport forever.

G.L.O.W. was a small, low-budget affair, part-vaudevillian variety show and part-wrestling match. What it lacked in technique it made up for in grit (and — in true 80s fashion — white people rapping badly).

Lighting up the wrestling world

In the 80s, opportunities for female wrestlers were scant. The WWE would occasionally introduce women into storylines, but rarely were they allowed inside the ring to compete. The Olympics didn't establish women's wrestling events until 2004.

Women's wrestling was considered a novelty and female matches were used as marketing ploys to help sell tickets for men's matches. Dee Booher, who played Matilda the Hun on G.L.O.W., was one of the few women who wrestled prior to joining the cast. In the documentary "GLOW: The Story of the Gorgeous Ladies of Wrestling," Booher recalls showing up to matches and being told that she couldn't wrestle a man. Instead, organizers let her wrestle a bear. As she tells it, she lasted longer than her male counterparts did.

Turning actresses into athletes

Casting for the show began in 1985. With few established female wrestlers available, the production staff turned to aspiring actresses. As one wrestler remembers it, the show put out an open call, but did not specify what the series would be about. After learning that the show would focus on wrestling, many women walked out of the audition.

Those who stayed were put through a physically and emotionally grueling training camp run by a stuntman and professional wrestler named Mando Guerrero. Guerrero was from a dynastic Mexican wrestling family. Under his tutelage, the women trained for eight hours a day, every day. Guerrero pulled no punches; in the documentary, one of the wrestlers recalls him placing an aspiring cast member in a sleeper hold on the first day of camp to show that he wasn't messing around.

By the end of the casting process, 36 women were chosen to participate in Season 1. Most were actresses and models hoping to break into the entertainment industry, but the open call also yielded dancers, stunt women, a phlebotomist and an Olympic shot putter from American Samoa.

The G.L.O.W. experience

In 1986, G.L.O.W. began filming at the Riviera Hotel in Las Vegas. The women moved into apartments down the street, colloquially referred to as "the G.L.O.W. House."

To wrangle their cast members, some of whom were as young as 19, producers implemented strict curfews. The women were required to remain in character whenever they were on hotel grounds and producers punished misbehavior with heavy fines.

From training camp to campy characters

The wrestling enthusiast and producer David McLane conceived of the idea for G.L.O.W., but credit for the show's campy tone and kitschy characters goes to director Matt Cimber. Cimber, who is famously known as the last husband of actress Jayne Mansfield, saw the show as a cross between character-driven sketch comedy and professional wrestling.

During training, Cimber assigned each cast member a character, loosely based on his first impression of the woman. These characters were cartoonish in nature, with names like Little Egypt, Susie Spirit, Jailbait, MTV, Americana and Babe the Farmer's Daughter. The wrestlers took these snap-judgment assessments and fleshed them out, adding costumes, elaborate props, accents and back-stories.

Subtlety was not the show's strong point: The characters were divided into groups of "Good girls" and "Bad girls" and the women were expected to fraternize only with characters of their same classification; failure to do so resulted in fines. Every G.L.O.W. match was a take on the classic struggle of good versus evil, with fresh-faced American characters like Susie Spirit and Americana squaring off against threatening foreign entities like the Louisiana voodoo queen Big Bad Mama or the ambiguously Russian Ninotchka. In these thinly veiled parodies of real life political issues, the good guys usually triumphed.

The rise and fall of the G.L.O.W. empire

Nobody expected G.L.O.W. to succeed — the show was essentially an infomercial, with wrestlers hawking products like Faberge shampoo in between wrestling matches and sketches. To the surprise of both the cast and crew, G.L.O.W. garnered a cult-like following with a demographic that encompassed everyone from hardcore wrestling fans to children. The documentary claims the show beat out male wrestling shows in the same time slot and it was not uncommon for thousands of people to wait outside the 200-seat showroom where the matches were held, in the hopes of snagging a ticket.

Shortly into its run, G.L.O.W. became a cultural sensation, landing the wrestlers cameos on hit shows like "Married With Children" and the opportunity to pose for Playboy. With the mounting ratings came increased pressure on the women: Director Matt Cimber was known for his particularly abrasive methods of motivating his cast, which included public humiliation and disparaging remarks about their bodies.

As the show reached its zenith, G.L.O.W.'s staff and audience pushed the wrestlers to fight bigger and harder — often at the expense of their physical well-being. The athletes suffered from physical injuries that long outlasted the show's four year run. At least one former wrestler uses a wheelchair to get around and another retreated to a residential treatment center after blowing out her knees.

After filming more than 100 shows, G.L.O.W. was abruptly cancelled in 1990. The cause of death was financial: Meshulam Riklis — an Israeli businessman and the show's main financial backer — pulled his money from the project. Per the documentary, Riklis provided no official explanation for his decision, but cast members speculate that his wife, the actress Pia Zadora, wanted to separate him from the young, nubile wrestlers.

47

The show's unexpected end came as a shock to its stars, who describe their relationship like a sisterhood. The women scattered after efforts to remount G.L.O.W. fizzled. Some stayed in the wrestling industry, working both in the ring and behind the scenes. Others acted or found work in other parts of the entertainment industry. It wasn't until documentarians began chronicling the show's journey in 2012 that the stars finally reunited for a long-awaited good-bye and some more awkward rapping.

Netflix's reimagining of the show will conclude after its fourth season, which is expected to air in 2020.

Hallie Grossman – Equals Fights Movement

The optics of intergender wrestling can be shocking. But those who participate say pitting women against men in the ring is a step toward equality.

Hallie Grossman is a staff writer for ESPN The Magazine. Follow her on Twitter at twitter.com/TheHallieG. Tim Fiorvanti contributed to this story.

This article was originally published on espn.com on August 16 2018.

In the middle of the night, at a quarter 'til 2, the audience fends off exhaustion and cold. The main ballroom in the Pontchartrain Center is cavernous, and as the thermostat dips into the low 60s, the men and women (mostly men) and children (two of them) lean forward, waiting for the show to go on. The venue is set up to house 2,500 people, but just 300 tickets have been sold. In the end, only about 170 fans have shown, so the faction that's here feels sparse, the event a little clandestine.

There's a bald man sitting ringside in a black shirt with bold white letters that blare: "POLITICALLY INCORRECT ... AND DAMN PROUD OF IT!!!" A group of seven friends who look to be in their mid-20s sit clustered together eight rows up in the bleachers, a sea of vacant blue seats in front of them. The room is mostly dark, save for the ring in the center illuminated by spotlight. There are no windows to the outside world here, and even if there were, the vista beyond, to Kenner, Louisiana, wouldn't offer much. An expanse of green fields. A smattering of shade trees in the distance. Downtown New Orleans is nearly 15 miles away, but with those fields and those trees blanketed in a velvety night, the city feels farther. This might as well be the ends of the earth.

Inside, as 2 a.m. draws near, the music picks up, a rhythmic pounding that crescendos in sync with strobing lights. It's a neon pink and green and yellow rave-like affair, and it's through a colorful cloud of smoke that Kimber Lee, royalty in the independent wrestling circuit, emerges. She's here in a homecoming of sorts -- returning to the indies after more than a year away in the WWE ranks -- to face "Hot Sauce" Tracy Williams at Lit Up. The show, hosted by Beyond Wrestling, is the promotion's first card featuring just men versus women, intergender matches from the opening bout until the final bell.

Kimber Lee runs the perimeter of the guardrails, reaching out to fans pushed up against the metal gates. She leaps over the turnbuckle and raises her arms, her sequined jacket and purple-and-black, bedazzled bikini set glinting in the spotlight. "Welcome back" chants break out. And when she squares off with Williams -- a svelte 192-pound man in miniscule black trunks -- the fans are unmistakably in her corner. For five minutes, they grapple and slam each other onto the canvas and trade kicks and expel grunts. Then Kimber Lee climbs to the top rope, launches herself through the air and slams her feet into the chest of a staggering Williams, sending him flying upon impact. Williams retaliates, picking up Kimber Lee and flinging her over his shoulder before spiking her to the ground. "Death Valley Driver!" the announcer hollers.

Seconds later, Williams clutches Kimber Lee in a headlock and the two wind up tangled, head to head, shoulder to shoulder. Kimber Lee punches Williams on his side, once, twice. A third time. After the fourth swing, a convincingly desperate heave to get him to loosen his grip, Williams stands straight, keeps Kimber Lee bent forward and winds his right arm back like he's wielding a hammer. He lets swing and his palm, wide open, collides with flesh. You hear the slap, the smack of broken skin, almost before you see it.

And then you do see it. You can't not see it. Between Kimber Lee's shoulder blades, just below her tattoo of a rose in bloom, blooms something new: a throbbing, bright-red handprint.

PHYSICAL RUIN IS part of this job description, and for the remaining weekend after Lit Up, Tracy Williams' open palm strike -- the evidence of a man physically beating up a woman while an accepting crowd looked on -- will burn a deep crimson on Kimber Lee's back. Depending on your vantage point, that handprint is either a token of honor and, perhaps, progress -- or a radioactive badge of shame, nothing but spectacle masked as progress.

Their match concludes after Williams locks his forearm around Kimber Lee's neck and yanks backward to submit her via a crossface; he keeps his belt, then gets booed for his efforts. A vanquished Kimber Lee staggers around the mat, raises her arms to salute the Kimber Lee chants, then ducks beneath the ropes to leave the ring. She hobbles along the path to the exit, clutches her jaw and steps through the thick black curtain that divides the public from backstage.

And there, on the other side, she stands up straight.

Kimber Lee, who goes by Kimberly Frankele when not in the ring, finds Williams and, like wrestlers do after every match, they huddle. They assure each other that, yes, they're both unharmed; yes, they both feel good about the how the match went. And then Williams explains himself, and that back slap.

"It was there," he tells Frankele. Her back was exposed; he seized an opportunity. "I'm sorry."

Frankele waves him off, assuring Williams that she would have done the same. It's their job as performers to leave safe spots open -- their chest, their back -- where opponents can deliver strikes carefully. "You're going to bruise," says Frankele of her chosen trade. "You're going to get hurt."

She laughs, because, really, she has been at this since 2009 and it's just one more bruise in a decade replete with them. And besides, she knows

51

Williams. They both trained under the same mentor; they know the lines they can and cannot cross with each other. "He wasn't supposed to hit me in the back like that," Frankele says, then shrugs. "But that happens. That's a move that's not fake."

Spend enough time backstage, and a kind of governance emerges. Everyone is on top of everyone back here, and between the embraces and the pleasantries, it feels closer to a high school reunion than a space where they're prepping to batter one another. There's the women's dressing room, where an array of carry-on suitcases are splayed open. ("PRO WRESTLING IS NOT A CRIME" trumpets a sticker on one black bag.) The wrestlers' makeup, their costumes and their snacks spill out onto a faux granite countertop. There's the men's dressing room just across the way. And there's the hallway. In this sterile, narrow corridor that stretches the length of the convention center, the wrestlers conduct their pre- and postmortems. Before their matches, they hammer out the storyline and moves they agree they want to execute. Afterward, they dissect how those storylines and moves played out. They are forensic analysts in Lycra and sequins.

Walk through the hall in those final, harried moments before Lit Up begins, and you'll find them convening, two by two -- wrestler vs. wrestler -- like Noah's Ark. Frankele and Williams practice their steps, knowing their story arc is a simple one. Williams owns the title belt; Frankele will try to wrest it from him. "Boom!" Frankele yells, then pretends to whip her head back. She mimics a series of punches; Williams pretends to sustain the blows. "Boom!" Williams says, and Frankele pretend-staggers for a few steps.

Down the corridor, about 20 feet away, another pair of performers, Deonna Purrazzo and Matt Riddle, go through their own paces. Neither has performed in an intergender match before tonight, and they decide their action will lean into that inexperience. Purrazzo will be the early aggressor, needling Riddle to fight. Riddle, the former UFC fighter, will be hesitant at first, knowing the power imbalance, until she frustrates him so much he swings back and outmuscles her. "Maybe it's like this," Riddle motions, and practices kneeing Purrazzo with his right leg. She nods and pretend-lurches a few steps.

"It's like a live-action movie," Frankele says. "We're stunt athletes."

Ask any intergender wrestler why he or she feels comfortable with the performances they're putting out in the world, why they don't balk at a man and a woman wreaking violence on one another, and they'll inevitably land here. Women will question the logic of being able to train and practice with men wrestlers but not actually face them in a match. They'll laud the empowerment they feel or the equality they seek to promote; Kimber Lee's catchphrase of choice is that she's the princess who'll save herself, thank you. But the heart of Frankele's argument is that she's just playing Kimber Lee. Frankele has seen the script and signed off on it, and afterward, she will even provide notes on the execution of that script, and so why wouldn't she feel comfortable? Why wouldn't she take up the intergender mantle?

"Wrestling is not fake. I hate that word," she says. Yes, the winner is preordained and the athleticism is choreographed, but it's still athleticism. "The moves are real. The bruises I have are real. I'm really landing on the concrete.

"But we're telling a story."

To a wrestler, they maintain this point. Frankele's trainer, Drew Gulak, calls professional wrestling "the craziest form of acting." Joey Ryan, another wrestler on Lit Up's all-intergender card, deems it performance art. "Everybody's in on it," he says. "Everybody knows."

And to those who would scream a woman could never beat a man? It's a moot point, these wrestlers insist. For one, they fashion their storylines to make room for that reality, that size and strength imbalances might exist.

Midway through their match at Lit Up, Williams throws Kimber Lee to the floor; she lands in a split, then wags her finger in rebuttal. Her point: Flexibility can counter brute power. For another, there's a transaction with the audience, wrestlers say. Even if it's an unspoken contract, the audience knows what this is and accepts it as such. They're in on the act. The fans walk through the doors of the Pontchartrain Center and suspend their disbelief to take in a performance. Like a Broadway show. Or a blockbuster movie. Or any work of fiction.

In this work of fiction, one man faces one woman. They've learned their lines. They've practiced their steps. At times, there are miscues -- say, a slap to the back that leaves a welt -- but that's merely part of the live-action extravaganza. Come on in, the water's fine!

When Williams' hand smacked Kimber Lee's back, the 170 fans drew a sharp, collective breath. She was a crowd favorite; the prodigal daughter returning. The masses were on her side, and so they responded in the only way that felt right. They gasped. Then they booed. But what if Kimber Lee hadn't been a crowd favorite, nor a prodigal daughter? What if they hadn't been moved by that fleet delivery of violence at all? Or what if they had been moved ... but reveled in it?

BEFORE SHE DREW adulation, Frankele faced a firestorm.

Three years ago, she stepped into another Beyond Wrestling ring, this time in Providence, Rhode Island, against another intergender opponent. Chris Dickinson picked up a folding chair while Kimber Lee kneeled in front of him. Dickinson lunged back, seeking leverage, hoisted the chair over his head, then swung down -- a wrecking ball set on demolition -- crashing it over her skull. He picked up her limp body, swung her onto his back, took off on a run -- Pazuzu Bomb! -- then threw her to the ground. She skidded toward the turnbuckle, a collection of beaten bones more than a whole body. And a fan in Providence that night captured the mauling on video.

The blowback was swift, and it was unrelenting. Angry viewers called the venue, then the city. Dickinson lost bookings and gained death threats. Fellow wrestlers joined the lynch mob too. "Guys that I trained with were like, 'Oh, you're gonna wrestle that Dickinson guy?'" Matt Riddle says. "'Try to hurt him.'"

Frankele, for her part, was floored.

"I was 100 percent fine. Neither of us had any idea it would go viral," she says. "We got to the back and it's, 'Oh my gosh, that was amazing! Thank you for taking care of me,'" she remembers telling Dickinson.

And that Pazuzu Bomb? She and Dickinson had wanted to push the boundaries even further -- a powerbomb from the top rope -- a notion that Drew Cordeiro, Beyond Wrestling's owner, vetoed immediately. "Absolutely not," he told them. "Way too dangerous."

The chorus was unswayed. At best, it insisted, intergender wrestling normalizes domestic violence. At worst, it glorifies it.

The optics, after all, are shocking. A petite wrestler such as Kimber Lee doesn't just fly through the air, they rocket. Against Dickinson, her head looked to ram into the ring bell -- though she and Cordeiro insist it didn't. Independent wrestling venues are small and private, and the events they house feel fringe, by extension. Illicit, even. And Beyond Wrestling's calling card as a promotion is an audience unrestrained by guardrails, so the fans are flush against the ring with no barriers. What this moment looks like, then, is a furtive congregation of gawkers bearing witness to, perhaps even sanctioning, a man pummeling a woman.

It's chilling. It's also incomplete.

To label intergender wrestling and the brutality it portrays as domestic violence is to fundamentally misunderstand what domestic violence -- against men or women -- can look like. "It's about a pattern of power and control," says Erica Olsen, a deputy director at National Network to End

Domestic Violence. "It's physical violence. It's controlling their technology. Controlling bank accounts. Ruining credit. It's a much larger, complex picture."

Weeks after Lit Up, Olsen watched video of Kimber Lee wrestling Williams, took in the moments when Williams grabbed Kimber Lee by her hair and when she retaliated with a kick to his jaw. "I have watched, unfortunately, so many videos of violent acts being committed against individuals. Some of those have been in the context of domestic violence in a partner. Some have been stranger assaults," she says. "This felt nothing at all like that for me." It was presented as performance, she says, and seemingly consumed like one.

But even art can create permission structures. Why doesn't this show of brutality open the floodgates to a more permissive, forgiving climate for violence against women? Consent, Frankele says. She not only agreed to get in those rings with Dickinson and Williams, she did so because she trusts them. When you train as a professional wrestler, you learn the right ways to roll and to fall and to brace yourself against the ropes. And you learn how to protect the person who steps into the ring with you.

"We have to challenge ourselves to respect the fact that consenting to be in this profession does not open the door to allow anyone to be abusive to you in any other space of your life," Olsen says.

It's why Stephanie Bell, who is an intergender wrestler and a survivor of domestic violence, feels she can be both.

Bell did not consent to physical abuse in her home. But she has consented to be in that ring, and she is exhaustively selective about who joins her there. "It's not just men, it's everyone," says Bell, who wrestles under the alias Mia Yim. "Who can I trust? Who's going to keep me safe?"

It is hard and it is complicated and it is fraught because two things can be true at once. It can be true that these women and men consent to be in a ring together and agree to inflict damage on one another's bodies. It can also be true that it is unsettling to see and hear it happen. Especially with children looking on, young people who are still forming their world views. Especially with potential survivors of domestic violence looking on, people whose worldviews already know abuse. But the root of the conflict is that violence is not a bug in the professional wrestling ecosystem. It's the feature.

"Research does suggest that exposure to violence as a form of entertainment can desensitize us to it," says Anastasia Powell, an associate professor at RMIT University in Melbourne, Australia, whose area of study has focused on policy concerning violence against women. "So there are some concerns to be had about entertainment that normalizes men's violence against women or displays it as not serious. But I think those same concerns apply to the glorification of men's violence against men."

And so maybe the reckoning isn't whether intergender wrestling normalizes or glorifies violence against women. Perhaps the reckoning is that professional wrestling normalizes and glorifies violence. Period.

IN THE MIDDLE of the afternoon, just a quarter after 3 o'clock, the crowd fidgets with anticipation and cold.

The Mercedes-Benz Superdome is cavernous, and as the thermostat dips into the low 60s, the men and women (in roughly equal proportion) and children (thousands of them), lean forward, waiting for the show to start. Exactly 78,133 tickets were sold, and as "RUSEV DAY" chants ring out from the upper decks, the assembly feels charged, raucous. It's mostly dark, save for the towering -- hundreds of feet high -- fluorescent pink, orange and green Mardi Gras mask at the top of a runway. There are no windows here, but if there were, the vista beyond would reveal a river of humanity flowing through the streets of New Orleans, spilling into the crevices and cracks of the city, making its way to this mecca. WrestleMania 34 might as well be the center of the universe.

It's three days after Lit Up, in the same city but a world away, and the WWE's annual Super Bowl-meets-papal-visit-meets-Comic-Con spectacular is in full swing. The sheer size and scope of WrestleMania -- it grossed $14.1 million this year and drew fans from every state in the country -- sheds light on one basic truth. The WWE is so ubiquitous and takes up so much oxygen in the professional wrestling kingdom that until the organization embraces intergender wrestling, intergender wrestling will stay relegated to the fringes.

There was a time when the WWE did not shrink from it. Chyna was the first woman wrestler to enter the Royal Rumble in 1999. Lita and Jacqueline and Jazz, all prominent women wrestlers in the early 2000s, squared off against men in the ring. But when the organization ushered in its "PG Era" in 2008, the mandate that came with its new family-friendly TV rating was clear. No bloodshed. Less gratuitous violence. Fewer edgy storylines. Intergender wrestling? Not welcome in this newly sanitized WWE.

"The thing that's troubling to me," says Beyond Wrestling's Cordeiro, "is intergender wrestling shouldn't be inconsistent with a PG era."

He chose WrestleMania weekend to host the promotion's first all-intergender card because, on the biggest wrestling weekend of the year, he knew it would be a special attraction -- and, by extension, an opportunity to showcase intergender wrestling with the nuance and consideration he thinks it should be afforded. Before Lit Up, Cordeiro sent a warning to all performers: "Absolutely no sexist humor will be tolerated." He doesn't view intergender wrestling as spectacle or taboo. He doesn't want others to consume it that way either.

Still, there are signs the WWE might yet come around to Cordeiro's doctrine, that the wall that presently divides the WWE and intergender wrestling might still crumble. WWE hopefuls have long feared that intergender experience would be a disqualifying mark on their résumé, but Purrazzo signed with the WWE in May with an intergender match and before her, Frankele, with a career full of such matches, signed too.

And then there was the brief interlude, a full 60 seconds, when intergender wrestling returned to the biggest possible stage: WrestleMania in New Orleans.

Just an hour and a half into the five-hour show, and 10 minutes into the night's most gripping match, Paul "Triple H" Levesque -- WWE's sculpted, Hulk-shaped 14-time champion -- throws Kurt Angle over the announcer's table. In his American flag singlet, Angle cuts a red, white and blue flash through the air, while Triple H goes back into the ring to check on his real-life wife and mixed tag-team partner, Stephanie McMahon. She's writhing on the mat, and just as he bends over her, behind his back, someone steps into the ring. And the crowd loses its collective mind.

Ronda Rousey waves her hands in a taunt toward Triple H -- come here, come get me. The UFC Hall of Fame champion doesn't want to fight Triple H's tag partner. She wants to fight Triple H. For half a minute, Triple H puts her off. He stares her down. He scans the audience -- the 78,133 fans who, at this point, have reached a shrieking boil. He smiles, then nods. It's an invitation. Rousey charges, and she's nothing but a flurry of punches and strikes, a tornado that leaves Triple H cowed in the corner. After the hailstorm, she turns around and beelines for the ropes. She slingshots off them to charge at Triple H again, blocks his kick, throws him to the ground, then rolls over him, jumps to her feet and lifts him over her shoulders.

Perhaps it's a thawing of the ice. Last November, Becky Lynch took on James Ellsworth on SmackDown; three months after WrestleMania, SmackDown would again feature Ellsworth in another intergender match on July 3, this time pitting him against Asuka. Perhaps it'll remain an anomaly; when discussing the state of intergender wrestling in the WWE, Levesque, the company's executive vice president, will downplay its viability. "It's funny, people ask me about that all the time, about intergender wrestling, and I'm a proponent of it when it works [like] Mixed Match Challenge or WrestleMania last year with us," he says. "But I don't believe that it should be the norm. The women don't need a man in the ring with them to become a prime spot on the card. They don't need that to be the main event [in WWE]. They just need another woman in there that's as great as they are."

For now, though, there is intergender wrestling on the sport's biggest stage. Or at least a flirtation with intergender wrestling. When Asuka and Ellsworth meet on July 3, and then battle again a week later in a rematch, the shows prove more farce than physical feat. The first ends in a double count-out when Ellsworth flees and Asuka chases him over the barricade; the second sees Asuka make quick work of a comically overpowered Ellsworth. Much like last November versus Lynch, the physical mismatch is presented as much -- if not more -- about Ellsworth's failings as an athlete as it is Asuka's prowess.

Frankele isn't watching on July 3, nor a week later for the sequel. She was released from the WWE in March -- she says the WWE didn't provide much explanation, just told her to keep working hard -- and she doesn't keep close tabs now that she's on the outside looking in. But she catches wind of the match online, and it leaves her cold.

"Yes, it's cool that they're making the woman look like somebody who could be that intimidating," she says. "But for someone like me, who works places where you see full-length matches of women really given time and a chance to put in some effort? It's a little disappointing.

"It's one of those things where you're just like, 'Oh, yay.' Then you're like, 'Oh. Kind of not yay.'"

Still, intergender wrestling remains the biggest fight, the biggest cause, of her career, Frankele says. "Maybe the reason everything lined up in the universe like this is because I'm supposed to go out there and make intergender an even bigger thing," she says. "And then I'm going to come back and be one of the people that wrestles the dudes in WWE.

"Never say never."

Manasi Nene - The Stare:
Empowerment in Women's Wrestling

Manasi Nene is a writer and filmmaker from Pune, India, who is currently working on a short documentary about Pro Wrestling Eve. Her Twitter is twitter.com/manasi_nene

Children should be seen, not heard, goes the common idiom. We like having them around, it gives us some kind of security. Give them an opinion though, maybe some actual emotions – things start getting inconvenient for the status quo. The same goes for women.

I went to a Catholic all-girls' school in Pune, India, and it's difficult to unlearn a lot of that behaviour. Walk with your hands behind your back, speak only when you're spoken to. Raise your hand when you want to ask a question – but only certain questions will be entertained. Especially questions like, "Where are all the female saints?", and "Why didn't Jesus have a sister?" Which, forgive me if I'm wrong, seem perfectly valid in an environment where you're told never to talk to boys because (it gets vague here) they're bad influences or something.

I'm all for children who won't treat my living room like an experiment in destruction. However, mix these expectations-from-children with expectations-from-women, and a different sort of toxicity starts to emerge. It's difficult to pinpoint – as a child, I was docile because of a fear of consequences, and as a young adult, quietness just arrived naturally. Young adulthood doesn't come with an announcement and entrance music, it just creeps up on you, like internalized misogyny or period cramps.

I'm Indian, and it's impossible for me to ignore that while talking about women's wrestling. According to a recent report by Thomson Reuters

Foundation, India is the most dangerous country for women. This was ranked on the basis of "healthcare, economic resources, cultural or traditional practices, sexual violence and harassment, non-sexual violence and human trafficking [...] human trafficking, including sex slavery and domestic servitude, and for customary practices such as forced marriage, stoning and female infanticide." It's unfortunate that such a loud proclamation, by an organization of this repute, is based on a poll and not research metrics. They asked 550 (unnamed) experts on women's safety to rank countries, there isn't any on-the-ground primary research that can back up this claim. But nobody needs primary research to know that even if a country isn't the baddest country on the planet, growing up there can still be a harrowing experience.

How much of this affects me, personally, on a day-to-day? Not all that much, fortunately. I went to college, I'm not going to be married off anytime soon, I can get away with swearing and punk politics, so I've hit the gender jackpot in a lot of ways. There's one thing I can't escape though – and though this is largely a cultural thing, I can't imagine it's much different in other places around the world. I'm talking about The Stare.

If you're a woman who likes walking with a straight back, head high, you will be Stared At. That's just the fourth law of Newtonian physics, I'm sorry, I don't make the rules, this is just a scientific truth we have to live with. The Stare, as practiced by at least two out of five men on any given road, exists to remind you that this space is not yours. It's the most subtle kind of power-play, you have to give it some props for that. You're not in any direct danger from The Stare itself, physically. All it says, really, is you're an anomaly here. Your presence makes things awkward, and we're not going to tell you to go away in the language of enemies. We're just going to stare, say that you look pretty, say that you should smile more. The Stare accompanies all cat-calling, but cat-calling doesn't accompany all the Staring (#notallStares).

I don't think I need to write much more about cat-calling; I don't imagine there is a female reader of this book who hasn't come across it, who hasn't felt declawed, defanged, derailed in the face of a compliment from the other side of the street, or seen a friend in the same state. This isn't an essay about cat-calling, though; this is an essay about The Stare. It's an essay about art imitating life imitating art, about leaning on each other, about being okay with breaking some rules, and looking things in the eye. It's an essay about The Stare, and not blinking when The Stare tries to mess up your day.

My first introduction to wrestling was through Total Divas. Not the most promising start, I know, but bear with me. Those were some cold days, and I needed a distraction and some adrenaline. You know those days where it's just you, a blanket fort and some television? The Real Housewives of Everywhere Else weren't really cutting it any longer, and I'm not quite sure anymore how I even came across Total Divas. I'm so glad I did.

Total Divas, for those uninitiated, is a reality show on E! Channel, in America. E! is best known for its celebrity news stuff, award-show-red-carpet-stuff, and original programming like Rich Kids of Beverly Hills, WAGS LA (and its spin-offs WAGS Atlanta and WAGS Miami) and every iteration of maintaining a steady pace with the Kardashians. I often explain Total Divas as The Real Housewives of WWE, but that's a bit of a misdirection since none of these women are housewives, and any wrestling fan knows that when something is advertised as being Real, reality is probably the salt and not the main ingredient. But I digress. The show was, and still is, unlike anything else on television.

Early regulars on the show were Brie and Nikki Bella, Natalya, Naomi, Paige, Summer Rae and (saving the best for last) Eva Marie. Later cast-members include Maryse, Lana, and Alexa Bliss. None of these portrayals really scream tomboyness, bruises, punk feminist brashness, over-the-top hilarity, sticking it to the status quo, all the things I have grown to love about wrestling. These women are badass in the ring, without a doubt, but a show based on the lives of wrestlers was strangely lacking in black eyes and impossible travel schedules. Their lives seemed to be more about clothes and brunches and make-up and petty schoolgirl squabbles, with a sprinkling of hashtag feminism.

Which was intriguing, to say the least. I couldn't pull myself away. This was a version of femininity I had never seen before – makeup and bruises weren't antithetical, here was a perfect marriage. One just helped the other shine. In my Puneri catholic school, we grew up with a fantastic dose of Catholic prudishness and Hindu don't-talk-to-boys-till-you're-married-ness, and here were women who couldn't reign in this flitting sense of freedom even if they wanted to. I won't go into the vacuousness of WWE's feminist PR (there's another essay in this book for that) – but hashtags aside, there was genuinely something cool about seeing these two modes being places side by side. The makeup and the bruises were both just part of the deal. These women knew they exist in a male-dominated, male-gazey world, and they dressed the part. This world of dresses and makeup is what I instinctively ran away from – I was always the tomboy, and being in a girls' school is an odd negotiation for us tomboys – but here they were using it to subvert deeper and deeper expectations. Nikki Bella has a fashion line, Paige has a makeup line, and neither of these is necessarily endearing to a tomboyish wrestling fan – but these women have *literally* put their necks on the line for storytelling, and that's probably more than what the smarkiest smarks could ever contribute. That's something you can't help but admire.

And to anybody who has grown up in a solidly gendered environment, like India, with exponentially different expectations and modes of being – Nikki Bella and Paige stand out. I watched six seasons of the show before watching any actual wrestling. Especially if there's nobody to explain things to you along the way, wrestling can be amazingly intimidating to get into. But I saw Paige go through hell and back because she loved her art, and there's really no going back once you see someone literally stick their neck out, for storytelling, for art, their passion. I wasn't expecting much – the women in the show spoke at length about #GiveDivasAChance and empowerment, but there's a certain cynicism that comes with growing up a woman in this space.

This space, meaning one where we have a whole festival in honour of Durga, the fiercest goddess in any pantheon ever, and yet we also have the "purdah" - literally meaning curtain, a practice in a lot of rural India where it's unseemly for a woman to show her face. This space, meaning one where's been a National Commission for Women since 1992, in an attempt to balance the legal scales in our favour, yet marital rape is still not illegal. This space, meaning one where we've had astounding pioneers in politics, education, warfare, sports – Indira Gandhi, Savitribai Phule, Laxmibai of Jhansi, Mary Kom respectively, among others - and yet they're outliers in a country where we've also got astounding rates of female infanticide and foeticide – sex-selective abortions, carried out largely because the family would prefer a male child, who can earn and provide, instead a female one (who, in a particular sociological context, largely in rural India, cannot earn, and whose (inevitable) wedding and dowry will likely mean a financial burden).

This cynicism comes, largely, through the sociological extension of a psychological concept, the Madonna-Whore dichotomy. In Freud's time, it translated as an inability of some men to mix desire and affection in a healthy way – your partner could either be a Madonna (saintly, pure) or a whore (devilish, impure). Rarely both, rarely would they understand women to be as complex as men. And it's a concept which can be extended today – in pop culture, only recently have we started seeing women as more than Damsel In Distress or Strong Badass Woman. In most mythology, you'll see goddesses sitting comfortably at one of two poles.

My big Feminist Moment came in 2012, with the "Nirbhaya" case. It's impossible to open a newspaper without reading about sexual violence, but this instance is the one that galvanized a country of 1.2 billion to actually do something. A young woman and her partner were brutally assaulted in Delhi, and it's one of the more horrific cases you'll ever see (I won't go into details here, but a quick google search will tell you about its cultural impact). Since then, "women's safety" has been the loud proclamation of every politician, social worker, artist, every well-meaning young woke boy. It became a catch-all for a thousand kinds of discrimination, active or passive, and soon after the concept of "respect" followed.

Respect women. Keep them safe. That's great, fantastic, thank you – that does nothing for the people who are there doing the attacking, it's just an illusion of safety for those being attacked. A dichotomy followed – young men respecting women as goddesses on some distant pedestal, who need to be protected, or the angrier underbelly of men viewing women with even more disdain because our anger at someone's death had the gall to disturb the status quo. Flash forward seven years, it's still impossible to open a newspaper without reading about sexual violence, and I still don't like being outside at night; and politicians are still bandying about this vague notion of women's safety that just seems like an elaborate excuse to keep us inside houses for longer. We celebrate Kali, goddess of destruction, once a year. An angry, articulate woman is still an aberration, and a largely unwelcome one at that.

In this environment, Total Divas becomes an intense sociological exploration. These women wear bruises and makeup with equal ease, they fully occupy the space between two poles instead of picking one over the other. I was more intrigued than inspired – I was still too much of a tomboy to really identify with these women, and they existed too comfortably within the male gaze for me. Makeup is great when it's about feeling good about yourself – it's a little less great when it becomes part of a compulsion to look pretty everyday, and then to look beautiful everyday, and then to look sexy everyday. Nikki Bella was trying to sell sex to the men and sex-positivity to women - but is there no version of feminine power without desirability? That's a question for better philosophers than me – I just wanted to see this empowerment that they kept talking about so much.

I didn't really expect much – the women on Divas kept talking about a Women's Revolution, and then got into increasingly silly fights that didn't smell of empowerment or even adulthood. There's a kayfabe-within-kayfabe rivarly between Natalya and Lana that culminates in Nattie throwing Lana's phone and clothes into the ocean, because Lana toilet-paper'd Nattie's room, because Nattie told her not to be a brat about picking rooms in a house they'd rented for the weekend. I knew wrestling was a carny business, and that they'd sell what needed to be sold. I was curious about women's wrestling but if Nikki Bella was the standard-bearer for it, I knew it would remain a passing curiosity at best.

Then I found Becky v Charlotte v Sasha at WrestleMania 32, and everything changed.

I'm not sure how I came across that match – the full version was on YouTube for a while, I must have typed "women's wrestling" into the search bar, and followed the rabbit hole. It doesn't matter how I came across it though, it's okay if I don't remember the particulars. The only thing I really remember is the shiver of electricity up my back, when I saw their entrances. Becky's heart. Sasha's swag. Charlotte's well-earned bitchiness. These aren't things you forget easily, especially when they're such outliers in your world. You don't forget your first frogsplash, your first suicide dive. When you're not used to seeing women raise their voice, let alone do dropkicks and armbars, you're not likely to forget irish-puns-metalhead vs pink-hair-swagass-acrobat vs biceps-barbie. And you're *definitely* not going to forget the fact that biceps-barbie's dad won her the match. You're *definitely* going to tune in for the next episode, to see what happens. You're *definitely* invested when each of Becky's kickouts gives you a physical euphoria, when you channel Sasha's confidence to deal with your own social anxiety, when you remember the ferocious grace of Charlotte's moonsault and finally, it hits you, that the makeup and bruises don't need to be enemies.

And that's fitting for a match designed around renaming the title, the division – this match would determine the first Women's Champion, and lay the Divas Title to rest. These people – *women*, not divas - are as human as you and me; they didn't emerge from the womb with a moonsault manual or boulder shoulders. These women have also grown up knowing The Stare. More than likely, these women have also grown up feeling unsafe. More than likely, these women have also been told to be quiet, been placed on pedestals they didn't ask for and been knocked down over things they didn't deserve.

And these women put all that aside, because they had a job to do. They put on their makeup, they put on their boots, they *fought*, and they made it look like the prettiest damn thing in the whole damn world. They knew the world would stare; so they figured out how to own it. They knew the world didn't expect a fight from pretty women; so they dolled up and hulked up and stepped up to the spotlight. The particulars of post-Man Becky, of Charlotte's lost momentum, of Sasha burning out for a business she loves so much – they don't matter so much in the long run. But knowing that they started small, and showed a generation how to *stare back* – that matters to me. Knowing that they *fight* back, and kick out after the toughest beatdowns – that matters to me. Knowing that these women, who started small, without boulder shoulders, without moonsaults, can be at the top of their business, by unleashing everything we have been taught to put away – that matters to me. Knowing that you can be godawfully beautiful and still kick ass, that matters to me.

Who cares if it's a story? It's still real to me, dammit – it doesn't matter who wins or loses, what matters is how they made me feel. Asuka doesn't stop being a badass because Charlotte broke her streak. Sonya Deville's idiotic booking cannot diminish the fact that she celebrates the weirdness of the outsider, and we need more of that. For all their annoyingness, I can't stop stanning The Iiconics. A common parlance in wrestling is that a good character is just yourself turned up to eleven – women's wrestling takes all the dots between makeup and bruises, and turns them into devious virtues. Alexa Bliss is as valid as Rhea Ripley. There's something very freeing about that.

And that's only with respect to one company, and one kind of storytelling. Let's not forget the indies, where women choose how to sculpt their characters. Let's not forget Pro Wrestling Eve and Shimmer, who aim to take wrestling out of a purely male gaze and showcase the most brilliantly badass women in the world. On the indies, you have your standard badasses – Mercedes Martinez, Rhea O'Reilly, Tessa Blanchard – but also people like Priscilla Kelly and Session Moth Martina, whose every appearance pushes the bounds of what's an acceptable version of womanhood. The glass gutter, if you will; an important counterpoint to the glass ceiling. Others have written more eloquently and with more authority; I can't really write much about the indies from my vantage point in India. Indian wrestling itself is fairly new and inexperienced, and I can't really say a women's wrestling scene even exists now that Kavita Devi is signed in Florida. It's going to take a long (long, long, long) time to embody the Sasha-Becky-Charlotte kind of swag here, especially while wrestling remains a largely blue-collar entertainment. Being in the public (male) eye is still just scary, and no amount of well-intentioned logic can change that for a while.

The facts don't change, and the Stare doesn't change. But these women have helped me change, and for the better. A lot of WWE's feminist rhetoric rings incredibly empty, and one can't ever ignore the carny-capitalist core of it. Is it really "hope" or "history" if they stage a women's match in Dubai or Saudi Arabia? Inasmuch as there's hope for monopolistic expansion of a television empire, inasmuch as any recorded events are history – they're not lying, so much as bending the truth for their PR purposes. The empowerment doesn't come from a company giving the women a Mae Young Classic or an Evolution, or scripting three women to put on the biggest match at the biggest event of the year and calling it progress. It comes from all the women that made themselves undeniable, moved tickets and merch, did their job better than anyone else in the world, man or woman, to a point where giving them the biggest spotlight at WM35 was the only logical business decision. The empowerment doesn't come from one company, or one pay-per-view, or one match. It comes from women carving out their own corner in this almost-entirely-dominated-by-the-male-gaze business, by being there and fighting and giving no quarter to the Stare, and asking no mercy from The Stare.

And now I feel like I can hold The Stare. I don't yet know if I can kick out, or fight back, and I definitely can't dropkick or moonsault or look as stunning as these women. I don't doubt that I'll get there, though. There's something about stories and characters that inspires us because if they can do it, so can you. In wrestling it feels even bigger – these characters are flesh and blood, not light on a screen or ink on a page. Interpret this however you want, that makes it more real. Of course this will still be within the male gaze, of course there will be stares. But if they can fight back, so can I.

And that will always make me stand a little bit taller, and talk a little bit sharper.
Woo!

Valerie Quartz - Wrestling and the Gay Community

Valerie "Baru" Quartz is a seamstress and the woman behind Daryl Apparyl currently residing in Phoenix, AZ. She is passionate about cats, kindness, and a good soft pretzel. Val make clothes for Daryls! (and people too) via etsy.com/shop/DarylApparyl and she is a part of the tarotsupercard.bigcartel.com project. Her Twitter is twitter.com/valcano.

If you told me three years ago that wrestling would be what helped me proudly embrace my sexuality, I don't think I would have believed you. I started watching wrestling because a roommate suggested it, and I figured it would be as fun to watch as any Super Bowl party I'd attended for the snacks and socializing. As someone who values community, my main motivation was the excuse to gather a group of people and share an experience together.

That's what wrestling is to me: a shared experience with others who are passionate about the art form and connect to it in diverse and meaningful ways. When my love for the sport began to blossom, many friends and co-workers were puzzled by my enthusiasm for such a violent and male-dominated form of entertainment. I was a 30-year-old woman, working as a 4th grade teacher, certainly not what most think of as the standard wrestling demographic. And I *was* reluctant at first. Wrestling has a reputation as a redneck sport, as something that wasn't for me. Would I be welcomed or condescended to? Would the fandom let me value wrestling more for its camp, glamour, and drama than for the technical aspects of the sport?

However, as I watched, I saw so many examples that went against the hyper-masculine wrestler stereotype. I was instantly drawn to the wrestler donning checkers and dancing to ska music who, in real life, used his platform to raise funds for a mobile medical clinic in Syria. I was deeply invested in the stories of hard work, friendship, betrayal, and finding the light within to overcome the dark. When I looked around, I saw that I wasn't alone, that so many others were connecting to these stories and having their own emotional and passionate reactions.

One of the biggest stories in the early days of this growing infatuation with wrestling was the reunion of the Golden Lovers, a tag team made up of Kenny Omega and Kota Ibushi whose saga and love story had been building for years. Though this certainly is not the only queer story of importance in wrestling, it's the first one I encountered. It touched me deeply. Seeing others on Twitter connect to this story in the same way was so exciting and affirming! I have always been a bisexual woman, but felt I wasn't "gay enough" to own that as part of my identity. The saga of the Golden Lovers put me in touch with others who were equally moved and had been waiting for queer representation in their media. I had found my people! I felt seen, validated, and proud of my sexuality. We were a group of people who had dealt so much with ridicule and alienation, but had chosen to become stronger and kinder as a result of those experiences. Whenever I sheepishly tried a new creative endeavor, the gay community on wrestling Twitter supported me and cheered me on. Reassuring talks of mental health and encouragement were prevalent and normalized among my mutuals. Wrestling introduced us, but we formed a community and thrived because we chose to take care of one another.

Before ALL IN, my friend Lisa (@evilpeach) put out an invite for an LGBTQ+ friendly meet-up called Y'ALL IN. Ecstatic for the opportunity to gather in person with my favorite corner of wrestling twitter, I ordered Y'ALL IN lanyards and made personalized badges with each attendee's name, twitter handle, and pronouns. We had so much fun that we repeated this event a year later in Dallas and called it the Y'ALL IN CLIMAX. Both of these days were full of smiles, excited conversation, and a strong sense of belonging. Folk brought friends, wrestling zines they had worked on, cosplay, and even a bulk order of folding fans to aid against the Texas heat. The opportunity to help create a safe space where one doesn't feel the need to explain who they are is incredibly valuable.

It is from the warmth and enthusiasm of this community that the Tarot Supercard Project was born. Thirty-five artists collaborated to make a wrestling-themed tarot deck. We drew inspiration from each of the 78 cards and how they were originally depicted, then matched them to wrestlers we felt embodied the spirit or visual representation. And yes, the first card we started with was "The Lovers" featuring Kenny and Kota! Because of the number of contributors, the project has a lot of heart and diversity when it comes to artistic styles and representation of what wrestling means to our community. The Tarot Supercard Project will also be contributing part of the proceeds to the Kaleidoscope LGBT Youth Center. This tarot deck is so special because it embodies the spirit of the gay community I found through wrestling. We are a group of passionate and creative individuals making connections, making ourselves visible, and making our community stronger with our talents and abilities.

Jason Norris - The WrestleMania 35 Experience, and the Fallout for the Women's Division of WWE

Book curator and editor. Jason is a lifelong wrestling fan who conducts wrestling interviews or argues with friends on The Holy Shoot Wrestling Podcast. He co-runs Europe's largest Meet Up group for wrestling fans called Watch Wrestling London. Tweet him at twitter.com/WrestlingLondon.

(Billie, the friend mentioned in this chapter, passed away unexpectedly several months after the trip. Knowing that going to a WrestleMania was on his bucket list makes me happy to have shared these moments with my friend. Rest peacefully Billie, you are missed.)

There she was, Session Moth Martina, in the Hooters by Penn Station, New York New York, on the day of WrestleMania 35. Friends and I had been 'victims' of the Martina attack/grind at a couple of shows back home in London and I was a big fan of her act. For context, you should know Martina comes to the ring with an open beer, a bag of cans, refers to having 78 kids and grinds on everyone from the referee to women in the front row. If anything Hooters was too classy for her character, she should have been outside with a can of Stella on the go while dancing on confused tourists. I would later see Martina play the sperm that was impregnated and went on to become Kris Wolf at Kris' retirement show in the Resistance Gallery a few weeks later (yes really). For now she was surrounded by the iconic beer and wings in the Hooters restaurant right by Penn station, the lunch stop for many that historic day.

We were in New York for a week for the full WrestleMania experience, and apart from twice bumping into Matt Riddle in two rather cool situations in an eighteen-hour period, we had not seen any wrestlers outside of the events we attended. I am told in New Orleans the previous year you could not move without tripping over a WWE or indy star, but New York is a vast place with events across the boroughs, and the last people I expected to see were UK indy scene regulars Martina, Chris Brookes and an (unmasked!) Kid Lycos.

The chance however to get a picture with Session Moth was lost due to people arriving and blocking me into out booth, while other fans were then going to the table to say hello before the group left. There was just too much going on and too much of buzz to get that photo, but we did say hello to Chris Brookes on his way out and wished him well. He explained that all the Indy wrestlers in New York were off to bars to watch the big show, and not spend their hard-earned money from the week on the expensive WrestleMania experience out in New Jersey. These are people that I have seen many times in the UK, and Martina's act is never going to play well on WWE TV, so it was a reminder of the wider wrestling world on the biggest day of the year. I cannot imagine someone who collapses in the ring and hulks up by having the ref pass her a can of beer, and then wrestles as if drunk, is ever going to make it to PG WWE programming in 2020.

I was ticking something off my bucket list. We were staying in Brooklyn, taking in Indy shows, WrestleCon, NXT, Axxess, RAW and the granddaddy of them all that is WrestleMania. You don't know what a WrestleMania is? Imagine if the NFL Superbowl, Halloween, the season finale of Game of Thrones and an AC/DC concert had an orgy and sold tickets. That is WrestleMania.

This year it was different for me. Rather than watching the big show the following day (it starts at midnight in the UK), a group of friends had organized themselves to have a week in New York to see this historic show, the first time in 35 years that women were the main event. I am not going to lie and say this was the only reason seven lads from London were going to be there, but all were fans of the women involved and wanted it to be the main event. This is the story of that day and a reflection on how all of the women on the show were treated; did WWE and the old man pull it off, or did they (metaphorically) shit the bed?

76

Before getting to New Jersey for WrestleMania we had the aforementioned brush with greatness that was Session Moth Martina in Hooters. Another highlight earlier that week had been my friend Broderick meeting his favorite and fellow Scot, Nikki Cross at Axxess, who also organized a grumpy Erick Rowan, James Drake and Zack Gibson alongside the waiting crowd to sing Happy Birthday to him. At the same Axxess my friend Billie and I were lucky to have photos taken with the super friendly Ricky Steamboat and Lana; I will let you guess what meant more to me as a lifelong wrestling fan who still thinks Steamboat vs Randy Savage is the greatest match ever (from WrestleMania 3). My friend Wes had managed to meet his long-time favorite Gail Kim at the WrestleCon event while the rest of us saw Tessa Blanchard at the Wrestling Revolver show in an intergender match, which confirmed us as huge fans for her. Now that is a true Horsewoman. Tessa was clearly becoming a huge star, we watched as a huge queue built at her convention table later, people waiting for her to arrive while Joey Ryan did the nice thing and set it up for her while he ate Cheetos.

Back to Sunday afternoon, the day of WrestleMania. The seven of us were now at Penn Station, on our way to Middle of Nowhere, New Jersey, the location of the Meadowlands Sports Complex. First thing we learned? New Jersey is not that close to New York despite what WWE tells you. We had to change at a station on the way for a special stadium service, which is where the wrestling fans were now merging into a mass of humanity, with lots of fun with Adam Cole (Bay Bay) and Uso chants on the platform and then on the train. I was quite proud that when an American guy tried to get a cheer for 'Bring back the attitude era' a couple of the younger lads in our group let out a clear 'NO!' These guys had missed that era, blaming their age of all excuses, but had caught up on those peak years and found it over rated with problems around the treatment of women, the racism and its general crudeness.

We got to MetLife Stadium early to take the show in, to be honest an event of this scale is a little intimidating and I like to get my bearings. Once all sorted we found our seats in the lower bowl and you soon learned you were going to need to look at screens a lot of the time due to the distance, but it was still a great spot to watch the entrances.

The now annual tradition of a women's over the top rope battle royal was the second match on the show, with a special moment as former ring announcer Lillian Garcia returned to WWE to handle the introductions of all involved. Most of the women all walked to the ring together without their own theme tunes playing, with Naomi the first to get a separate entrance. I found this odd as she was doing nothing at this point even despite winning last year, whereas Asuka was the second to get her own walk to the ring, which made much more sense. Asuka, the former world champion. The woman who beat Becky Lynch at the Royal Rumble just months before. The woman who beat Lynch and Charlotte Flair in a ladder match. The clear favorite, at least she was being featured for the start of the match.

There were some early highlights such as a crazed Nikki Cross and surprise entrant Candice LeRae getting some attention, before Asuka warmed up by eliminating both. The Riott Squad showed great teamwork while Sonya Deville rocked a rainbow flag in her back pocket, but on the downside Dana Brooke looked awful throwing herself over the top rope, and after her warm up Asuka went missing for most of the match. She awoke when it was down to 'three' but in an upset Asuka was thrown out and Sarah Logan seemed to win, before Carmella appeared from under the ring. She had been forgotten about for the entire match and stole the victory in what appeared to be a crowd-pleasing moment, but for fans upset with how Asuka had been pushed to one side in recent weeks this was a hard pill to swallow. At least the match was better than the men achieved later with Braun and the Saturday Night Live guys.

An hour later the main show kicked off with pyro and the expected big event mood setting, followed by our host Alexa Bliss appearing on stage. She was the first woman to be given the hosting honor at WrestleMania and she looked like a natural as her charm worked for the waiting audience. The crowd was happy to see her, despite her mean girl character it seems most people were fans and appreciated her efforts. Then she was given credit for bringing out Hulk Hogan, who received a mix response from the crowd, something he faces at all shows since racist comments were made with a less than full apology offered. Not the kind of stink you want on your host, but Alexa went all in, posing with Hogan before disappearing for the first of many outfit changes.

The next involvement of women on the main show was the appearance of the HOF class of 2019 on stage, featuring Torrie Wilson as the designated women entrant of the year at the main ceremony the previous night. WWE seems to have a policy of one dead person, one manager, one group and one woman among the acts they induct each year, and it was Torrie's time. She may never have been Madusa or Sensational Sherri in the ring for WWE, and for many her dog barking and lingerie matches were a part of a very different (attitude) era, but there was no doubt that Torrie was a star that worked hard and drew fans. The most important inductee of the night was instead a woman that fans had campaigned for to get the honor. The late Chyna (Joan Laurer) made it as part of the D-generation-X faction, but not on her own, this year. While it was great to see this much-deserved recognition, really Chyna needs her own moment. Shawn Michaels gave a minute to acknowledge Chyna, to huge fan applause, but the induction the previous night had mainly been the men goofing off, while the arguments against her getting the spotlight continue to ring hollow. Weak excuses related to her leaving on bad terms and appearing in pornographic movies have been offered, when male stars with even worse relationships with WWE, and well documented controversies, have had that hall of fame moment.

The first big women's match on the main card was for the new tag titles. In fact, only two matches on the entire main card featured women and both were centered on title feuds, no other storylines were ongoing to justify other matches on the main card. That time on a very long show was apparently needed for a 25-minute Triple H hardcore match and backstage comedy spots with the two guys from Saturday Night Live that few people in this international crowd knew of.

This match also featured eight of the roster, with stars such as Sasha Banks and Bayley, Nia Jax and Tamina, established tag teams, and the return of Beth Phoenix to team once again with Natalya Hart, someone that could still go and show up most of the roster. We ended up with an upset as The Iiconics, an enjoyable but still a comedy act, won the belts by taking advantage of the damage Beth has inflicted champion Bayley. Both Billie Kay and Peyton Royce looked genuinely moved to tears following the victory. It was a shame in the months to follow they disappeared from television, while most people remember this match for the rumored tantrum of Sasha Banks in the locker room before she took time off (which was never confirmed to actually have happened but created lots of clicks for wrestling news sites).

The next major contribution to the show from a woman was the return of Carmella, alongside R-Truth, for a dance break. While these can be fun at smaller non-TV shows, it was close to midnight by this point and we were waiting for our main event after that preshow had started seven hours ago, so really people just wanted this moment to end.

Midnight. The main event production had now started. This was getting really late when the show takes place in a hard to access part of New Jersey. Parents have brought their young girls and boys to see this historic moment, and many of them missed it. I sat and watched the rows around us start to empty as I heard one dad tell his kids 'We'll watch the rest tomorrow, we have to get you home as its school tomorrow morning'.

Hell, one of my fully-grown adult friends sat elsewhere said he fell asleep during this down time as so many struggled to keep their energy up.

And so, the main event. The historic moment we had been waiting was due to start, but first Charlotte had to arrive by helicopter and via a red carpet for the Queen. In addition, Ronda needed her theme song played by Joan Jett. At least they were getting impressive entrances, but happening an hour earlier would have been ideal after a long period of nothingness adding to the late time for the bell to actually ring. Becky got more of a 'woman of the people' entrance and the crowd was with her to full applause, clearly keeping something in reserve for their hero. Then the bell finally rang.

The match had the usual issues that you get from a three-way contest, where one of the three usually has to take a big move and be kept out of the match for a little bit, until they swap with someone, and repeat. Each woman in this match is an accomplished performer so it was enjoyable, with some good use of tables and signature spots each is known for. Then it just ended. Out of nowhere. The crowd was completely deflated as we tried to work out what was going on, as we had all seen the crucifix leverage pin by Becky onto Ronda, and we had all seen that Ronda's shoulders were not down for a full three count. It was messy conclusion to a match that had been building to a bigger finish than this.

It was such an underwhelming moment, such a lackluster finish. People had waited for this, they wanted Becky to tap Ronda out, and that was the storyline as they each favored an armbar submission, neither being know for their pin attempts. We watched the replays and everyone got up to leave as Becky celebrated and we cheered, but it was not the moment we wanted.

Ideally, the show would have ended an hour earlier with a clean victory for Becky. Instead, the show was five and a half hours following a two-hour preshow, and while we wanted to give Becky what she deserved, many of her young fans had gone home and most of those remaining were getting tired while starting to work out if they were going to make the train out of New Jersey. Thousands ended up stranded in New Jersey as a torrential storm hit and the trains had stopped running due to the late finish, while my group made one of the last trains back to New York.

We had enjoyed WrestleMania and were finishing out night in an Irish bar with shots at 2:30 in the morning. We had been to a WrestleMania and most of the show had been great fun, but man was it a slog at times and did it end with a whimper when it should have been a crack of thunder.

Coming out of the show, quite a lot changed and some opportunities were missed. The battle royal win was ignored and Carmella kept doing comedy with R-Truth, while Sasha Banks disappeared off TV for months as rumors circulated about her ever returning (she did eventually). While the Iiconics had a run with the belts it amounted to nothing with little TV time to build their act, before Alexa Bliss and Nikki Cross formed an odd couple tag team that actually worked really well and won the titles. The fans eventually accepting Alexa as a babyface, rather than a faker waiting to betray another friend as she had done in the past, seemingly won over by the enthusiasm rather than the naivety of Nikki. Nia Jax also disappeared from TV due to surgery, while Tamina just disappeared as she had a habit of doing. Ronda Rousey also went from being one of the biggest stars in the company for the past year to seemingly quitting wrestling despite the hype of a multi-year contract, indicating in interviews her focus on now starting a family. Charlotte Flair, seen as the star of the women's roster for several years, was a mess of booking as she flipped from bad to good, and we think back to a bad queen again, with two forgettable title reigns on SmackDown along the way (one lasted 5 days, the other 5 minutes). With a record ten championship reigns for WWE, all since 2015, each seems less relevant rather than legacy building for Charlotte at this stage.

Coming out of WrestleMania however, a new Man had been anointed, with Becky truly being given the ball. She held the major women's championship for a record period of time, headlined shows around the world, sold a lot of merchandise, was the number one draft pick come October and remained the champion as 2019 ended. WWE definitely has not aced this test, with misses including the lack of an all women's event or tournament as seen in 2018, and the continued male dominated shows in a country such as Saudi Arabia, a pure cash grab at the expense of their integrity. There was also more focus put on Seth Rollins and new shiny toy The Fiend, with diminishing returns, as the year progressed.

The Man is still the story of 2019 for WWE, beating all challengers, and via their development system WWE looks set to bring through some world class performers to pair her with in 2020. It will be the coming year when we truly learn if this was a short-term endorsement or if the women get to move beyond firsts such as WrestleMania main events and make such occurrences the norm.

Manasi Nene - The Boss and The Bard:
Reflections on Shakespeare and Pro Wrestling

Manasi Nene is a writer and filmmaker from Pune, India, who is currently working on a short documentary about Pro Wrestling Eve. https://twitter.com/manasi_nene.

Thou know'st thy part. Thou art not a bit-part player, of ever-decreasing import to the stage. Forsooth, good madam!

Thou art but a mortal, ready to wear the clothes of something else entirely. Something imaginary, something unreal. Yet, this seems more real than the rest of your life. The theatre, it's a story you can control, with a beginning, middle and an end. You've always loved books; they offer this kind of simplicity.

But what you really love is being there with the story, with the crowd roaring, analyzing everything you do, cheering at all the right moments. It's tense, it's dangerous. Romeo and Juliet die at the end, as does Macbeth, as does Desdemona, everyone knows this. But in the comedies, everyone always gets married and lives happily ever after. Everyone knows this.

You're about to get to the stage. Play, alarums and drums, to herald your alive. Sing choir, sing! Sound alive, lest thy part be anything less than spectacular.

Spectacle, that's what this is. The "spectacle of excess", in the words of that worthy nobleman, Roland Barthes.

Welcome to the world of pro wrestling.

Odd idea, right? The most enthusiastic person you know, w.r.t pro wrestling, is your five-year-old kid brother, whose other big loves are football and mud. The most enthusiastic person you know w.r.t Shakespeare are the irritating aunties from the posh part of town, the ones who are two feet away from becoming crazy cat ladies and they always correct your grammar, even when you explain that language isn't fixed in stone.

They're drawn by the same thing(s). These aren't (necessarily) just the tights and muscles.

"But it's not real" doesn't really ever count as a valid critique of pro wrestling. It's as real as Shakespeare is. It's as real as Harry Potter. In fact it's probably more real than Harry Potter, which had magic, dragons, and a grown man with a vendetta against a young boy. My letter from Hogwarts never arrived. But it's still real to me, dammit.

Wrestling doesn't have magic. It has bodyslams, sure, but it's all still a dance, which is choreographed around conflict. In classical literary theory, this is necessary for catharsis – the resolution after the hero's journey. Your protagonist (whether it's Hamlet or Hulk Hogan) has to go through an undecided amount of drama, before emerging either victorious or defeated. That's how stories work everywhere. That's why you care about them. Or at least, that's why I care about them. Sure, they're all made up. But it's still real to me, dammit.

In the big wonderful world of literary criticism, the "carnivalesque" is probably my favourite concept. It's about doing things you're not allowed to. It's about doing things you're not supposed to. Like making poop jokes. Or making fun of your boss. Or genderbending. Or making fart jokes. There's a rich history to this, there really is.

You know why the carnivalesque is called the carnivalesque? Of course you do, let me not insult your intelligence. It comes from the simple spirit of a village carnival.

And you know what else comes from village carnivals? You guessed it, wrestling.

Theatre before Shakespeare was more in the tradition of "morality plays" - plays based on the Bible, that taught you how to live. There were very clearly defined good and bad characters. Of course this bled into other performance traditions, especially the drama that emerged right afterwards.

The baddest bad guys, though, were the wrestlers. The ones who'd challenge the whole village. And it would be a really big deal, when someone beat them. In fact, that's how Orlando starts out in As You Like It. Eventually, carnival-capitalists realized there's more money to be made off crowds, so they started turning these fights into dramatic spectacles. Somewhere along the way, this really blew up. So then we're at a point where everyone knows that theatre is staged - literally, it happens on a stage - but nobody except a select few know that wrestling - or, to use a better term, pro-wrestling – is staged.

This is the same kind of logic (or leap of logic) that takes place when parents try to tell their kids about Santa Claus. Someone is in on the fiction, and somebody else isn't. Everyone knows that other forms of fiction - movies, books, fake news - are fiction, so it's not a big deal when you cry during The Notebook. But to be surprised at a plot twist in a wrestling match? There's going to be some smartass who tells you it's all fake. Wrestling is as fake as Shakespeare, but it's also as real as Shakespeare. Both have grown from the carnivalesque and from morality plays - there's a clear sense of good and bad (usually), there's a clear sense of authority. The most important, though, is that there's a clear sense of spectacle.

There are stories being told, in front of you. Now that performance art is past the age of GG Allin and John Cage, it's time to see how these stories are told. Lit-crit has to keep up with the times, yo.

The "hero's journey" is one of the most enduring analytical structures in any kind of storytelling. It's not just found in epic poetry with quests and treasure, but pretty much every story ever told. There's a hero/ine, and s/he wants a thing. It's difficult to get this thing, so your hero/ine must devise ways of overcoming obstacles (often placed by, or embodied by, other characters). In the end, by the end of the narrative, the hero/ine may or may not have the thing. As the audience, you really want them to get the thing, so you're as emotionally invested in this as the character is. And thereby hangs a tale.

That's what makes any narrative tick – Frodo really wants to destroy the ring, and Sam and Gandalf really want to see this happen, but Smeagol and Saruman really don't want to let this happen. Of course they all have other motivations as well, but this conflict-of-interest is what drives everything along. The world-building is undoubtedly a huge part of any narrative, but there isn't any world to build if you don't have compelling characters travelling through them.

Macbeth wants to be king. But Macduff wants to take him down. Much the same way as any wrestler wants the belt, and other wrestlers want to take him/her down.

Though wrestling does run on the idea of "face" vs "heel" (the good vs the bad), every match is essentially a step in the race to the championship belt. We're invested because we want to see our favourite wrestlers win. The faces are noble characters, who play fair, but keep falling prey to the wiles and slyness of the heels. And unlike Tolkien's world where we rarely get to see the "dark" side in action, wrestling shows us the journeys of both characters, the good and the bad.

Deviousness is itself turned into an art.

And for anyone who has ever cheered a heel, I'm sure this sounds familiar.

Imagine this : your father is a very powerful man, and your brother is very powerful as well. In fact, he's the most eligible bachelor in all seven kingdoms because he's handsome, he's rich, and he's better at using his sword than anyone else around. You're pretty, that's about all you have going for you. You aren't going to get the land, the title, the gold, nothing. All you can hope for, is a good husband. There's this guy you really like, but he's taken. Also your father is trying to wage war against his people, so that someone else - let's call him Bob - can take over the throne. Bob's not your type, but he's okay.

Bob gets the throne, and now he's the most powerful man in the seven kingdoms. Great! Except, none of that power is yours. You have three children, destined for greatness, and you love them with the ferocity of a lion. You want the best for them. Bob and his clowns aren't going to be able to do that. Plus, Bob has a drinking problem, and goes to bed with a different woman every night. You don't mind this, you expected it. But court is a mess, and you keep cleaning it up. You've never got any real power - you're a woman, and people hold it against you. Horrible things happen your brother and father. Your older son is poisoned (presumably by your slimy other brother), your daughter is shipped off to a strange land, and your youngest son becomes horribly infatuated with a woman who wants nothing more than to take over your position in court. She's not too great for your son, either.

So when you do finally blow up a sept or two in the season finale of Game of Thrones, it would probably be a moment of major catharsis.

Then comes another — younger, more beautiful — to cast thee down and take all thou hold'st dear.
Characters are defined by the ethical choices they make, in good times and in bad. Mostly bad, because we can never have nice things. You'd

never have any interesting fiction, if nice things kept happening. The protagonist and the antagonist have opposing interests, and as the audience you're given the privilege of following one's thought process right till the end.

There aren't that many narratives with a bad person as the protagonist. Sure, there are antiheroes, and they're a narratological blessing - but it's rare to find a coherent explanation of why the antagonist wants what s/he wants. We just know them because they are not the protagonist. Because they stand in the way. But they also have a rich sense of ethics, of motivation, just as the protagonist does. We just don't get to see it.

What wrestling and Shakespeare teach us about villains, that isn't so easily evident in more subtle narrative art, is about the ethical logic of the fictional world. There's a fixed set of rules that one is expected to adhere to. The good adhere to it, the bad (often) don't. The stage, it's its own universe. You can't hit people with steel chairs, unless you're on stage. You can't employ murderers to take out your rivals, unless you're on stage.

I mean, you can, but then people would just hate you very, very much. You'd probably go to jail, because as a populace, that's the ethical rule we've written for ourselves.

Lady Macbeth just wants to see her husband become more powerful, and she supports him as much as she can – you can't fault her for that. You can fault her for murder, treason, if that's your ethical backbone. Everyone is pretty violent, conflict is what makes stories tick. But everyone isn't violent in the same way.

In Shakespeare's more "royal" plays (the historical plays and the tragedies) it's impossible to run away from violence and murder. You can't run from violence in the ring, either. It's difficult to be any kind of "good guy" if you've spent half an hour beating someone up. Offstage, you'd go to jail for that kind of violence. But on stage, because it's incorporated into the ethical logic of the fictional universe, that sort of violence is fine.

The "heel" must prove villain to two completely different entities - the hero and the audience. The audience must also revile him/her, otherwise what's the point of the performance? And the hero must also revile him/her, otherwise what's the point of the script?

And that's where it gets interesting.

Shakespeare had to be entertaining, in whatever way he could. He had to make some ca$h for his company, The King's Men. He had to beat out that bore Marlowe and that brat Ben Jonson.

What he seemed to have done right was establish character conflict in the first act, if not the first scene, and from there the stakes keep getting higher and higher, until the end. Your "protagonist" side will either win or lose, that's that. Maybe both - Richard 3 and Macbeth both got what they wanted, and also pretty gory endings. Cosmic justice, some would say. The actors are contracted to fulfil their role in the story, production after production, and they know exactly what's expected.

Pro wrestling, however, is a strange circus world that just goes on and on and on, with character journeys going on far beyond title reigns. But they also have to make some ca$h for the company, and they do it the same way Shakespeare did - by establishing character conflict, and raising the stakes. Richard III and Macbeth are pretty solid heels - the plays work because you're not a fan, but you follow their journeys anyway. There's no illusion, that they are good guys - they're power hungry murderers, plain and simple. You're supposed to hate them. The more you hate them, the more invested you get.

When a performer goes out of his/her way to antagonize someone, there's a method to this madness. In wrestling, the faces and heels want the victory/the championship belt, and both go about procuring it differently. One is supposed to make us love them, and one is supposed to make us hate them. The heels are there to break all kinds of made-up rules. It doesn't always work. But when it works, it works because their villainy gets us to care. And if you're a grown adult wearing outlandish costumes and performing your outlandish act for a different crowd every night, that's saying something. And heel-turns and face-turns, they're part of the game. Remember Snape's face-turn in Harry Potter and the Half-Blood Prince? A lot of people will still glorify him, for turning from villain to hero in such a swift move. And remember Macbeth's heel-turn? He started off as a good guy, but we still remember him as a villain.

Both these fictions work because the audience isn't just involved in the protagonists - both Shakespeare and wrestling work as performances because they also get you emotionally involved in the stories of the antagonists. With drama building on both sides of the conflict, the catharsis isn't a happy side-effect. The point, however, is the creation of the largest spectacle possible.

I mean, there's a reason that Roland Barthes, the ultimate posterboy of literary theory, called this the "Spectacle of Excess" - this grandiloquence which must have been that of ancient theatres, it's more common than you'd think. This goes back to the most spectacular of myths - David v Goliath, Ram v Raavan, Tom v Jerry, etc. If you have a really good goodguy and a really bad badguy, then you've got a really big show. If you have a really big show, then you have lots of ca$h. This is something that all artists, starving in their garrets, have made great use of.

Especially William Shakespeare. With his saccharine-sweet goodpeople and his cartoonishly evil badpeople (who always had better lines) and his amazingly high stakes, he knew exactly what he was doing.

Except, he wasn't very forward when it came to the wimmenfolks. We can cut him some slack - a proper mass sensibility w.r.t the rights of women wasn't born until almost two centuries after Shakespeare, when Mary Wollstonecraftwrote A Vindication on The Rights of Woman in 1792. And even then, it took a while to catch on.

"Speaking a discourse isn't the same as living its dictates", says Julie Crawford, a Professor of Humanities at Columbia (in a video called Women's Contribution to Shakespeare Productions, which you can find on YouTube). Though she's talking about gender in Shakespeare - especially about The Taming of The Shrew, this also applies amazingly to wrestling.

Shakespeare has his share of "strong female characters" - Lady Macbeth (from Macbeth), Kate (from The Taming of The Shrew), Cleopatra (from Cleopatra and Anthony) and Rosalind (from As You Like It) often get cited as examples of Shakespeare's brand of proto-feminism.

But they're being played by dudes, in a theatre full of mostly dudes, where the power is mostly held by dudes, these strong powerful women get married to dudes, all the punchlines and plot-twists end up showing that dudeness=power, and the little bit of power that these women have come not from them being powerful, but from them being married to someone big and even their best traits are all masculine.

So um. Yay, feminism?

Wrestling feminism has been having a bit of a moment, with the Women's Revolution / Evolution and whatnot. Only one promotion, admittedly, is making such a big deal out of it. But since this promotion is the biggest, most visible one that's the one I'll be focusing on. Older promotions tend to range from bad to terrible, with respect to women. Other playwrights don't have a phenomenal track record over Shakespeare either, so it all seems pretty fitting.

Let's start with my favourite, Lady Macbeth. She gets to cut some killer promos against Duncan - but she's essentially a glorified valet for Mr Macbeth. She doesn't hold any power. It's tough to call her a "strong female character" if she has no power. Same with Rosalind, and Katharine, and Beatrice. Just because they have nice, meaty lines - they're able to speak the discourse - doesn't mean they can live the discourse. They're all born into powerful families, or marry into powerful families.

Repeat after me: this isn't power.

For example, let's flashback to Lita. The baddest-ass lady wrestler of a generation, she was a teammate of the Hardy Boys, Matt and Jeff. Then Kane, a fire-undead-demon-thingy-dude, kidnapped Lita and tied her up backstage. Next show, she was pregnant. Then she miscarried because Kane fell on her. Then she cheated on Matt with Edge, turning her into Edge's stupid valet. Then she had to simulate sex onstage, and there's an angle about giving up her career because her boss wanted her to do a spread in Playboy, and she didn't want to.

Sure, Lita is a badass. She does really cool moonsaults and suicide-dives and butt-kicking and general punk-rock things..

But where is the power?

To Shakespeare's credit, though his plays never allowed for a true "strong female character", he allowed for lots of gender bending. He locked down on its performativity far before Judith Butler came along, and he got something right.

To use litcrit-phrasology, the non-teleological nature of this play could actually be a boon. Maybe Lady M doesn't need the pressure of ending up the champion. Maybe Rosalind and Viola and Katharine and Beatrice just really don't mind falling in love with their respective men at the end, and undoing an entire script of hard work. It doesn't work for me. Maybe it's me. (Maybe it's Maybelline.) That the primary feature of most women in wrestling (until fairly recently), and pretty much all Shakespearean women, is their beauty, doesn't sit right with me. This transfers power to the people beholding their beauty - and their judgement of this performativity - rather than keeping it with the performers. It's not that men don't have this pressure, because they do. But men (from literally any man in Shakespeare to literally any man in wrestling) are known for their strength, not their looks. It's sad that toxic masculinity ends up conflating them. Still, it's not like they have to fight off a tradition of bra-and-panty matches, or not being allowed to act in Elizabethan and Jacobean theatre.

The dramatic beats in Macbeth are fairly translatable to the world of pro wrestling. It's my hope that through this last bit, I've been able to show how the two worlds are linked - as a student of Literary and Cultural Studies, every kind of storytelling is pretty valid. Bodyslams are a bonus.

Macbeth and Banquo, the #1 contenders for the Tag title, have a pretty cool match against the Thane of Cawdor and his pesky Norwegian sidekick. Then, in the main event, Macbeth wins the Intercontinental Title. On his way back, he sees three fans, holding signs -

MACBETH FOR #1 CONTENDER.
MACBETH FOR INTERCONTINENTAL CHAMP.
MACBETH FOR WORLD CHAMP.

And also there's some stuff about Banquo.
Macbeth can't believe this at first - but yeah, he's already the IC, what's to stop him becoming world champ? Duncan and his stable, that's who. Lady M, his trusty valet, urges him (in a shockingly amazeballs promo) to take out Duncan via nefarious means. Now that Duncan's weak, it's pretty easy for Mr Macbeth to challenge him to a retirement match, and win the title for himself.

Except, now he's turned on his good friend Banquo as well, who ponders whether or not he should join a rival company. Seeing him in the audience one day really freaks Mr M out, so he tries to take out Banquo and his son via nefarious means, too. After all, he is the world champ, which inevitably means he must be invincible.

Or so he believes. He sees more signs in the audience, telling him nobody from his promotion can beat him. This is great news, because there is no way a good storyteller will randomly conjure up a character who can take the protagonist down, because it fits in so well with the general deus-ex-machina kind of trend that all these resolutions follow. No way at all.

So Macbeth goes around terrorizing the locker room until - gasp! - someone from the rival promotion is here! Of course, there is a terrific match between the two, and the injuries Macbeth suffers means he can't wrestle anymore. Give it up for the new world champion, Macduff!

And then the story keeps going on, and on, and on.

At least, this is how I see it. Maybe you don't. Maybe you do. Maybe promos and bodyslams aren't your thing - which is absolutely fine. Maybe the iambic pentameter isn't your thing, and that's fine as well.

But good stories? They're for everyone. Forms and stories change over time, and it's quite cool to try and keep up with them all. Some are about murder and some are about romance – but all the good ones boil down to some conflict.

Oh, you don't agree?

Fight me.

Sarah The Rebel - Breaking into the Indy Scene: a US Experience

Sarah the Rebel is also known in some parts of the wrestling world as Sarah Wolfe, but perhaps you know her best as Razor on the AXS TV show Women of Wrestling, the promotion owned by original GLOW founder David McLane.

Sarah covers her start in professional wrestling, the schools she has been to, training with New Japan, her time as a manager/valet, how she became involved in WOW, and her views on the current representation of women in AEW, NXT and WWE. Follow her at twitter.com/SarahTheRebel.

Interview conducted by Jason Norris

Who the hell do I think I am?

You may have seen me as Razor on WOW - Women Of Wrestling - which airs in the U.S. on AXS TV. I was also part of the Occult Couple, managing and teaming with Tyler Bateman as Sarah Wolfe at various indie shows, most notably Championship Wrestling From Hollywood (CWFH) which you can watch on the Fite TV app. I now go by the name Sarah The Rebel, a nickname I used from my livestreaming days on Twitch, since the Sarah Wolfe persona was created specifically to team with Bateman and we are no longer teaming.

On the non-wrestling side of things, most recently I was in Scotland for the Edinburgh Fringe Festival and then Las Vegas as part of the Spiegelworld production The Atomic Saloon Show. Another indie wrestler, Barbie Hayden (Abilene Maverick on WOW) is also a part of the show; it's been a very interesting experience using my wrestling skills for a very different

type of performance art.

Getting Started in Wrestling

I first discovered wrestling when I was flipping through the channels one day as a kid and came across Chyna on my television screen. I was like 'who is this amazing amazon who looks like Xena?' Then I eventually saw Luna Vachon and Miss Jackie and I was hooked. I loved how strong and powerful they looked, and I remember how frustrated I used to get that these women rarely got to win compared to the super hot model types like Sable. I hated Sable as a child because I felt that she couldn't wrestle but was being pushed over women more technically sound than her just because of her looks.

One time, years later, I was hiking with my then-boyfriend. We saw this jacked lady with huge arms and shoulders. I said 'Wow, I want to look like that!' and my boyfriend looked at me and said "Oh but not that muscled, right?" So I guess men aren't as into muscled women unless they have that particular fetish, whereas for myself, I see jacked women and all I can think is 'Woah I want to know all about this warrior on my television screen!'

Watching when I was younger I created this persona for myself and I was going to be a wrestler, but then I hit puberty and I looked down at my chest and said, 'Oh no, my boobs aren't big enough to be a wrestler' and I gave up on my dream.

Fast forward many years and I was working in the video game industry as a writer and PR specialist. I was at E3 and I ran into Xavier Woods from the WWE. He and I got to talking because we both love video games and he told me that there are wrestling schools. I had no idea about any of this because all I knew about wrestling was WWE. My closest moment to being a part of a WWE show even as a kid was when Eddie Guerrero rode my brother's low-rider car to ringside in my hometown, and I still didn't get to go to the show because he said it wasn't for little girls. I hadn't even seen an independent show when I met Xavier, I didn't even know what the indie scene was. I went home that night and looked up wrestling schools and found Santino Bros, but I still didn't sign up. Xavier invited myself and my podcast (Women Wrestling Friends) co-host Tamara Brooks to an episode of RAW. When we got back to the car there was a flyer on the car and it was for Santino Bros, so I took it as a sign. I went to the school and I asked 'am I too old?' and they said, no, so I asked 'am I hot enough?' and they said, 'yes, and you don't have to be super hot anymore anyway.' I signed up and that was about three years ago.

The Training Process

While I would like to say it was onwards and upwards from this point, it was not that easy. Wrestling training is hard, very hard. I quit the first time I trained because I pulled my back out and then I healed it and I came back and the other side of my back went out and I couldn't move. I couldn't even go to the bathroom without assistance or go down the stairs, that's how much I couldn't move. I thought, 'Well, I'm just not tough enough to be a wrestler', and I had this fear now because of the intense pain from both of the injuries. I quit and did a bunch of Pilates training to strengthen my back, which had become weak from a decade of working on video games and sitting at a desk all day hunched over at my computer.

I built my back up and then I eventually came back and went through training again, and it went a lot better. The most intense training I went to was later in the New Japan LA dojo, which I did in Spring 2018. I was the only woman in the class and the trainers did not change anything for me. The number of reps I did, the weight that I lifted, everything was the same as the men. That was probably the most intense thing I have ever done in my life, and I had to do it while sick. I was so sick the entire time;

I had tissues stuffed in my nose during the exercises. I remember at the very end I found out from some of the guys that they had used me as motivation. Anytime they wanted to quit, they would look at me and see that I was still doing my squats, tissues in my nose and all. They thought they couldn't quit as long as I was still going.

I don't believe that you should just train at one school and be done with it; there is so much to learn from different people, hence the New Japan dojo experience. If you are in another town and you have the opportunity, you should go to another school and train, so I always work on improving myself. I also trained at the WOW dojo, which was a third style of training. In each of the schools they teach you different ways of doing things, there is not just one way. I'm now at the FSW school and even here there is one thing that has been routine at every other school I've attended and they do it differently at this school. It's always good to expand your horizons when you train.

WOW was a chance to train in a women-only environment, but that is extremely rare in the U.S., like EVE in the UK. If you go back to the names I mentioned when I was growing up, every woman in the WWE was also training and wrestling men. The only other all-woman school I know of was Fabulous Moolah's school back in the day.

I had my debut through Santino Bros as a manager. Santino Bros considers you a semi-pro once you debut with them, so that was considered my wrestling school graduation. I had my first wrestling match with WOW during their first season in the Fall of 2018 and since then I've wrestled for places such as GLAM, OVW and CWFH.

Women of Wrestling

WOW has been running on AXS TV for two seasons, and it has been great to be a part of the show. I first became a part of WOW when a friend sent me a job ad for an all-women wrestling company looking for a writer. I work as a writer in my spare time, and since I loved wrestling it seemed like a dream job. I reached out and thy loved that I actually knew about wrestling and had a depth of knowledge about writing for wrestling fans. I started the job and you can see my writing in most of the wrestler profiles on wowe.com.

A few months into the job, WOW announced that they were having auditions for their new season. I asked if I could audition, knowing that they might consider it a conflict of interest to have a writer also wrestling for them. They said I could audition. I later found out that Selina Majors (the head trainer) had a conversation with David McLane (the founder of WOW) and told him 'If we don't let her audition, she's going to wonder for the rest of her life what could have been.' Luckily he agreed with her and of course I landed the part because character and story based wrestling is my favorite kind of wrestling.

Even before I "discovered" WOW, I wanted to be a part of a show like this. I remember one time I was cutting a promo and my trainer was filming it, and when I finished he said "Wow you sound just like a GLOW girl! That's what you remind me of." I almost cried when he said it because it was actually my dream. I wanted so bad to be this huge over-the-top character that you really don't get to see anymore, especially not in WWE. All the other major companies seem to want grounded realism.

For anyone who doesn't know, David McLane also created the original GLOW. So working for WOW was the fulfilment of that dream to work for a company that values women's wrestling and big personalities. McLane truly believes in women's wrestling and has been trying to create new shows ever since the end of GLOW in the eighties. Now with the team-up with Jeanie Buss and the AXS TV deal, his latest show WOW might be the one to finally live up to GLOW's popularity.

Razor, my character in WOW, is the leader of a girl gang called the Psycho Sisters. Razor grew up on the streets, she didn't have a very good home life and she basically created a place where other women who were not accepted for who they are could all work together and have a safe-haven. The motivation is pretty similar to the motivation of any Batman supervillain really. It's to get money, it's to get fame, it's to get glory, it's to be able to do whatever you want without anyone being able to say anything to you.

It's been amazing to be on WOW. There is literally nowhere else on TV in American where you can see women's wrestling with storylines that aren't focused on boyfriends and mean girl betrayals. Our storylines are more like 'this lady is a voodoo lady and she's turned this other person into a voodoo puppet' or 'this person is a rapper and she's got to do this to prove to herself that she's ready'. There are so many different stories. It's women of every shape, size, color, nationality, LGBT representation, everything is on there. You can be a star, you can be in the running for the world championship, whether you're black, whether you're white, whether you're skinny, whether you're fat. There is nowhere else where women are treated like this as wrestlers on TV in America. In addition to the great stories and larger-than-life characters reminiscent of GLOW, we have the modern high standard of athletic wrestling. You can watch something like the Tessa Blanchard versus Reyna Reyes match and realize that we are not just fun and games: there is serious wrestling in several different styles, from strong-style to lucha to old-school southern style grappling.

I've had a lot of people ask me if I'm a star now. It's a weird question to me. I get recognized every once in a while, but it's hard to feel like I'm a celebrity of any kind. But I do know that most women that I know have imposter syndrome and imposter syndrome for anyone who doesn't know is when you don't believe that you are what you are, and you think that people will realize you are a fraud. For example, one time I was on a podcast and at the time I didn't have a job and they asked how I wanted to be introduced. I said it didn't really matter as I wasn't doing anything, then my friend on the show pointed out that I'm a published author, which I had totally discounted. That same thing happens in wrestling. I think for some of us, we are signed wrestlers on television but AXS is a smaller channel and there hasn't been as much press about us as the likes of AEW. It's easy to kind of downplay the impact of it, but we are signed wrestlers on television and people can watch women's wrestling and find the channel in many ways. It is still a big deal and I'm very thankful to be a part of WOW.

Being a Manager/Valet

I was in a manager class at Santino Bros, well actually it became a referee and announcer and commentary and manager class. They called it the wrestling advocates class. One of the women who would pop in a bunch was Jezebel Romo and she has just decades of experience being a valet and being a manager to a lot of different wrestlers. I got a lot of info from different people including the wrestler I ended up managing, Tyler Bateman; he has 17 years of experience in the industry. Everyone was very willing to share knowledge and to give tips and feedback. As far as the character of Sarah Wolfe, they came to me after the manager class finished and said 'Hey, we've got somebody for you to manage.' They asked 'How would you feel about it being Tyler Bateman?' Tyler was my boyfriend at the time and I said, no, I didn't want to manage him as I felt he didn't need a manager. He's excellent on the mic and he's excellent in-ring, an all around awesome wrestler. 'Why would he need a manager?' I asked. However, they had an idea for this very romantic storyline that we were going to create, funny enough with his real-life ex-girlfriend.

That intrigued me because I love storylines, especially the "garbage" kind involving kidnapping and weddings and those sorts of things so once I heard what they wanted I decided to do it.

They asked what name I would manage under, and I didn't really know but I wanted it to sound goth. Sarah Wolfe just worked. I didn't think the character would stick because I honestly thought that Tyler Bateman was so great on his own that nobody would ever want a manager with him as an act. I based my character off of his character. Bateman was known as the King of the Crossroads, the devil himself. He wore a long black coat and a top hat and it was very dark and kind of Jack the Ripper-like. So I molded Sarah Wolfe after that and that's why she was so dark and supernatural themed.

Bateman signed with Ring of Honor and I decided that it didn't make sense to continue as Sarah Wolfe, since she was never really "me". I'm transitioning to a new character bit by bit. Her name is Sarah The Rebel and so far I've managed Shogun Jones and Funny Bone as this new persona. I also work as a manager at Hoodslam's GLAM in Oakland as a character named Tia Mott, although I recently started wrestling as that character as well.

So I have a few manager characters. Tia Mott was due to Hoodslam asking me for a character and then we kind of built it together, she became the mother of monsters, she's basically like a swamp witch, a creepy monster lady. It's different from Sarah Wolfe, who's supposed to be more sexy and seductive and goth. This character is more like grungy, spit green mist in your face, a real creepy creep.

Being a woman in the male dominated world of professional wrestling
The hardest part is it seems like a lot of guys I have met in the backstage, off camera part of wrestling really don't take it seriously that they should

hire women to work for them. They really don't think it's a problem that they don't have women writers, that they don't have women on commentary that they don't have women directors or women producers. They don't see it as an issue, and that's been the most frustrating thing to run into because it's a huge blind spot for them because these men don't notice that they'll tell the same story over and over and over again for their women wrestlers. Then when they can't tell that story they have no new ideas and let the women go. Versus if you actually had a woman in the writing room, a woman backstage, a woman in a position of power who could say, 'Hey, did you know women do other things?' I think we would get better stories.

Women don't just go for massages and feud over men. We do a few other things. We are just as dimensional as the guys are. But for some reason, guys really don't see the blind spot there. I hate to use it as an example, but the new NWA Powerr show that's out on YouTube, the two people I know backstage who were in charge are both white men, the announcers are white men, the commentary team are white men, the backstage interviewer is a white man, the vast majority of the wrestlers on the roster are white men. They probably didn't even notice that they did that and it's because you tend to hire people you know, you tend to hire friends. To give them credit Eddie Kingston is one of their big personalities and they did have women's matches after that first episode and one of those women (Ashley Vox) even repped the LGBT flag on the show so again I don't think this sort of thing is on purpose. But a woman did not speak for the entire first episode. In the second episode it took thirty minutes to hear the first woman speak. This blind spot is frustrating for me to watch. I wish more promotions could recognize that part of the reason their stories are stale and part of the reason they aren't coming up with new things is because they won't give women a seat at the table to bring another   perspective.

I think that's why WOW is so amazing. The two people that created everything are a man and a woman. Then they also have women writers, and women PAs. There's women in so many backstage positions. And it works because there have been times when someone has pitched an idea that might be inappropriate and we've had someone there to say 'Hey, did you know, that is a little insensitive. What if we did this?' and the thing they suggest is ten times more creative than the original ideas and way less offensive.

As far as the male wrestlers, so many of them trained with women so they know what we're capable of and they don't have issues with us. The biggest issue they might have is sometimes it doesn't seem fair that a rookie woman wrestler can make more money than a rookie male wrestler, but that's because there aren't as many of us, that's just a supply and demand thing. So my biggest gripe is not with the wrestlers at all, it's with the people who book shows and who manage and create companies.

AEW, NXT and the Use of Women

At the time of this interview (I'll always hope this can change) AEW is not backing up its statement before the shows started that it would include more women's wrestling. They usually have one woman's match on a show, so that's not really that interesting to me. It's disappointing because you can't turn around and say 'We're going to be so much better than WWE and different than WWE' and then the only place you're different is in promoting smaller white men that the WWE would not push. To be fair, they could potentially have wanted many more women but they were unavailable due to contracts etc. At the same time, look at a company like Impact, which does so much with a pretty small women's roster in comparison to WWE.

WWE's NXT had the Mae Young Classic; I was at the second taping and watched Triple H interact with the women in the tournament. It's very clear that he believes in the women and he thinks that they're equal to the male wrestlers. And if you think back to his relationship with Chyna you can see the hints that he's maybe always felt that way about women wrestlers and wanting to give them a place to shine. The women given time in NXT are definitely killing it, even if I prefer WOW overall.

Women in a Wrestling Crowd

It doesn't matter where you are, it's generally not great if there's a bunch of guys at shows. Even NXT, which is taped at the same location, Full Sail, every week with a regular crowd, has been called out about their racism recently due to their response to the Asian wrestlers. I was very surprised by some of the things people were saying in that crowd. I've noticed that there is a group of wrestling fans in any crowd that like to be a part of the show a little too much. They're the fans that have their own "gimmicks", dressing up in costumes every show or having crazy signs etc. This type of fan often tries to make the crowd laugh at their jokes or otherwise tries to insert themselves into the show. Sometimes that results in them saying fucked up things just to try and get a laugh.

It is really frustrating. I think Kelly Klein was just talking about some fan at a Ring of Honor show who was just calling her fat and ugly the whole time and just kept yelling it out, and that happens at any show. It doesn't matter if it's an all woman show, any show where there's a bunch of guys in the audience has the potential to do that. I know that promoters have to make money, but there have been promotions that have taken a stand and said 'Hey, guess what?' if you say the F word in here you're getting kicked out. If you say a slur at our wrestlers, if you touch our wrestlers in an inappropriate way you're getting kicked out', and those promoters are getting a lot of support from the rest of the fans. I wish that promotions would be a little more proactive and make sure that it's a safe and comfortable environment for everybody. I don't claim to know the best way to do that though. I almost want to put those rowdier fans in their own little glass box where they can't bother anyone but themselves but where they can still enjoy the show.

There are always going to be guys that take everything a woman does as an invitation to say sexual things or to try and touch her. On my podcast, Women Wrestling Friends (which you can find on iTunes), one of the little ways we try to fight back against this entitled mindset is by talking about male wrestlers the way guys talk about women wrestlers, just to make people uncomfortable. I think giving them an idea of how jarring it can be will help them understand the issue with it.

Heather Bandenburg - Breaking into the Indy Scene: a UK Experience

Heather grew up wanting to be a writer, and then accidentally became a lucha libre wrestler aged 21. Since then she has launched herself fully in to a series of adventures, including writing feminist narratives on wrestling; and running an immersive cabaret show called I Need to Cher.

Heather covers her start in professional wrestling, appearing on big lucha events in the UK, the current representation of women in wrestling and what led to her publishing Unladylike: A Grrl's Guide to Wrestling (London: Unbound 2019). Follow her on Twitter at https://twitter.com/Ranabitesback.

Interview conducted by Jason Norris.

Who the hell am I?

I am Heather Bandenburg, alias Heather Honeybadger when I referee for Pro-Wrestling EVE. As a masked character I am also known as La Rana Venanosa in Lucha Britannia, I started off as a poison dart frog and then upgraded to Queen of the Sewer. I am an angry woman, I like wrestling, and I write about it.

Unladylike: A Grrl's Guide to Wrestling, and the world of wrestling books

My book is called Unladylike: A Grrl's Guide to Wrestling and it's available on the big book sites. It's part life story of an unlikely wrestler and part beginners guide to women in wrestling.

The book was crowdfunded on Unbound, which was really the only way I could get it published because the big publishers couldn't see where it would sit in Waterstones – so it was a long road to get here. The book's concept started about three years ago when I got sick and I couldn't wrestle for quite a while, and I was going a bit mad. Since about age 10 I had always wanted to write a book and for years I'd dabbled with all of these ideas about what I could write about, and it turns out that the fates decided I was going to write a book about wrestling.

I started writing fiction, a bit like a *Whip It* version of wrestling - a teenage girl leaving her tiny town and running away from home to pursue her wrestling dreams. Then I met Milly McKenzie and Candyfloss who were *actually* 16-year-old women who wrestled, and I was thought I cannot write this book, it's their story. So I just ended up writing essays for the likes of The Guardian and The Huffington Post about feminist issues within wrestling as there was nobody else doing it at the time. The book came a lot later after I had established exactly what 'non wrestling audiences' (aka. The rest of the population) would be interested in reading about.

While working on my freelance writing, I became quite frustrated that there weren't many women writing about wrestling, the field was just completely dominated by male voices. That's really hard to see when everyone is throwing around the words 'women's wrestling revolution'. Things like *Glow* were coming out and outside the wrestling world the industry looked like a hard-femme paradise, but there are *still* so few female voices outside of the ring, and even fewer of them speak to women.

Glow created this new audience of young, angry women over night that had a sudden interest in wrestling, and there are no books that are written for them. I wanted to buck this trend by writing a book written by a woman for a non-wrestling audience, that instead of thanking about things from the past like the Attitude Era and Hulkamania, talks about the physical experience of becoming a wrestler that is not in the WWE. The closest to this on the market is AJ Mendez's book which is really good, particularly as she is an absolute champion for people with mental health issues. But there's also a tell-tale line early on in the book where she writes "I assume you must know about wrestling or why are you even reading this book? For a bet or something?" It's not a dig at the reader – she is just aware of the reality that books by female wrestlers really only tend to get one kind of audience, and a small one at that.

Starting my Wrestling Career

So just to be clear, I didn't really know anything about wrestling when I started. At my first wrestling training class I couldn't tell you who The Undertaker was.

I used to do stand-up comedy and back in 2011 I did a gig at the Resistance Gallery, a dive bar in East London that also doubles as a wrestling venue. Vanderhorne, who runs the place, saw my act and asked if I wanted to come to a free training session. This was on the basis that he needed more women in his promotion 'Lucha Britannia' and also I clearly didn't mind making a total tit of myself. So I said 'okay sure' and I turned up with my best friend, Rebecca Biscuit, to give it a go.

We both hated exercise, neither of us even had gym clothes, so we polled up just in pajamas. The London School of Lucha Libre has always been open to anyone who wants to come but then it was more people who actively sought out wrestling, rather than stumbling across it.

I remember that we were both terrified but everyone was so nice, the coaches and the students were really encouraging – but it also appealed to me more than any other sport I'd tried before. If you are a woman you've generally been told your whole life not to take up too much space and not to make too much noise. If you are into sports in school, they offer you netball, maybe football if you are lucky, and gymnastics. This class was the total opposite.

Before I went wrestling training, I had never 'play fought' before in my life, it turns out I loved it. I suddenly had this hobby where I could fall over and be clumsy without being embarrassed. My coaches praised me for being a loud and noisy character, something I was shunned at in so many places. I was immediately addicted.

Learning how to Wrestle

For most people the only wrestling training they have seen is the equivalent of a montage scene in a film. Of course not many people have a clue, unless they've tried it themselves, just how hard wrestling training is. This included me.

Starting with zero knowledge, it took 3 years of working my ass off before my first match. The physical fitness and discipline didn't come naturally to me. Not only do I have dyspraxia, (so falling over I am great at, but telling left from right is a challenge), it meant I also had to learn everything about wrestling. People could tell me to do a stunner, but I didn't know what a stunner was. I started with the same basics as everyone else - learning to bump, learning to roll and learning to do a character but I would then have to go home with a list of the most basic wrestling things to look up online.

My teachers would always reference past PPVs, like WrestleMania, so I thought if I just watched all of them like a series, I would 'get' wrestling. So I started with WrestleMania 1, and imagine watching WrestleMania 1 when you haven't watched any wrestling before. It's a really long show to start with, and obviously part of me loved it but another part of me thought 'well this was racist'.

I went back to my coaches and told them that I didn't like WrestleMania. I think before then they had not realized just how clueless I was, and they also saw that I just needed a wrestler that I could identify with. As a

111

slightly overweight feminist, Hulk Hogan or Steve Austin were never going to be my heroes, I needed someone I could empathize with. They gave me the name of Bull Nakano and I went into YouTube to find her, and it got to the point where I was just clicking on her name and I didn't care who she was wrestling, I watched it all. I went back her early days when she was just 17, and she was wrestling with Dump Matsumoto. That was when I realized there was a future for me in the ring, because as far back as the 80s the stars had been screaming furious banshees, I'd found my tribe.

Over the years I've trained, I've seen hundreds of people try wrestling and not succeed for one reason or another. Even people who have a background in dance or martial arts, or who are as muscly as a great white shark, can do the physical part but then struggle at being a character, or engaging a crowd.

I had the opposite problem, from day one someone could be like 'do a promo as a box of fried chicken taking down vegans' and I could do that without thinking about it, but if someone asked me to do a press up I couldn't manage one. I think the main thing I learned in 3 years from starting to wrestle to being in the ring for a match was just learning about the humbleness needed to become a wrestler, like helping to put up the ring up for those shows. I don't think you can do it any other way, I don't think you can learn about being a wrestler until you've done it the long and hard way.

My first match

My first match was against my now-husband, so an intergender match. I had been ready for ages but I was nervous because I wanted to be a feminist character, but back in 2012 if you were a feminist you were usually automatically a heel, and I just did not want that.

I realized that if I wrestled a really horrible man I would be a face (a hero, as opposed to a heel/villain). Fraser volunteered to help me, because he has the opposite problem that he never gets to be the bad guy because he's usually smaller than everyone else. The angle was that we were having a fight because I had taken over cooking on the barbeque and had over stepped the gender divide. My dad was in the audience this was the first time my dad met my new boyfriend – Fraser took his top off and threw it in my Dad's face. We had the match and it went great, then we went to the pub and had a lovely time.

Building a Career in the Ring

Even though my career has been almost a decade long, I should be clear that I've not progressed as far as I would have liked in wrestling. Mainly because I had cancer so have been in and out of the ring for about four of those years. I guess I would say I am up to 300 matches for Lucha Britannia and Burning Hearts.

The highlight of my career would be when I wrestled for Lucha Libre World at the iconic York Hall on the same show as the legends Hijo de Santo, Cassandro El Exotico, Silver King (RIP), Lady Apache and Chika Tormenta. It was such an honor to be able to meet the legends of *lucha libre* – they were all so humble and encouraging, even though most of them never removed their masks, even for the tube ride down.

I can remember so clearly waiting in the wings, and as they announced me I stepped out in to these lights and just spat water on everyone, I felt like a cross between Beyoncé and the Green Goblin. In my head I told myself, 'I'm just going to hold on to this moment, it doesn't matter what else happens, I've been here'. There's no way of describing the rush of being in the ring somewhere like that. I think that's why people continue to wrestle, because it's hard and it hurts but we get those moments.

Strangest Wrestling Events

The weirdest wrestling event I performed for was with Lucha Britannia, 15 of us were shipped out to a private party in Berlin for 24 hours.

We landed at two in the afternoon and had an hour in the ring, and in Germany the rings are different, they have this slightly slippery surface so that made it harder than usual. Then we went for dinner, which was like some kind of weird school trip where I had to explain in German to the waiters about a million different dietary requirements. The show we were in was part of a huge art installation, so when we got into our gimmicks at about nine we had to be hidden in this tiny room waiting until one in the morning. There was nothing on offer to drink except Red Bull and gin, and eventually everyone cracked so when we were either a bit tipsy or wired on caffeine. The people around the ring had no idea what was about to come out, so we did this match in front of these crazy drunk Germans while they played Queen over the top.

There was this amazing moment when Cara Noir jumped out of the ring to leave and this enormous German woman picked him up like a baby and just put him back in the ring and sternly going 'NO! Again!'

We all were paid quite well for it, we wrestled three matches and then we were just at this massive party in Berlin and then we all got a flight home at six in the morning.

In general, the corporate gigs are always weird, because there are people who have no idea what they are watching, they don't know how to react. There's been times where people have literally tried to climb in to the ring to take selfies during a match; and other times when they've stayed about 10 foot away from the canvas because they're terrified. Ultimately, wrestling is a spectacle like no other so I try to explain to people new to wrestling is that it's a violent pantomime, and once they understand that it's a lot easier to get them involved.

Why are you passionate about wrestling?

One of the reasons why I wrote Unladylike is because I have been trying to figure out why I love wrestling. I gave up and stopped wrestling twice because of illness and for better or worse I've always returned to it, despite it being dangerous and difficult. But wrestlers cannot retire, we find it impossible.

Look at Ric Flair and Terry Funk - classic examples of guys that have struggled with the same thing. Terry Funk has retired 72 times! You would think it is just like these big guys that have got the grandeur and a big career, but the fact is most wrestlers find it hard to stop. I'm trained by Greg Burridge, who is an indie legend in the UK, even though he's officially retired, once or twice a year he just needs to get back in the ring and do a match. Even during this interview, I'm 3 months pregnant, but I'm already talking to people about when I'll be back training.

I suppose one reason is because wrestling gives you the chance to completely forget who you are - it's freeing. To be able to have people suspend disbelief and control them in the way that you want to, and to be this strong superhero, why would you not want to keep doing that as long as possible?

I love wrestling for those kind of existential reasons, but also because it is an industry where you can enjoy it without making it big, it's ultimately a very DIY, community based type of art. I've never dreamt headlining WrestleMania or anything like that. I think another reason why I wrote Unladylike is the celebration of non-famous wrestlers like myself, and most of the people I've worked with. We are an incredibly important breed - one in 100 trainees will get as far as having their first match; so just being in a show is an achievement.

I hate the idea that you have failed as a wrestler unless you get on TV or make it to the WWE network, because it is just not true. There are so many great wrestlers that have been and gone in the ring that have not had half the screen time and recognition they deserve. Wrestlers, if nothing else, are passionate.

How the World Reacts to Female Wrestlers

Another thing with Unladylike was it gave me the chance to research women wrestlers. I have been looking at people like Lola Gonzales and these women were never in the WWE. The fact is they had a big impact due to their skills even though they never got on that big screen. The stories of these women need to be told, so I wear the fact I'm a female wrestler as a huge badge of pride – it makes me unique.

When people hear I'm a wrestler, it doesn't matter if they are a man or woman, they will always ask 'really, you? You don't look like a wrestler'. Maybe it's because I have a vagina or because I'm a size 12, but apparently I don't look like one. Then they ask if wrestling is real, and it depends on how much I like the person as to what I reply. Usually, I ask them to imagine if you are standing in a ring in front of over 200 people in your pants and then a giant person jumps off a 6-foot turnbuckle and you have to get kicked in the face by them without getting hurt. Then tell me what is fake about that experience. If I don't like them, I will just change the subject.

But to be honest it's those who are existing wrestling fans that I find hardest to talk to, and this isn't me trying to tar people with the same brush, it's just my experience that you have to prove yourself to be worthy of being a wrestler. While marketing for my book, quite often male fans, on hearing that I've been a wrestler for 7 years, will feel the need to explain women's wrestling to me, and why women are so liberated. I find this quite harsh because they just assume that I am not as knowledgeable about wrestling because I am a woman, even though it's literally my life. I think other female fans would say similar things. Wrestling has people that consider themselves the gatekeepers of knowledge which can be daunting. One of the biggest achievements for me with this journey of writing a book was that I did a 2-hour talk on wrestling, and at no point did I feel like an imposter, I felt confident in my knowledge throughout. It's only taken me a decade to do it, but I finally feel like I know what I'm talking about!

The fact is that this kind of imposter-syndrome is part of the battle women have to get taken seriously. Women have been fighting for recognition as long as wrestling has existed, not just as wrestlers but also as decision-makers in the industry.

Just because you can name every single WWE pay-per-view it doesn't qualify your opinion to mean more. I feel that is still a thing, this whole gatekeeping mentality, not seeing people as proper wrestling fans or proper wrestlers until they cross a certain level. And if you're a woman the gate posts are moved even further away.

Women's Wrestling in WWE

My opinion is WWE is so behind the rest of the wrestling world. They are trying so desperately to catch up and I think you can hear what the fans want but for some reason they still seem to think their fans are all bigoted men and write storylines with this in mind. No queer characters, no inter gender wrestling, storylines for women that are usually just about petty squabbles rather than truly weird stuff. Essentially women are still not allowed to be ugly in the WWE, they still need to be saleable for sex, and

I think this is a massive limitation – there is no female Bray Wyatt, or a interesting heel of that nature – why?

And in regards to inter gender wrestling, I think that attitudes are changing but there are still excuses slowing us down. The big thing that people will always argue to stop women fighting men is domestic violence. But I think conversely, by having less women in the ring you are suggesting they cannot be strong. I hope my son grows up to be slightly terrified of woman and knows that they can kick his ass. Because I think if more women see these role models like Becky Lynch beating the shit out of someone bigger than her the problem will solve itself.

Fantasy Booking and Favorites

My dream opponent would be Cassandro the Exotico because he is my favorite wrestler of all time. He also has taught me a number of times and is a good friend – the LSLL fairy godmother in fact.

He is so tough, you'd have to be if you're the first openly gay male wrestler to hold a world heavyweight belt. As a teacher and wrestler he's remained humble despite his huge level of skill. To me it wouldn't be about my glory, it would be the honor of essentially wrestling with my teacher. However I'm just saying that, I think I'd be too intimidated to even lock up with him I love him that much. In fact when he trains us I always mess up because I'm so keen to impress him.

My tips on becoming a wrestler

My main recommendation for training is try it, because you could surprise yourself. I've been really lucky to be taught by three different schools, and the main ethos of all of them is that they welcome everyone.

But also, if it turns out your place isn't in the ring, it doesn't mean you can't be part of that family as a fan and a supporter of wrestling. It doesn't matter if you are a woman and you are a female wrestling fan, your voice is valid, and I know sometimes it can be hard if you are in very male environment to have an opinion, but hold on to it and write about it and talk about it. Seek out women who also like wrestling because they are out there.

And to everyone, not just women, if you think you want to try and be a wrestler the hardest thing is walking through the door. You will know immediately and either think this is horrible, or you might be like me and feel this is the best decision you ever made.

Heather Bandenburg - Why We Need to Talk About Stereotypes

This is an extract from 'Unladylike: A Grrls Guide to wrestling' (London: Unbound 2019). After the interview for this book, Jason and I had an off mic discussion about harmful stereotypes in wrestling. Mainly it was Jason naming WWE stars that I didn't know had done incredibly dodgy gimmicks, within wrestling, and me guffawing in disbelief. But though we shouldn't take ourselves too seriously in this industry of 'violent panto', it's important that we look at what the ramifications our creations have. Sure, it's not politics, but it's also 2020 – there should not be sexism or racism in wrestling.

I found that very few people within wrestling address this quite problematic aspect, so this extract talks a little about why we need to talk about stereotypes.

-   Heather Bandenburg

One thing I have gathered so far in my vibrant but limited wrestling career is that in-ring characters are never subtle. They require a 100 per cent commitment from the performer not only to tell a story of good versus evil, but to portray this while doing something dangerous. The wrestling ring acts as an arena wherein the frustrations and joys of the audience are mapped on to it. It is a spectacle that suspends disbelief. In the same way that we can accept that the violence in wrestling is fake, if it entertains us, we will believe a character is a person's real nature (providing they act engagingly enough).

Before you add the death-defying moves and the pomp of rippling muscle, it is the battle between 'good' and 'bad' that remains the most integral component of the performance. The audience must know which wrestler corresponds with which side of their moral compass, and this compass is intrinsically linked to the society around them. A wrestler portrays their goodness or badness through their costume, their music, their facial expressions, and even through the way they enter the ring.

They then have roughly fifteen minutes to tell a whole story so exciting that the audience are out of their seats. There is no script, there is no time to rehearse, and there is no editing suite. There is no time for the audience to reflect on the bad guy's abusive childhood and how this relates to him carrying the head of a bear into the ring. Nor is there time to explore the self-image of the woman in the gold bikini who high fives the kids in the front row. One is good, because she's pretty and happy; and one is bad, because he's tortured and deranged.

We need to talk about stereotypes because as soon as you accept their use in indicating good and evil, it becomes a slippery slope of assumptions.

Let's take an example: the voodoo witch doctor. This is a character that re-occurs again and again in wrestling – evil, mysterious and powerful – and usually with negative connotations of Afro-Caribbean culture. In the Gorgeous Ladies of Wrestling (GLOW), a women's only promotion in the 1980s, every character had gimmicks like porn monikers. The character Black Magic, a 'voodoo priestess' blew dust in opponents' faces. In the 1990s, the WWE bought in Papa Shango. These characters are both widely considered to be two of the most racist characters in wrestling industry, though still remembered fondly by fans. Why? Because Papa Shango, with his skull make-up and top hat, is a 'relatable' stereotype of a black person written by, and for, a white male audience.

However, using these past examples is a bit like shooting fish in a barrel. What about now, in the lovely, left-wing, mutually supportive UK wrestling circuit that I inhabit? Well, to date I've seen three 'witch doctor' gimmicks (names changed for discretion).

1.   **Mogli**: the white, skinny boy who got knocked unconscious at a show I went to in Tooting. He walked to the ring to the sound of didgeridoos, talking nonsense and pointing at the audience with what

appeared to be a curtain rail with some fake fur stuck to the top (the kind that you get for a pound a metre on the market). His entire body was painted blue. Throughout the match I was thinking, what would happen if he walked out the door, a few feet away, into the High Street? His costume wasn't black-face, but it was close.

2.   **El Mortaria**: a wrestler for Lucha Britannia. I started to meet him outside of his gimmick early on in my training, and he was always happy to teach me, and once gave me a safe-as-fuck tombstone pile driver very casually on a Tuesday night with no prior warning. It turns out that the 'monster heel' of the promotion was a very quiet, cynical man, who drove a van for Asda and had a huge selection of Christmas jumpers. However, in the ring he would put on a ripped white suit, paint his face like a skull, and suddenly would resort to smiling terrifyingly, instead of speaking. If you wanted to talk to him, you had to do it before the make-up was on, because afterwards he became someone else. He would walk along the top rope and do flips, which considering he was almost seven foot tall was impressive to see. He was something undead, a bit like a zombie. He didn't speak in an accent or pretend to be something other than a terrifying scare-crow filled with evil.

3.   **Isata the Voodoo Queen**: I met Isata a few years later, when she was on a show I was presenting. Unlike the other two characters, Isata is black, and has strong family ties to a country where 'witchcraft' is still practiced. Backstage, she was a bubbly delight but she transformed, fully, when in the ring. She was the whole shebang, covered in white make-up and talc, her tongue pierced, with white contact lenses, and screaming into the faces of the terrified audience. I never asked her directly, but she told Italian Vanity Fair in an interview: 'Isata is not a racial stereotype; I wear the make-up of my mother's matriarchal village in Nigeria where women are revered. If people think that me representing this element of my cultural past is offensive they need to think about what they're saying.'

Isata created her character based on something that she deemed to be a powerful reflection of her own identity. I think a woman crafting a character is very different to a person simply being given a character based on the color of their skin. It is very different, as well, to a white person deciding to just 'try on' voodoo for a cheap boo – although this is still how some gimmicks are created in wrestling.

Why am I using these specific examples? Because though I know two promotions in the UK that are run by a woman. I know of none, however, that are run by a person of color. Wrestling on the whole is written by one group of people: white men. This is why we need to talk about stereotypes, we need to examine where and why wrestling remains such an un-diverse community. The only way to change the problematic bits is to give someone else a go at deciding who wins and loses.

Shannon Vanderstreaten - "Blinded by the Light that is Your Velveteen Dream": Queer Villainy in Professional Wrestling

Shannon Vanderstreaten is a graduate of The University of East Anglia's Gender Studies MA, where they completed a dissertation on femininity on Total Divas, which can be found on Academia.edu. Shannon's previous informal writing on wrestling can be found at their blog, You Know It's Fake, Right? https://youknowitsfakeright.wordpress.com/. They are currently pursuing a career in social work.

Villainy, in both professional wrestling and other entertainment media, has oftentimes been coded as queer. A character such as Dustin Runnels' Goldust was perceived by the audience as a 'heel', or villain, because of his performed queerness. The audience of the 1990s brought negative attitudes towards queerness to the wrestling ring, and heteronormative values and ideology were reasserted by their participation in the performance by reacting 'correctly' to his character by booing him. In a more contemporary setting, performers are bringing more nuance and subtlety to characters that might be interpreted as queer, to which audiences are responding more positively, thus demonstrating a change in how queer villainy is being portrayed in the ring. Patrick Clark's persona Velveteen Dream in WWE's NXT brand began as a seemingly queer-coded heel, yet despite his egocentricity and in-ring viciousness, became a fan favorite after his Rivalry of the Year with Aleister Black in 2017.[1] The performance of Dream's masculinity is very clearly modelled

---

[1] 'The 2017 NXT Year-End Awards were presented on the NXT TakeOver: Philadelphia Pre-Show' *WWE.com* [online] (27th January 2018) https://www.wwe.com/shows/wwenxt/nxt-takeover-philadelphia-2018-01-27/article/2017-nxt-year-end-award-winners (accessed 14th April 2019)

on the gender-defiant Prince, allowing for an interesting investigation into the intersections of Blackness and queerness. Queerness in professional wrestling is slowly being incorporated into compelling storylines, but the problem remains that actual queer talent (neither Clark nor Runnels identify openly as queer) remains marginalized. As well as this, the queer performance of wrestlers is often limited to a feminized appearance akin to drag: once they are in the ring, masculine violence is enacted to quickly reassert heteronormative gender values. Queer villainy is acceptable as a performance, but only when it is sanctioned by a heteronormative power.

The idea of queer-coding is central to many arguments in this essay, and so it must be defined. As a concept, it explores the ways in which negative attitudes, ideas, and stereotypes about queerness are written into different forms of media. This is frequently discussed in relation to Disney films. Li-Vollmer and LaPointe write that "children's animated movies are the source of a cultural pedagogy, functioning as educator, moralist, and cultural encoder"[2] and also that "movies and other mass media can and do present images of how gender has been performed, is performed, and should be performed."[3] In their investigation of male villains in ten different animated films, Li-Vollmer and LaPointe find that the antagonists have "delicate physical features that invoke ideas of traditional ideals of feminine beauty."[4] The contrast between Scar and Mufasa in *The Lion King* is given as an example: "the slim face and pointed chin of the vengeful lion Scar is shown in close-up with his noble brother Mufasa, whose face is broad with a huge, heavy jaw."[5] Scar's appearance does not fit traditional hegemonic masculinity, and so his character is pushed into the role of the villain. Li-Vollmer and LaPointe also move on

---

[2] Meredith Li-Vollmer and Mark E. LaPointe. 'Gender Transgression and Villainy in Animated Film' in *Popular Communication*, Vol. 1, No. 2 (2003) pp. 89-109, p. 94
[3] Op.cit, p. 90
[4] Op.cit, p. 97
[5] Ibid.

to the villains' language and non-verbal gestures. Staying with *The Lion King*, Scar's feminized appearance is accompanied with camp movement: he "demurely extends a limp wristed hand as he says 'oh I shall practice my curtsey.'"[6] In a scene where Mufasa is trying to reassert his authority, Scar is seen as a queer threat to heteronormative power. When children watch Disney films, they are being educated on gender norms, as the vast majority of the villains portrayed on-screen transgress societal boundaries on masculinity and femininity. The logic follows that children will decode the media in the 'correct' way, aligning themselves with the heteronormative heroes and police non-normative forms of gender they encounter.

Li-Vollmer and LaPointe's work on queer-coding in children's animated films can also be applied to performers in professional wrestling. The villainy of Goldust's character is intricately bound up with his performance of queerness. Before his debut match with Marty Jannetty in October 1995, Goldust uses his promo to tell the audience that "tonight, there will be lights, camera, and ooh, so much action. Mr DeMille, I'm ready for my close-up."[7] By referencing Gloria Swanson's character in the 1950 film *Sunset Boulevard*, Goldust is establishing his gimmick as that of a Hollywood starlet, thus positioning his character in the realm of drag. His appearance of a long blonde wig, exaggerated gold and black make-up, and ostentatious gold and feathered gown also adds to the dragged up nature of his character. Bradbury writes "Runnels's 'camp' performance as a smouldering starlet [...] undermines the conventions of what a traditional 'masculine' wrestler 'should be' [...] in his debut Goldust channels a Marilyn Monroe or a Jayne Mansfield and performs

---

[6] Op.cit, p. 101
[7] *Goldust's WWE Debut,* [YouTube video] September 20th 2013
https://youtu.be/3j9KFh_5cDs (accessed 15th April 2019)

a striptease in the middle of the ring."[8] Newton writes that "homosexuality is symbolized in American culture by transvestism,"[9] meaning that "Goldust's cross-dressing operates as shorthand for the audience of his sexual desire for men."[10] As his entrance music plays, Vince McMahon on commentary calls Goldust "bizarre."[11] Following on from the pay-per-view debut, on his WWF[12] network television debut, Goldust was given the moniker of "The Bizarre One."[13] His character is consistently Othered and made to seem strange because of his performance of queerness. Commentary continues to play up the unusual nature of his character: Jerry Lawler quips "he's gotta be a little intimidating, a little scary, a little spooky!"[14] Goldust is positioned as "intimidating" because of the queer threat he poses to the other (masculine) wrestler in the ring. Queerness is something "scary" to heteronormative society, and so he is feared by the audience, who respond appropriately to this queer threat by booing him.

Despite the fact that Goldust enters the ring with a highly feminized appearance, he discards his costume to wrestle in a more typical, tight-fitting one piece. His tough, masculine wrestling style juxtaposes the initial femininity: "the ease with which Goldust shifts from bewigged starlet commanding the gaze of the crowd to attacking Jannetty in the

---

[8] Janine Bradbury, 'Grappling and ga(y)zing: Gender, sexuality and performance in the WWE debuts of Goldust and Marlena' in *Performance and Professional Wrestling*, edited by Broderick Chow et al. (Abingdon: Routledge, 2017) pp. 107-117, p. 108

[9] Esther Newton, *Mother Camp: Female Impersonators in America* (Chicago: Chicago University Press, 1979) p. 3

[10] Bradbury, 2017, p. 110

[11] *Goldust's WWE Debut*

[12] Mathaeus Abuwa, 'Here's why the WWE changed its name from WWF' *Sportskeeda* [online] n.d. https://www.sportskeeda.com/wwe/heres-why-wwe-changed-its-name-from-wwf (accessed 15th April 2019)

[13] Goldust makes an entrance worthy of Hollywood: Oct. 30, 1995, *WWE* [online] n.d. https://www.wwe.com/videos/goldust-makes-an-entrance-worthy-of-hollywood-oct-30-1995 (accessed 24th March 2019)

[14] Ibid.

opening seconds of the match undermines any readings of Goldust's effeminacy as passive and inert."[15] Judith Butler's work on drag here is particularly important: "in the place of the law of heterosexual coherence, we see sex and gender denaturalized by means of a performance which avows their distinctness and dramatizes the cultural mechanism of their fabricated unity."[16] One of the roles of drag is to "draw attention to the artificial, constructed, and performative nature of masculinity and femininity as social categories and blurs the lines between these binary oppositions that in the popular imagination, are often perceived as dichotomous and mutually exclusive, as well as biologically encoded."[17] Within the wrestling ring, often presumed as a place of hegemonic masculinity, Goldust's character exposes gender to be performative in nature by switching between masculinity and femininity. Mazer writes that "professional wrestling explicitly and implicitly makes visible cultural and countercultural ideas of masculinity and sexuality. Wrestling's apparently conservative masculine ideal is constantly undermined through the parodic, carnivalesque presentation of its opposite."[18] It can also be said that "Goldust's in-ring appearances permit a multivalent deconstruction of gendered 'reality'. His is a performance (wrestling) of a performance (drag) of a performance (gender) that discards and occludes a reading of essential masculinity."[19] I would go further and suggest that attention to the character of Goldust as a Hollywood starlet continues to highlight the constructed, theatrical nature of wrestling. The WWE and professional wrestling might aggressively assert masculinity as the norm, but this assertion still allows for other types of (queer) masculinity to materialize.[20] Professional

---

[15] Bradbury, 2017, p. 110

[16] Judith Butler, *Gender Trouble* (New York: Routledge, 1990), p. 187

[17] Bradbury, 2017, p. 110

[18] Sharon Mazer, *Professional Wrestling: Sport and Spectacle* (Jackson: University of Mississippi Press, 1998), p. 14

[19] Bradbury, 2017, p. 110

[20] Mazer, 1998, pp. 89-90

wrestling exposes the very constructed nature of gender and its performance, and thus perhaps it can be considered to be a queer medium because of this.

Professional wrestling is also akin to a drag performance with regards to the audience's participation in the spectacle. In his research, Keith McNeal explored "the interactive dynamics that take place between drag queens and audience members."[21] Many critics of wrestling have written that without the audience, the spectacle of wrestling does not work properly. Di Benedetto writes "responses from the attendant masses, who are more than passive audiences but rather active participants, are as important as the athletics."[22] Koh continues this by saying that audiences are "in a relatively powerful subject position. Matches and storylines are structured around their visibly active participation through, for example, their cheering and booing of heroes and villains."[23] This interactivity all these writers have noted then is clear in the ways in which fans respond to Goldust after his match with Jannetty. After gaining the victory in his debut match, the camera pans to the crowd who are booing his win. They quickly disappear from sight when the lights of the arena go down to leave a single gold spotlight on Goldust as he exits. Smith writes that "to receive a 'pop'- a strong reaction, positive or negative, from the audience-wrestlers must establish who their characters are, what that character represents ('babyface' or 'heel')."[24] As we have already discussed, it is

[21] Keith E. McNeal, 'Behind the Make-Up: Gender Ambivalence and the Double-Bind of Gay Selfhood in Drag Performance' in *Ethos*, Vol. 27, No. 3 (September 1999) pp. 344-378, p. 349

[22] Stephen Di Benedetto, 'Playful Engagements: Wrestling with the attendant masses' in *Performance and Professional Wrestling*, edited by Broderick Chow et al. (Abingdon: Routledge, 2017) pp. 26-35, p. 26

[23] Wilson Koh, 'It's What's Best for Business: Worked Shoots and the Commodified Authentic in Postmillennial Professional Wrestling' in *Quarterly Review of Film and Video*, Vol. 34, No. 5 (2017) pp. 459-479, p. 460

[24] Tyson R. Smith, 'Passion Work: The Joint Production of Emotional Labour in Professional Wrestling' in *Social Psychology Quarterly*, Vol. 72, No. 2 (2008) pp. 157-176, p. 161

Goldust's queerness that establishes him as a heel. This gimmick "provides the crowd with an opportunity to vociferously and vocally reject queerness [...] in his early performances, Runnels would not only cross-dress, but would often flirt with and sexually tease his opponents, an act that would solicit audible homophobic slurs from spectators in ringside seats."[25] Here, the importance of audience participation in the spectacle of wrestling becomes crucial. Gender is policed in professional wrestling by the audience, who perceive Goldust's appearance as wrong, bring their ideas of normative gendered behavior to the live event, and express these ideas in reacting 'correctly' and negatively to his character. In his seminal piece 'The World of Wrestling', Roland Barthes states that "in America wrestling represents a sort of mythological fight between Good and Evil (of a quasi-political nature, the 'bad' wrestler always being supposed to be a Red.)"[26] Exploring Barthes' piece in the context of the 1990s, however, the "quasi-political" nature of wrestling has moved from the Communist as villain to the queer individual as villain.

Sam Ford believes that "wrestling fans' ability to 'become so involved in the theatrics' might lead to 'true catharsis, that they bring pent-up frustrations into the arena where they release them vicariously. Professional wrestlers may be performing a social service by acting as a safety valve for emotions which under other circumstances might result in socially unacceptable violence.'"[27] However, the wrestling ring is still clearly a place where to a certain extent, heteronormativity remains constant. The fans are still coming to the ring with negative societal expectations about queerness and queer people. The spectacle, rather than performing a "social service" of keeping queer people safe in the

---

[25] Bradbury, 2017, p. 112

[26] Roland Barthes, 'The World of Wrestling' in *Mythologies* (1957) trans. Jonathan Cape (London: Vintage, 3rd edition, 2009), p. 12

[27] Sam Ford, 'He's a Real Man's Man: Pro Wrestling and Negotiations of Contemporary Masculinity' in *The Routledge Companion to Media Fandom*, edited by Melissa A. Click and Susanna Scott (Abingdon: Routledge, 2017) pp. 174-183, p. 175

'real world', merely reinforces the violence that people want to see inflicted on queer people, as Goldust is still Othered and booed by the crowd. One of the clearest examples of homophobic behavior by both the WWE and the crowd was Goldust's feud with Jerry 'The King' Lawler. On a 1997 episode of Raw, the pair were to have a first round match for the King of the Ring tournament. Beforehand, Lawler cut a scathing promo on his opponent:

"It seems our sissy friend is having a little identity crisis. First he was Dustin Runnels. Then he was Goldust. And now he wants to be the King Of The Ring. We all saw you out here, with tears running down your face, wonderin' why your old man- Oldust- don't love you any more. Well I know Dusty Rhodes, and he told me why. It's because you married the biggest gold digger in Georgia, then you put on a woman's wig, then you went around the ring kissing men like a flaming f*g."[28]

While the article referenced is about WWE leaving this scene on the Network, the corporation has since been removed it from their streaming service. Nonetheless, the crowd erupts into an enormous cheer for Lawler after he uses the slur "fag."[29] Oppliger writes that "homophobia has little to do with taboo sexual acts and everything to do with the enforcement of acceptable male behavior, including the suppression of feminine qualities."[30] While Goldust's wrestling is still masculine, and he remains in a heterosexual relationship with his wife Marlena, he is still vilified by the audience for his feminized appearance and "sissy" behavior. There were (and to an extent, are) limitations to how progressive queer

---

[28] Michael Sidgwick,'10 Moments You Can't Believe WWE Left on the Network' *WhatCulture* [online] (25th May 2017) http://whatculture.com/wwe/10-moments-you-can-t-believe-wwe-left-on-the-network?page=4 (accessed 14th April 2019)
[29] 'Goldust vs. Jerry 'The King' Lawler- Raw- 5/26/1997' *Dailymotion* [online] (11th May 2011) https://www.dailymotion.com/video/xinhkf#.U6rcewATy00.reddit (accessed 15th April 2019)
[30] Patrice Oppliger, *Wrestling and Hypermasculinity* (Jefferson: McFarland and Company, 2004), p. 100

characters can be in the ultra-conservative business of professional wrestling, and to how the audience will respond to them. After this promo, Lawler would cheat to win and defeat Goldust in their match, which the crowd cheer for. Even though Goldust would continue an attack on Lawler post-match, the role of the audience cannot be understated in ensuring Goldust's heel status, even though he unfairly lost. As they boo for him in this segment, he is still positioned as the queer villain. The message underlying this is that heteronormative masculinity ultimately prevails over the queer Other, despite gaining some violent vindication after the fact.

We now move to look at the WWE's modern day attempt at creating a queer character. Patrick Clark Jr, known professionally as the Velveteen Dream, became a prominent figure in WWE's developmental brand NXT during his feud with Aleister Black in 2017, which was voted by viewers as the brand's 2017 Rivalry of the Year.[31] The performance of queerness can definitely be seen as being an integral part of the storyline. However, this feud once again demonstrates the importance of audience participation in professional wrestling in establishing (or championing) queer characters. Despite the writers of the feud intending for Velveteen Dream to be the heel and Aleister the face, it was Clark's unique charisma and talent in-ring, as well as his promos and character work, that led him to becoming a favorite of the fans. The modern day audience gets behind Velveteen in this feud: perhaps something they would not have done had this gimmick been introduced two decades earlier. It is important to note that Velveteen's gimmick is based very much on Prince. The musician was known for a "gender transgressive" appearance on stage: "he wore eyeliner, high heels, and outfits that often included ruffles, lace, crop tops,

---

[31] 'The 2017 NXT Year-End Awards were presented on the NXT TakeOver: Philadelphia Pre-Show'

spandex, and velvet."[32] Like Goldust, the writers of NXT attempt to establish Velveteen's villainy through outrageous costuming, but this would actually become part of the reason why the audience would gravitate towards him.

The importance of speech is a critical focus on the feud between Black and Dream, as at the centre of their rivalry was the fact that Aleister refused to acknowledge Velveteen, or "say his name."[33] Warden writes that "spoken language is intricately bound up with the body, a fact we unconsciously acknowledge every day when we open our mouths and use our larynx, lips, tongue and diaphragm to articulate our thoughts."[34] Speech is something physical, and something that can be violent: this is important to consider when thinking about the active and physical nature of professional wrestling. The ability to cut compelling and entertaining promos that build a story between competitors is crucial. The feud begins when Aleister Black enters the ring to speak for the very first time: up until this point, his character had been silent. As Black is delivering his promo, which states his intention to go after the NXT Championship, Velveteen Dream's music hits. On commentary, Mauro Ranallo describes Dream as "a man that's the polar opposite of Aleister Black."[35] The use of purple in Dream's entrance lighting, as well as him wearing purple sunglasses, are all a nod to Prince. Dream enters wearing hoop earrings and a velvet crop top, a notably feminized appearance compared to Aleister's dark coloured suit. The juxtaposition of Dream's muscles with a feminized costume sees a "paradoxical masculinity" being presented, where "reverence for the traditional signs of masculinity and the

---

[32] Twila L. Perry, 'Conscious and Strategic Representations of Race: Prince, Music, Black Lives, and Race Scholarship' in *Southern California Interdisciplinary Law Journal*, Vol. 27, No. 549 (2018) pp. 549-592, p. 551

[33] *NXT (Episode 415) (WWE Network*, 11th October 2017)

[34] Clare Warden, 'Pops and promos: Speech and silence in professional wrestling' in in *Performance and Professional Wrestling*, edited by Broderick Chow et al. (Abingdon: Routledge, 2017) pp. 17-25, p. 17

[35] Ibid.

violation of those signs"[36] are simultaneously at work. Dream is not presented as stereotypically masculine, but he is not as overtly queer in his costume as Goldust either. In modern WWE, it might be said that queer villainy has become much more subtle, though still exposing gender as a performance.

Black remains stoic as Velveteen tells him that he has "walked through darkness only to be blinded by the light that is your Velveteen Dream."[37] Darkness and light remain an important motif throughout the feud, with Dream bragging about being a star and wanting to have the spotlight and the attention of the audience on him. As he speaks to Aleister, Dream leans in closely to his face, focusing on his mouth, as though he is going to kiss him. Instead of basking in the "experience" of Velveteen Dream, Aleister kicks the microphone out of his hand, and sits cross legged in the centre of the ring, which elicits cheers from the crowd. However, Velveteen recovers, drops to his knees, leans in again towards Aleister's face (eliciting another extremely positive and excited pop from the crowd), but then slithers out of the ring, all the while maintaining eye contact with his opponent. Although we can see that Velveteen's queerness is far less obvious than a character like Goldust, his character's Otherness is still present. The swift act of violence against him quickly re-establishes Aleister Black as the more masculine competitor, and might be considered an instance of queer behavior being policed.

The feud would continue on NXT television for the next two months. The next encounter between the pair would be Dream beating up Black's opponent Lio Rush before their match began. Aleister stands on the ramp, watching as Velveteen gyrates his hips while staring intently at Black, who then delivers his finishing move, the Purple Rainmaker, to Rush.[38]

---

[36] Brian Pronger, Brian. *The Arena of Masculinity: Sports, Homosexuality and the Meaning of Sex* (London: GMP, 1990), p. 145
[37] *NXT (Episode 412)*
[38] *NXT (Episode 414)* (*WWE Network*, 4th October, 2017)

Once again, the character of Velveteen Dream is clearly established as being modelled on Prince. Interestingly, this gimmick of 'being Prince' was tried with Patrick Clark a year prior to this feud, but the crowd are audibly unimpressed as he walks down to the ring.[39] The trouble with the original gimmick was that it ultimately lacked subtlety: Clark begins one promo "NXT Universe, we are gathered here today to get to this thing called NXT Takeover: Toronto." The spoken intro at the beginning of Prince's 1984 track "Let's Go Crazy" begins "Dearly beloved/We are gathered here today/To get through this thing called 'life."[40] WWE's use of his lyrics was uncreative and cheap. The Velveteen Dream is still modelled on the type of queer Black masculinity Prince embodied, but there is a different angle to Dream: his main goal is to have the spotlight and the attention on him. This is a more fully realised character than just imitating Prince, which is why the Velveteen Dream is far more engaging and compelling than Patrick Clark's initial incarnation. Mazer believes that "while the professional wrestling performance always presents a version of masculinity that is sanctioned by the dominant culture, its presentation of alternative masculinities as concurrent proposes a community of men that is inclusive of a wide range of identities and behaviors."[41] Prince is the public figure that provides the "alternative" masculinity that Mazer discusses. The racial similarities between Clark and Prince must be noted: Prince might be considered the most public example of a queer Black masculinity, and to perform a queer Black masculinity means to imitate him in some way.

---

[39] *Shinsuke Nakamura is interrupted by Patrick Clark: WWE NXT, Oct. 19, 2016* [YouTube video] October 19th 2016 https://www.youtube.com/watch?time_continue=76&v=5vItnjtsyG0 (accessed 21st April 2019)
[40] 'Let's Go Crazy' lyrics, *Genius* [online] n.d. https://genius.com/Prince-and-the-revolution-lets-go-crazy-lyrics (accessed 21st April 2019)
[41] Mazer, 1998, p. 90

As the feud progressed, Velveteen would continue to come to the ring during Aleister's matches, even stealing his jacket at one point, but he was still not able to get the attention of Black.[42] Taking and wearing Aleister's jacket might be a form of drag for Dream's character: as we have already established, Velveteen's masculinity can certainly be considered 'alternative' to hegemonic norms of masculinity. However, the same can also be said for Black's Goth character. Mazer notes that "rather than prescribing limitations to masculine behavior, professional wrestling recognizes [...] and, it might be argued, even encourages the unleashing of masculinity expressivity in all forms."[43] One of the reasons this rivalry was so intriguing is because the types of masculinities featured in the feud, both queer and of a non-hegemonic sub-culture, are not often seen in professional wrestling. Ford believes that wrestling writers should be "proposing alternative storylines which value new types of stories and new types of faces and heels (wrestling parlance for heroes and villains), or even a greater moral complexity in what constitutes being a face and a heel."[44] This rivalry was so interesting because it was something different. The new types of heel and face that Velveteen and Aleister respectively performed were queer in that they were not traditionally what an audience would consider heels or faces. Aleister's character of a brooding Goth, is not what the audience expects of the face, but is extremely popular anyway. The queer villainy of Velveteen, rather than being reviled in the way Goldust's character was, manages to eventually garner the sympathy of the crowd.

The final encounter between the two on television before their pay-per-view match would be the apex of the homoerotic nature of the feud. As Black walks to the ring for his scheduled match, Velveteen Dream rises from the dry ice of Aleister's entrance and ambushes him from behind. Velveteen ties Aleister up in the ring ropes, and slaps Black's face,

---

[42] *NXT (Episode 416) (WWE Network*, 18th October, 2017)
[43] Mazer, 1998, p. 90
[44] Ford, 2017, p. 179

demanding that he say his name in a scenario that evokes elements of bondage and domination. Commentary describe this exchange as "the most vulnerable we have seen Aleister Black in NXT!"[45] According to Henricks, wrestling "provides 'alternative scenes of dominance and submission' through the presentation of moments when either one contestant or the other is very far ahead."[46] Despite Velveteen being the more feminized character, he shows a great amount of in-ring aggression and masculine power as he stands over Aleister Black. As we already saw with Goldust, by attributing this masculinity to the character, the queer threat of Velveteen is neutralized to some extent. Sammond writes that in wrestling, the practice of BDSM is "ostensibly stripped of its overtly sexual connotations [...] s/m in wrestling emerges in submission holds that test the endurance of wrestlers [...] to absorb as much pain as they can."[47] Aleister is shown to be able to "absorb" the pain of Velveteen's slaps in a submissive position, but the overall domination has sexual implications. Pronger muses that "masculine wrestling is revealed as nothing but an appearance that must yield to erotic reality."[48] Aleister would be submitting to Velveteen's domination by saying his name. The promo Dream cuts a few days before the pay-per-view match further emphasises the sexually charged nature of their match: "Aleister Black, gotcha! [...] The Velveteen Dream is on your mind. And in Houston at Takeover, when all that's dark comes to the light, The Velveteen Dream will get what he wants, when your lips say my name."[49] Again, speech and the mouth are a key motif in the feud. Speech in professional wrestling has violent power. The domination that Dream wants is rooted

---

[45] *NXT (Episode 417) (WWE Network,* 25th October, 2017)

[46] Thomas Henricks, 'Professional Wrestling as Moral Order' in *Sociological Inquiry*, Vol. 44, No. 3 (1974) pp. 177-188, p. 180

[47] Nicholas Sammond, 'Introduction: A Brief and Unnecessary Defense of Professional Wrestling' in *Steel Chair to the Head: The Pleasure and Pain of Professional Wrestling*, edited by Nicholas Sammond (London: Duke University Press, 2005) pp. 1-21 , p. 11

[48] Pronger, 1990, p. 146

[49] *NXT (Episode 419) (WWE Network*, 8th November, 2017)

in language, but he is clearly willing to use sexualized violence to play mind games with Aleister in order to get what he wants.

This eight week feud culminated in a pay-per-view match at *NXT Takeover: War Games*. Velveteen walks to the ring wiping his mouth, once again drawing attention to the importance of lips and speech in this feud. As he enters the ring he takes off the leather coverings to his trousers to reveal his trousers with both his and Aleister Black's faces on them, with "Say My Name" emblazoned across the crotch.[50] The commentary team reference 'Ravishing' Rick Rude,[51] another wrestler who "often wore his opponent's likeness on his crotch or buttocks […] his aggressive conflation with masculine and feminine, of gay and straight aesthetics was extraordinarily successful in generating what can be recognized as genuine heel heat: spectators hated him."[52] However, instead of rejecting Velveteen's mind games, the crowd pop for this costume choice and chant for him. Dream then tells Aleister "they know my name! You're gonna say it too!"[53] In the same way that Rick Rude used this style of clothing as a heel tactic, Velveteen's non-conformist fashion choices demonstrates how queer villainy in professional wrestling has progressed to be more about subtle character work. However, it might be said that Velveteen is not considered a traditional heel, given how much the crowd are on his side during this match. The audience might believe that queerness is not an attribute to fear in our contemporary times, and so change the writers' direction on where Dream's character was going, once again demonstrating the importance of the audience in this medium.

Like Goldust, Velveteen also conflates the masculine and the feminine with an aggressive, powerhouse style in-ring. Nonetheless, he also adds

---

[50] *Velveteen Dream makes his fashionable in-ring entrance: NXT Takeover: WarGames* [YouTube video] 18th November 2017
https://www.youtube.com/watch?v=u4qb7e1ErwA (accessed 17th April 2019)
[51] *NXT Takeover: WarGames (WWE Network,* 18th November, 2017)
[52] Mazer, 1998, p. 94
[53] *NXT Takeover: WarGames*

a certain flair to his moves, further adding to his character's development as a "flamboyant upstart."[54] His Death Valley Driver (later named the Dream Valley Driver) is different to other wrestlers as he cartwheels out of it,[55] his Swinging Spike DDT incorporates a twist rather than just a vertical drop like the original move.[56] Professional wrestling is a form of world building: every element of a character, from costume to promos to the way an individual wrestles, has to be in sync. It therefore makes sense that Velveteen's wrestling, while aggressive, is still queer in some way.

After an evenly contested and exciting match, it would be Velveteen's showboating that would cost him the victory. Ultimately, Aleister was able to win the match with his finishing move Black Mass, a spinning heel kick, which cuts off Dream telling Aleister his name one last time.[57] For Barthes, defeat in wrestling "is not a conventional sign, abandoned as soon as it is understood; it is not an outcome, but quite the contrary, it is a duration, a display."[58] It could be said that Velveteen's loss only lasted a short "duration", for Aleister gets a microphone, turns to his dazed opponent, and says "enjoy infamy, Velveteen Dream," thus granting him the acknowledgement he has been wanting for the past two months.[59] Barthes also says that "what wrestling is above all meant to portray is a purely moral concept: that of justice."[60] It was right that Aleister should win the in-ring battle: it maintained his undefeated streak, and he conducted himself 'properly' by not engaging in sabotage or mind games in the way Velveteen Dream did in the build to the match. Nonetheless, Nigel McGuiness astutely points out that by Black saying Velveteen's

---

[54] *NXT Takeover: WarGames*

[55] *Velveteen Dream- Death Valley Driver* [YouTube video] June 15th 2017 https://www.youtube.com/watch?v=WRkCF_FGPWk (accessed 22nd April 2019)

[56] *Velveteen Dream- Swinging Spike DDT* [YouTube video] November 19th 2017 https://www.youtube.com/watch?v=iiCBjmOOkmA (accessed 22nd April 2019)

[57] *NXT Takeover: WarGames*

[58] Barthes, 1957, p. 10

[59] *NXT Takeover: WarGames*

[60] Barthes, 1957, p. 10

name, "both men won."[61] The idea of justice that Barthes believed to be central to wrestling is queered in itself: neither man ultimately triumphed over the other, because they each got what they wanted. The queer villainy of Dream is simultaneously neutralized as an overarching threat by being physically defeated, but also at the same time, the final part of the feud is Aleister uttering Velveteen's name. In ending the rivalry like this, Velveteen Dream's queer character is therefore established as a massive talent that is not going to be vanquished so easily.

Part of the queerness of Velveteen Dream is related to Patrick Clark Jr's success in the business as a Black man. In 2015, Clark took part in WWE's reality TV series *Tough Enough,* but was eliminated by judge Hulk Hogan. Hogan justified his decision as the elimination being his way of "setting [Clark] up for greatness,"[62] despite Clark performing well in the episode.[63] Given that Hogan was fired by the WWE two days after this because of racist and homophobic comments,[64] it might be implied that race was a factor in Clark's elimination. For his championship match at *NXT Takeover: War Games II* against Tommaso Ciampa, Velveteen came out dressed as Hollywood Hulk Hogan,[65] but still added elements such as black and white feather boas and earrings, as well as his Prince-esque sunglasses, to be in keeping with his own character's queer appearance. Even the New World Order (NWO) logo, Hogan's World Championship Wrestling (WCW) faction, was changed to OVA, to fit with Velveteen's

---

[61] *NXT Takeover: WarGames*
[62] Christopher Jeter, 'Velveteen Dream proving that he's the star Hulk Hogan said he wasn't' *Daily DDT* [online] (18th November 2018) https://dailyddt.com/2018/11/18/velveteen-dream-proving-star-that-hulk-hogan-said-he-wasnt/ (accessed 25th March 2019)
[63] *Tanner and Patrick's war (of words) continues: WWE Tough Enough Digital Extra, July 14th, 2015* [YouTube video] July 14th 2015 https://www.youtube.com/watch?v=6ccl24gkJ4w (accessed 23rd April 2019)
[64] 'Velveteen Dream proving that he's the star Hulk Hogan said he wasn't'
[65] *Velveteen Dream makes a Hollywood entrance: NXT Takeover: WarGames II (WWE Network Exclusive)* [YouTube video] 17th November 2018 https://www.youtube.com/watch?v=UMuOqcszfV8 (accessed 22nd April 2019)

signature phrase, 'Dream Over.'[66] Christopher Jeter writes that "not only did Dream come to the ring dressed in Hollywood Hulk Hogan attire, which alluded to Hogan's late-90's renaissance in WCW, he also used Hogan's signature three punch-big boot-leg drop comeback as part of HIS fire-up sequence."[67] This appropriation of Hogan's costuming and wrestling style is a way of queering wrestling's racist past. As Perry establishes, "the bodies of Black males have long been the subject of fear and derision. The Black male body is both subjugated and feared."[68] Black masculinity in wrestling is often limited to the character of the 'monstrous athlete.' Bobby Lashley being Donald Trump's prize fighter at *WrestleMania 23* is a good example of this. Velveteen Dream, while still only in the developmental brand of WWE, has already been highlighted as a future star by many members of the old guard.[69][70] This queering, it could be argued, is a reflection of the changing business as a whole, where the new talent appearing in the WWE is more racially diverse. Jeter continues "not only is Dream one of the most charismatic and athletically gifted young wrestlers on the WWE roster, but he has also effectively used smark[71] terminology time and time again to advance many of his feuds, subverting the very criticisms Hogan levied against him."[72] Clark

---

[66] *Velveteen Dream makes a Hollywood entrance: NXT Takeover: WarGames II (WWE Network Exclusive)*

[67] 'Velveteen Dream proving that he's the star Hulk Hogan said he wasn't'

[68] Perry, 2018, p. 586

[69] Raza Kazi, 'Shawn Michaels has handpicked one NXT star as his protégé' *Give Me Sport* [online] n.d. https://www.givemesport.com/1249749-shawn-michaels-has-handpicked-one-nxt-star-as-his-protege (accessed 23rd April 2019)

[70] Felix Upton, 'Triple H on Velveteen's Potential: "It's Scary How Good He Will Be"' *Ringside News* [online] (17th November 2018) https://www.ringsidenews.com/2018/11/17/triple-h-velveteen-dreams-potential-scary-good-will/ (accessed 23rd April 2019)

[71] Slang that describes a 'smart mark.' In wrestling terminology, a mark is someone that views the wrestling product within the confines of kayfabe (the reality in which wrestling exists), whereas a smark has 'inside' knowledge of the wrestling business and uses this to pick apart or critique booking decisions.

[72] 'Velveteen Dream proving that he's the star Hulk Hogan said he wasn't'

represents the future of the business, perhaps meaning that there is now room in professional wrestling for queer characters and people of color to carve out a space for themselves to be taken seriously.

The performance of queer villainy in the WWE has progressed over time, as societal norms have become marginally more accepting of queerness. When Goldust was performing in the 1990s, his character was reviled by the crowds for his femininity, whereas in our contemporary age, Velveteen Dream is loved by fans for the queerness he performs. Despite existing in separate historical eras of the business, however, the femininity of both characters is seemingly neutralized by their aggressive and masculine in-ring performances. Nonetheless, the character work of both Velveteen and Goldust still demonstrate the ways in which professional wrestling "expose[s] the vulnerable and uncertain construction of masculinity."[73] Queerness is still seen as threatening the hegemonic masculinity of the wrestling ring, even though it frequently reveals the performative nature of gender. It could be said that "nowhere in the sports world is homoeroticism implied more than in professional wrestling,"[74] which is definitely seen in the Velveteen/Aleister feud. While having queerness partially represented in the biggest wrestling company in the world by an interesting and nuanced character such as Velveteen Dream is a positive step forward for the corporation, WWE still only have one openly gay person on their entire roster in 2019.[75] Perhaps it is too much to expect a billion dollar corporation with links to the Trump administration[76] to present us with carefully written queer storylines featuring openly queer talent.

[73] Sammond, 2005, p. 13

[74] Oppliger, 2004, p. 97

[75] Brock Koller, 'New Jersey's Daria Berenato taking risks, making history on path to WWE' ABC Action News [online] (28th June 2015) https://6abc.com/sports/njs-daria-berenato-taking-risks-making-history-at-wwe/812066/ (accessed 23rd April 2019)

[76] Feliks Garcia, 'Linda McMahon: Senate confirms former WWE executive for Small Business Administration post' The Independent [online] (14th February 2017)

Spenser Santos - The RiSE of SHIMMER and the Renaissance of Women's Professional Wrestling

Spenser Santos is a Visiting Assistant Professor in the English Department at the University of Iowa. They have been a wrestling fan since birth, and have incorporated pro wrestling as an object of analysis in literature classes. Twitter - twitter.com/SaintRidley

On November 6, 2005, the landscape of women's wrestling transformed forever. A ragtag group of 18 wrestlers banded together with Ring of Honor commentator and manager Dave Prazak to put on the first ever SHIMMER show. The wrestlers came from all over, and they had in common a frustration with the limited roles available for them in the North American wrestling scene at the time. Quite often they would be the only woman booked for a show and, rather than perform opposite a man in the ring, they would be relegated to valet duty. Prazak was the glue bonding the women of this first show, as he worked alongside them and heard their frustrations. From their desire to wrestle and Prazak's connections with Ring of Honor, an idea was born: SHIMMER Women Athletes.

SHIMMER is a small outfit. Most often they run out of the Berwyn Eagles Club, a small venue in a Chicago suburb configured to seat some 220 or so fans. They tape four shows over the course of a weekend and hold tapings twice a year (they are currently transitioning to two shows over the course of a weekend). Three times a year on occasion. Otherwise, the only other shows SHIMMER puts on are their WrestleMania weekend

https://www.independent.co.uk/news/world/americas/linda-mcmahon-confirmation-donald-trump-cabinet-wwe-ceo-small-business-administration-a7580226.html (accessed 27th April 2019) shows, usually held in a nightclub or other similar venue. The tapings are marathon feats of endurance for the wrestlers and fans alike, and yet many fans return season after season. What draws them isn't spectacle (they could get that in WWE, AEW, or other larger promotions), nor even necessarily the quality of the wrestlers' work. SHIMMER is home to exceptional wrestlers, but so are many promotions. What SHIMMER brings to the table that no other promotion can is its history.

When SHIMMER was founded, women's wrestling as a field was in perhaps its worst slump ever. The British independent scene did not have many women of prominence, nor the promotions to foster their growth (Saraya Knight would found Bellatrix Female Warriors in 2006 and Pro-Wrestling: EVE would not be founded by Dann and Emily Read until 2010). Women's wrestling in Mexico was not much more than a side act, considered less valuable than the minis (not a dig at the minis, as many fantastic luchadores have been part of that division like Mascarita Sagrada and Mascarita Dorada). Part of the problem for both Britain and Mexico was a reflection of the broader problem faced by North America at the time. North America was a desolate wasteland for serious independent women's wrestling. But what about Japan, where women's wrestling had always been strongest? Japan was in the midst of a complete collapse of the women's side of the industry. SHIMMER came about in the middle of all of this, and the promotion strove to offer what had not been on offer in American wrestling rings for fifty years: quality women's wrestling.

Since SHIMMER's emergence, numerous other independent women's promotions have cropped up around the world. Mixed-gender promotions have poached from talent highlighted by SHIMMER and built divisions around them. Promotions like TNA and WWE changed their approach to women's wrestling. Little by little the wrestling world has grown more hospitable to women, and even in Japan *joshi puroresu* has rebuilt and begun to thrive once more. In order to properly contextualize what SHIMMER was fighting against and striving to achieve, it is imperative to understand the highs and lows of American and Japanese women's wrestling prior to 2005. Only then can the SHIMMER project be put into perspective and its contributions to women's wrestling as a whole be understood.

Light: Mildred Burke and the Birth and Heyday of *Joshi Puroresu*

In the early television era as the 1940s gave way to the 1950s, professional wrestling received a surge of interest from women. Television meant augmenting the flash and pageantry of the sport, and personalities like Gorgeous George emerged and created the world of gimmicks that professional wrestling is based on today. The rise of television brought a larger female audience, with women comprising roughly 60 percent of live audiences in many cases and as much as "90 percent of the TV wrestling audience."[77] While women's wrestling was never quite a mainstream attraction in the United States even at this time, this period marked the height of women's wrestling up until the present resurgence. American women's wrestling was primarily the purview of Billy Wolfe and his troupe of wrestlers, and they drew crowds and made money off Mildred Burke as champion.

So what happened to American women's wrestling to bring it to the point where SHIMMER needed to be founded? In part, the breakup of Billy Wolfe's dominance over women's wrestling doomed the women's side of the industry. Wolfe's stranglehold on women's wrestling meant there was only one group to book women from: his group. And Wolfe was not well-regarded, in large part because he sexually exploited his wrestlers. In the words of Freddie Blassie, women were often booked as "curiosities,

[77] Jeff Leen, *The Queen of the Ring: Sex, Muscles, Diamonds, and the Making of an American Legend* (Atlantic Monthly Press, 2009), 156.

like midgets and freaks" to appeal to a "sick, deviant taste."[78] Of Billy Wolfe, the common perception among the mainstream men in the business was that they "thought of him as a pimp."[79] Wolfe was also not part of the boys' club of the NWA, and many male wrestlers saw little reason for women to fall under the NWA's purview. Lou Thesz, in his autobiography, claims that while he had nothing against the idea of women wrestlers, he "never met one – a wrestler, that is" during his career because they were performers working to titillate male audiences. Thesz recalls that he was happy when the NWA ruled that he did not have to appear on cards where women were promoted.[80] Although women's wrestling was a profitable venture, it certainly was not part of the mainstream of the sport for audiences or fellow wrestlers.

More damaging to women's wrestling was the end of Burke's reign. She and June Byers, whom Wolfe had crowned champion while Burke was injured, wrestled in a shoot match (a legitimate wrestling contest) on August 20, 1954 to determine the undisputed World Women's champion. The generally-agreed upon story is that Burke went down when her knee dislocated 16 minutes into the first fall, then wrestled to a stalemate in the second fall until the match was ended at 63 minutes. On the strength of her victory in the first fall, Wolfe was able to hit the press and get the story out that June Byers was the new champion, though Burke maintained her claim that she had not been beaten in two falls and thus had never lost. As Dave Meltzer put it, "Byers was never able to draw like Burke" and the popularity of women's wrestling dwindled with the split between Burke and Wolfe.[81] Two years later the NWA pulled its own double cross on Byers, crowning a new champion without involving

[78] Freddie Blassie and Keith Elliot Greenburg, *Listen, You Pencil Neck Geeks* (Pocket Books, 2004), 33.
[79] Freddie Blassie, *Listen, You Pencil Neck Geeks*, 34.
[80] Lou Thesz and Kit Bauman, *Hooker* (Crowbar Press, 2011), 151-52.
[81] Dave Meltzer, *The Wrestling Observer Newsletter*, April 3, 2017.

Byers in the match (just as Byers was first declared champion by Wolfe): The Fabulous Moolah.

Moolah's tenure as top dog in women's wrestling was almost entirely enabled by her ownership of the championship and the rights to promote women's wrestling on NWA cards. She would eventually sell her championship to Vince McMahon, who promoted the new WWF Women's Championship with Wendi Richter as the new face of women's wrestling.[82] Moolah kept women's wrestling in the United States at the side show level and never strove to grow it, content instead to use her stable to prop herself up. The declining popularity of women's wrestling in the United States seemed almost permanent, as nothing WWF did (and they were the only promotion to even attempt anything with women's wrestling) from the 80s until the arrival of SHIMMER made any difference.

McMahon's experiment with Wendi Richter didn't take off. He tried again in the 1990s with Alundra Blayze, but the effort was half-hearted and ended with Blayze's contract not being renewed while she was still champion, leading to her famously trashing the belt on *WCW Monday Nitro*.[83] Women in wrestling became relegated to the role of bikini models, objects of lust for the male viewing audience. Some women made the effort to become good wrestlers, but the role carved out for them was limited at best. As Dave Meltzer explains:

> But no matter who came along, the women's match at the house show was a quick throwaway prelim match that was far more about pretty women in skimpy outfits than wrestling. While some of the women were reasonably good, that wasn't why they were there, and there were far better women working outside the main roster who never got a call. Some of them were very pretty in real

---

[82] Dave Meltzer, *The Wrestling Observer Newsletter*, June 29, 2015.
[83] James Dixon, *Titan Sinking: The Decline of the WWF in 1995* (History of Wrestling, 2014), 206-7.

world standards, but John Laurinaitis would tell people, "We're looking for 10s." Natalie Neidhart had been wrestling for years before she ever got a chance, and that's with being part of arguably the most famous wrestling family in North America. Sara Amato (Sara Del Rey), one of the best woman wrestlers in the country over the past 15 years, was hired by the company as a trainer, with the idea she didn't have the looks to be a main roster performer, without even testing it out by giving her a shot.[84]

WWF/WWE's vision of women's wrestling, explained above, was part and parcel of the branding of the women as Divas, a separate designation from the men who were branded as Superstars and one which was designed to marginalize. Divas, as Sasha Banks explained in an interview with Chris Jericho, were supposed to wrestle a style that was feminized and sexualized. It meant they had to "be girly, do hair pulling, do catfights," she said.[85] Divas were restricted from competing in some of the types of matches that the men could compete in, and they were given limited time and training. Diva matches were popularly seen as an opportunity by fans to go to the bathroom or restock on snacks, as nothing significant would happen. After all, there weren't significant stories being told, so nothing significant *could* happen.

Where the industry in the United States had fallen off a cliff, women's wrestling in Japan had thrived for decades leading into the 1990s. Mildred Burke may have been blacklisted in America following the shoot with June Byers, but she toured Japan beginning in November 1954. Her first excursion to Japan drew 15,000 to see women's wrestling on November 19, 1954 in an event that was televised and which elicited both approval for putting on a good show and disapproval for being too tame

[84] Dave Meltzer, *The Wrestling Observer Newsletter*, June 9, 2014.
[85] Jericho, Chris, "EP168 – Sasha Banks," *Talk Is Jericho*, Podcast audio, August 12, 2015. https://omny.fm/shows/talk-is-jericho/tij-ep168-sasha-banks

compared to the likes of Rikidozan.[86] This first Japan tour sold out three shows at the then-new Kurama Kokugikan Hall (which in 1984 was torn down and replaced as the main site of Sumo wrestling by Ryogoku Kokugikan, also known in English as Sumo Hall), and Burke would reflect that this was "the biggest moment" of her life.[87] The early Burke tours would lay the foundation for what would come: All Japan Women's Pro Wrestling.[88]

All Japan Women remains, nearly 15 years after its death, the single most successful women's wrestling promotion in history. It had the best financial backing (time will tell if STARDOM will be the recipient of more financial support as of its acquisition by Bushiroad on October 17, 2019), the longest tenure at just shy of 40 years, and significant boom periods which included the most-attended women's wrestling show of all time, Big Egg Wrestling Universe.[89] Founded in 1968, the promotion held a de facto monopoly over women's wrestling in Japan until competition began to spring up starting in 1986. Its audience was, during its heyday, primarily young women, though as this audience aged out of interest in the wrestlers television ratings declined until the final AJW broadcast aired in 2002. And even in Japan, where women's wrestling thrived, there was a stigma attached to it, as Dave Meltzer described after his 1987 visit

---

[86] United Press, "15,000 See Girls Grapple," *The Pacific Stars & Stripes*, November 21, 1954. https://i.redd.it/rosb4dtpw3x11.png

[87] Burke wrote that she was "pioneering women's wrestling in Japan, breaking through centuries of tradition instead of the simple prejudice" she had overcome in the United States. Jeff Leen, *The Queen of the Ring*, 243.

[88] She had also, prior to the match with Byers, been instrumental in establishing women's wrestling in Mexico during the 1930s and 1940s. See Ricardo Cárdenas Pérez, "Representaciones y roles femeninos en el cine mexicano de luchadoras," *Balajú* 7 (julio-diciembre 2017): 43-44.

[89] Big Egg Wrestling Universe drew either 32,500 or 42,500 fans to the Tokyo Dome, for a gross revenue of over $8 million. Dave Meltzer early gave figures of 42,500, though he and other sources now agree on 32,500 for attendance. See Meltzer, *Wrestling Observer Newsletter*, November 28, 1994 and LaPrade and Murphy, *Sisterhood of the Squared Circle*, 314-17.

to Japan: "The people who attend the men's matches do not attend the women's matches in Japan. It is a completely different audience and in fact the Japanese fans and reporters that we met couldn't even understand why we were so interested in the girls [*sic*] card. There is a definite negative stigma about the girls, at least among the wrestling fans probably because the show is so obviously designed at mainly reaching teenage girls."[90] With the proliferation of competing promotions, bad real estate deals by the family that owned AJW throwing the financial backing of the company into disarray, and declining television ratings, the road turned bumpy for the venerable promotion after the final boom of the early 1990s.[91]

By the middle of the 1990s, All Japan Women was just one of many promotions and had lost its sterling reputation. Its competitors, such as Ladies Legend Pro Wrestling and JWP Joshi Puroresu, as well as ARSION, GAEA, and others were often its equal, and none quite reached the heights that AJW had once achieved. In order to maintain some level of draw, co-promotion of events between All Japan Women and the other promotions often took place, though these seem to have contributed to further erosion of interest, and more importantly of the scene. The Quebrada news archive for AJW lists for November 30, 2001 Nick Higley's thoughts on AJW's announcement of a working relationship with the struggling ARSION: "this is a last gasp desperation move to save the promotion. Somebody should have told Rossi Ogawa that the last two companies to co-promote with AJW (JWP and NEO) were forced to shut down temporarily after the interpromotional period ended."[92] What was once a revered institution was in its final years only able to survive by cannibalizing the competition without generating growth. The market for women's wrestling in Japan was at its lowest point ever, and the scene

---

[90] Dave Meltzer, *Wrestling Observer Newsletter*, December 21, 1987.

[91] Dave Meltzer, *Wrestling Observer Newsletter*, June 12, 2017.

[92] Higley, Nick, "11/30," *Quebrada News Archive*, November 30, 2001. http://www.quebrada.net/news/NewsAJW5.html

was on the verge of collapse. ARSION was the first to die in 2003, followed by GAEA and AJW in 2005 and Jd' in 2007. LLPW continues today, though smaller than it was in the 90s, and many small promotions were founded in the wake of the mid-2000s collapse, with no true successor to AJW evident. Joshi wrestling has been firmly a niche interest in wrestling fandom since the mid-90s and completely out of mainstream thought since the demise of AJW (again, it is too early to tell what the Bushiroad acquisition of STARDOM may mean for the industry).

The collapse of Japanese women's wrestling in the early to mid-2000s marked the lowest point in women's wrestling globally. The West had virtually no outlets for women interested in actually performing as wrestlers, and Japan was in a state of serious contraction which meant that there simply was no possibility of building back up any time soon. The world of women's professional wrestling was shrouded in a darkness that threatened to be absolute and eternal. What it needed was a way forward.

SHIMMER like a Girl

If 2005 was the nadir of women's wrestling worldwide, it was also the year where things began to lurch back into a positive direction. In 2017 Dave Prazak recalled how SHIMMER was born. He had been booking the women's division in IWA Mid-South and after getting together with Allison Danger, Rain, and Lacey. Together they decided the time was right to put together a women's wrestling DVD series. This was the height of popularity for DVD as a distribution model for professional wrestling, and focusing on women's wrestling would bring a unique spin, which Dave considers a must for any start-up independent promotion: "if you're going to promote independent wrestling you need to have something unique to bring to the table rather than just be another of the dozens of – actually hundreds, probably, it is hundreds – hundreds of other promotions around the world."[93] SHIMMER was certainly unique, and it had the backing of a major promotion in Ring of Honor for DVD distribution. Women's wrestling had been an interest of Prazak's since AJW's last boom period of the early 90s, and he wondered why a women's wrestling product focused on athleticism and competition like that had never taken off in North America. The goal of SHIMMER, as he explained to Bryan Alvarez a few days before SHIMMER's debut show, was "to see what the female wrestlers of the United States can do if taken seriously and not relegated to taking each other's clothes off."[94]

When SHIMMER started, there was no certainty that it would ever be more than the one weekend event. After a year, Dave Prazak reflected that nobody really knew what would come of it. It could have just been the "one taping that we did in early November of last year and people wouldn't buy the DVD and people wouldn't support us live and maybe the Ring of Honor fans wouldn't take women's wrestling seriously and not give it a shot."[95] What began with a single two-volume taping on November 6, 2005 would grow to 117 volumes and counting. SHIMMER's taping schedule would morph over time, taking over an entire weekend for a four-volume taping for the first time with volumes 23-26 on May 2-3, 2008. The four-volume weekend became a standard for SHIMMER, allowing them to maximize the value achieved for the promotion's expenditures, particularly on airfare. SHIMMER pays for the wrestlers who aren't Chicago locals to fly in, Dave Prazak explains, "so the only way that we can make this profitable is if we film several shows worth of content out of every plane ticket that we have to buy."[96] The

[93] Brian Tramel, "Dave Prazak, Episode 20, Season 3," *Shooting the Shiznit*, May 27, 2017. https://player.fm/series/shooting-the-shiznit/dave-prazak-episode-20-season-3
[94] Bryan Alvarez, "November 1, 2005 Figure Four Daily," *Figure Four Daily*, November 1, 2005.
[95] Bryan Alvarez, "November 8, 2006 Figure Four Daily," *Figure Four Daily*, November 8, 2006.
[96] Brian Tramel, "Dave Prazak."

four-volume weekend would become a standard for SHIMMER for the next decade, through volume 117.[97]

Even a year into SHIMMER's existence, there was a perception that there were promotions taking SHIMMER's gimmick. Prazak was unsure there were a lot at that time, but he did note APW's annual Chickfight tournament and NECW's World Women's Wrestling shows and how all were united in their desire to elevate the perception of women's wrestling.[98] More promotions have since sprung up to continue that mission across the U.S. and Europe: Bellatrix Female Warriors, World Women's Wrestling (2006-2010), WSU (2007), Pro Wrestling Women's Alliance (2007-2013), Femmes Fatales (2009), Pro-Wrestling: EVE (2010), SHINE (2012), Queens of Combat (2014), RiSE (2016), and Women's Wrestling Revolution (2016) among others. SHIMMER wrestlers have contributed heavily to these promotions, as founders and as talent. Mercedes Martinez, for instance, feels that she has contributed to the popularity of Women Superstars United (formerly Women Superstars Uncensored) where she was champion for three years.[99] Without SHIMMER, WSU may not have gotten started, and without Martinez's standout performances in SHIMMER she may not have been in a position

---

[97] SHIMMER announced via Facebook on October 27, 2019 that they would move to a two-volumes over a weekend model beginning with volume 118, keeping the usual schedule of Spring/Fall tapings with a Wrestlemania weekend show as well as an annual Summit collaborative show on Summerslam weekend. Ultimately, the financial burden both for SHIMMER and for fans (whose tickets were priced according to the two-shows-in-one-day model) were the key factor. For more details, see the announcement post on Facebook:
https://www.facebook.com/groups/273879149381647/permalink/1974055126030699/.

[98] Bryan Alvarez, "November 8, 2006 Figure Four Daily," *Figure Four Daily*, November 8, 2006.

[99] Matthew Hollie, "Bellatrix vs. SHIMMER Countdown: Interview with Mercedes Martinez," *The Barbwire Blog*, September 6, 2013.
http://thebarbwireblog.blogspot.com/2013/09/bellatrix-vs-shimmer-countdown_6.html

to wrestle in the Women's J-Cup tournament that inspired Sean McCaffrey to begin the promotion in the first place.[100] McCaffrey wanted WSU to be a WWE to SHIMMER's more pure wrestling focused product, a promotion based on stories and characters. What he created was a bit more ECW than WWE, and as Jon Harder notes, WSU was an innovator right along with SHIMMER.[101]

SHIMMER's reputation, though, was well enough established by the time WSU came along that a promotion like WSU could take the chance of doing a more character-based, violence-focused women's wrestling promotion in the United States. SHIMMER had been no stranger to stipulation matches (Cheerleader Melissa and MsChif's falls count anywhere and last woman standing matches showed SHIMMER was willing to bloody its hands), though those were special occasions in SHIMMER. WSU would push that to the limit, building off SHIMMER's example that women's wrestling could be taken seriously on its own in America.[102] Along with SHIMMER, WSU was for years at the vanguard of a push for women's wrestling legitimacy in the United States. They held the first women's WarGames match at *Breaking Barriers 2*, and for several years WSU held the record for longest women's match in history. Burke and Byers had held the record with their shoot, but Mercedes Martinez and Angel Orsini broke it with a 70-minute match (later

---

[100] Sean McCaffrey, "In Praise of Mercedes Martinez," *SLAM! Sports*, July 13, 2007 http://slam.canoe.com/Slam/Wrestling/GuestColumn/2017/07/13/22737816.html.
[101] Harder particularly touts WSU's way of selling iPPVs for a niche product. See Jon Harder, "The MiC's WSU: Vastly Underrated Yet Influential," *Hardway HQ*, December 2, 2016 https://www.hardwayhq.com/single-post/2016/12/02/The-MiCs-Women-Superstars-Uncensored-Vastly-Underrated-and-Very-Influential
[102] WSU would go on to put on many ultraviolent matches and deliver many firsts in the industry, including the first women's WarGames match (which ended when Mercedes Martinez's team surrendered as Jessicka Havok raised a machete over her head) and two of the three longest women's matches in wrestling history (Angel Orsini vs. Mercedes Martinez on June 6, 2009 for 70 minutes and Mercedes Martinez vs. Lexxus on August 6, 2011 for 73 minutes).

surpassed in WSU by Martinez and Lexus at 73 minutes on August 6, 2011).[103]

Where SHIMMER has remained largely stationary and focused on its own style of wrestling, promotions aside from WSU have also taken their own spin off SHIMMER's proof of concept. SHINE is likewise relatively stationary, bouncing between Florida and New York, but has been focused on iPPV as a model of distribution. Pro-Wrestling: EVE launched one of the earliest subscription streaming platforms for a women's wrestling promotion with EVEonDemand and have put together the most attended all women's show in European history with their first Wrestle Queendom show.[104] More recently, RISE has become a touring show and the destination for some big matches, including the current recordholder for longest women's wrestling match in history.[105]

One of SHIMMER's more lasting legacies is its commitment to training the next generation of women in wrestling. SHIMMER once operated its own wrestling school in conjunction with ROH. The SHIMMER Wrestling Academy officially opened for business in 2008, offering dedicated classes for the numerous women who had inquired about how to train and become professional wrestlers.[106] The school remained in business until SHIMMER and ROH severed ties in the middle of 2011.[107]

---

[103] *Women Superstars Uncensored Presents: The Longest Women's Match in History*, DVD, Women Superstars Uncensored, 2011.

[104] Jamie Greer, "Pro Wrestling EVE Announces Women's Dream Match for SHEvivor Series," *Last Word on Pro Wrestling*, November 21, 2018 https://lastwordonprowrestling.com/2018/11/21/pro-wrestling-eve-announces-womens-dream-match-for-shevivor-series/.

[105] Mercedes Martinez vs. Tessa Blanchard for the Phoenix of RISE Championship in a 75 minute Iron Woman match at RISE 10 – INSANITY, https://www.youtube.com/watch?v=apoJgbkKRb0.

[106] Brad Dykens, "SHIMMER Wrestling School now open!," *Online World of Wrestling*, September 11, 2008 http://www.onlineworldofwrestling.com/shimmer-wrestling-school-now-open/.

[107] "F.A.Q." *SHIMMER Women's Professional Wrestling*, July 2017 http://www.shimmerwrestling.com/p/faq.html.

In August 2016, RISE was founded to help fill a much-needed gap in the American women's independent scene: that of a developmental system.[108] Part of the need for RISE came as a result of women's wrestling gaining traction among the major promotions once again, most notably in WWE.

With WWE waking up to women's wrestling once again, it is fair to say that SHIMMER's greatest legacy has been its effect on not only the independent scene, but the major promotions as well. The Knockouts Division of TNA was started in October 2007, centering around Gail Kim (who had been severely underutilized in WWE) and Awesome Kong (who had been appearing for SHIMMER for a year and a half by this point) as the premier feud of the new division. Under the previous NWA affiliation TNA's women's division was treated as less than a joke and comparable to the worst excesses of WWE's own treatment of women's wrestling (for example, Leilani Kai was stripped of the NWA Women's Title for refusing to defend it in NWA-TNA when the company's presentation of women was so horrendous). Now, however, the Knockouts division was knocking it out of the park and became one of the most vibrant and exciting parts of TNA's programming.[109] And while there have been ups and downs since the initial explosion of the Knockouts division, it remains one of Impact Wrestling's greatest strengths. It is such a strength, in fact, that Tessa Blanchard is poised to challenge Impact World Heavyweight Champion Sami Callihan at *Hard to Kill* on January 12, 2020 in a match where Blanchard is widely considered the favorite to become the first woman to hold a major

[108] Kevin Harvey, "Official Announcement: RISE 1 – IGNITE!," *RISE-Wrestling.com*, August 6, 2016 https://rise-wrestling.com/2016/08/06/official-announcement-rise-1-ignite/.

[109] Laprade and Murphy, *Sisterhood of the Squared Circle*, 222.

promotion's World Heavyweight Championship and break the gender barrier.[110]

Comparatively slower than TNA/Impact to catch on to the trend, WWE has also taken cues from SHIMMER and significantly altered their approach to women's wrestling. Gone are the segregation of the roster into Divas and Superstars (though women's matches remain othered with the gendered designation men's matches do not receive), the matches focused purely on sex appeal, the limitation of characters to variations on crazy and/or bitch archetypes, and the arbitrary limitations on wrestling style.[111] The Divas Revolution (later the Women's Revolution, most recently the Women's Evolution) has been part storyline and part real change behind the scenes in WWE, as the company has sought to capitalize openly on getting on board the women's wrestling bandwagon. In 2017 and 2018 WWE hosted a 32-women tournament, the Mae Young Classic, and featured numerous independent wrestlers from around the world as well as their own homegrown wrestlers. A look at WWE's current rosters reveals a significant number of SHIMMER alumnae as well (roughly 42% of the company's overall women's roster): 7/14 women on Raw (including current Raw Women's Champion Becky Lynch and Women's Tag Team Champion Asuka), 4/13 women on Smackdown (including current Smackdown Women's Champion Bayley), 6/15 women on NXT, 4/9 women on NXT UK (including current NXT UK Women's Champion Kay Lee Ray), and 7/15 current Performance Center Recruits.

---

[110] Tessa would not be the first woman to win a men's heavyweight championship. Mercedes Martinez became the first woman to win the AWS Heavyweight Championship on January 26, 2019, and Meiko Satomura had a brief run with DDT's KO-D Openweight Championship in the fall of 2018. Should she win, however, Tessa will have won the most prestigious men's championship of any woman to win one.

[111] Related to what Sasha Banks said about wrestling like Divas (see note 9), Michelle McCool relates how she and Melina got in trouble for wrestling a match that was "too good for girls." https://www.youtube.com/watch?v=7r3fWH8tX-c

And the influence is working. WWE's women's divisions have been the talk of the industry, particularly where one Becky Lynch is concerned. Lynch main evented WrestleMania, winning both the Raw and Smackdown Women's Championships against Ronda Rousey and Charlotte Flair. A SHIMMER alumna has taken the industry by storm, labeling herself "The Man" as a testament to how she has become the top dog of all professional wrestling.[112] Becky Lynch finding her edge in WWE came as a result of an attempted heel turn, a turn toward being a wrestling antagonist. The fans wouldn't have it, but the edge remained and made Lynch even more popular. Now, she sits atop the company as one of its clear faces and shows no signs of the crowd turning on her as it has for other faces of the company like Roman Reigns, John Cena, or Seth Rollins. Lynch's popularity and more importantly its endurance feels not quite like, but most akin to the popularity of Hulk Hogan in the 80s, or Steve Austin and the Rock in the 90s (without the corresponding explosive growth in TV viewership those men had achieved). Nevertheless, a woman is The Man and many fans would argue the women's division is the strongest reason to keep watching WWE at all.

The future of women's wrestling

In her unpublished biography, Mildred Burke wrote that the restoration of women's wrestling would bring a revival to the entire sport. "That's what happened in the dirty thirties," she wrote, "when I hit those post-depression rings in the shimmering robes and eye-popping tights. The whole game was uplifted, interest surged into the sport and with it came new fans and new money."[113] SHIMMER Women Athletes came about at an all-time low point for women in the industry. Japan, the only region

---

[112] Justin Barasso, "Becky Lynch Reflects on One Year as 'The Man,'" *SI.com*, November 4, 2019 https://www.si.com/wrestling/2019/11/04/wwe-becky-lynch-man-one-year-anniversary.
[113] Leen, *The Queen of the Ring*, 278.

with a vibrant scene, was undergoing a significant collapse that it in many ways is still recovering from. In the rest of the world, the outcomes looked bleak. Mildred Burke's hopes for a revitalized state of women's wrestling on a major national level looked to be nothing more than the fervent wish of an elderly woman who yearned for better days for her spiritual daughters.

Today, however, Burke's vision seems closer than ever to coming to pass. A woman is The Man in WWE, while another is poised to take the men's World Championship in Impact. Intergender wrestling is on the rise in many promotions, promoting a message that women can compete just as well as men not only amongst themselves but directly too. What was once a stagnant aspect of the wrestling business, as few women had opportunities to even wrestle and thus little reason to train as wrestlers, has now become a vibrant and ever-growing swell of talent with numerous promotions ready to accommodate the influx of women. At the center of it all, shimmering and shining like a beacon in the darkness of 2005, was a small promotion based in Berwyn, Illinois. By proving that American joshi is possible, as Allison Danger said in conclusion to SHIMMER Volume 1, SHIMMER gave hope and impetus to women's wrestling worldwide.

Giselle Francisco and Reginia Walker aka The DeadassGirls Podcast - Wrestling Never Sleeps: The Emergence of Indie Wrestling in New York City

Two flagrant NYC chicks talking about Wrestling on DeadassGirlsPodcast, follow them on Twitter at twitter.com/DeadAssGirls

If you ask someone to list some of the most notable things associated with New York City, wrestling would certainly not be one of those things mentioned. Home to several independent wrestling schools and promotions, New York City is beginning to make its name in the regional wrestling scene. And although it has a long way to go, the list of stars that have emerged from the NYC indie wrestling scene is a good indication that The Big Apple might be the place an up-and-coming wrestler should take a bite out of on their way to sports entertainment stardom. Like its pizza and bagels, the flourishing wrestling scene in New York City will be one that natives and newcomers alike might be boasting about for years to come.

To an avid wrestling fan, New York City is often thought of as the "birthplace of WrestleMania", having hosted the 1st inaugural WrestleMania pay-per-view in Manhattan at MSG(Madison Square Garden) on March 31, 1985; which was the largest wrestling event on closed-circuit TV. Treated as a star-studded event with pop star Cyndi Lauper, Mr. T and Liberace; the World Wrestling Federation (now World Wrestling Entertainment) introduced wrestling to a wider audience at one of the most iconic event venues. Fast forward to 2019, New York City has hosted many other wrestling events, such as Extreme Championship Wrestling (ECW) and Ring of Honor (ROH) at the Hammerstein Ballroom, tapings of Raw and SmackDown at MSG and Barclays Center in Brooklyn, as well as Impact Wrestling at the Melrose Ballroom in

Queens. While WWE and ECW are considered to be the "major leagues" of professional wrestling, the introduction of ROH, Impact Wrestling and others have made a splash, akin to Rob Van Dam off the top rope.

One of the most notable independent wrestling promotions, Ring of Honor is a Baltimore-based wrestling promotion, which was founded in 2002. While its roots are not New York born, Ring of Honor has developed a dedicated fan base in the Empire State, after they hosted the 13th annual G1 Supercard pay-per-view at Madison Square Garden in 2019. Marred in controversy, due to rumors of the event being cancelled due to competition and involvement of WWE, the New Japan Pro-Wrestling collaborated event became the first non-WWE wrestling event to be held at MSG since 1960. The next well-known indie wrestling promotion is Impact Wrestling. Originally known as Total Nonstop Action Wrestling, the wrestling promotion was founded in 2002 by former WWE wrestler Jeff Jarrett, who wanted to create a wrestling company that did not heavily rely on television screening and only on pay-per-views. While Impact Wrestling is another wrestling promotion that is not actually New York City based, they too have grown a loyal Big Apple fan base with their occasional TV tapings at the Melrose Ballroom in Queens, NY; which draws a mixed crowd of content creators, independent wrestlers and hometown fans.

While Impact Wrestling and Ring of Honor are considered to be "major" indie wrestling promotions, there are a few New York based indie wrestling promotions that have been garnering some attention. House of Glory, commonly and affectionately known as HOG, was opened by Jonathan Figueroa, a Puerto-Rican born wrestler who went by Amazing Red in his indie wrestling career. After a stint in New Japan Pro Wrestling and Total Nonstop Impact, the high-flyer founded the Queens-based wrestling school in 2010. A highly regarded wrestler, who has been praised by the likes of Eddie Guerrero and Seth Rollins, Amazing Red trains all inspiring wrestlers from every walk of life. Amazing Red and his HOG team have emerged into the New York City wrestling scene with its many NYC shows, which have featured several indie and WWE wrestlers, such as Ricochet, The Young Bucks, Joey Janela, The Broken Hardys, The Lucha Bros and LAX. There is also Battle Club Pro, a Bronx based independent wrestling promotion that was founded in 2016, and has hosted many wrestling shows in unique locations throughout the five boroughs Schoolyards, high school gymnasiums and dive bars, anywhere that fits a ring can host a Battle Club Pro match. Still a relatively young wrestling promotion, Battle Club Pro has featured several up-and-coming indie wrestlers that are becoming very well known, such as Jordynne Grace, Ethan Page, Shane Strickland, and Austin Theory – the latter who in 2019 signed with NXT; WWE's developmental program. While not much is known about the indie wrestling promotion, it has managed to create a fan base of NYC creatives that have constantly shown support for the independent brand by promoting it on several social media platforms, such as Instagram, Twitter and Facebook.

Now, if you are looking for a truly NYC indie wrestling scene, then look no further than BCW, or Brii Combination Wrestling. Often known as BCW, this New York based indie wrestling company was founded by Anthony Cole aka Flex in 2016. Located in Brooklyn, NY this small, yet emerging wrestling company has been known to put on exciting shows in local church basements around the metropolitan area. Although the roster for the indie company is comprised of relative unknowns, Faye Jackson, the reigning BCW Women's Champion has become a fan favorite with her powerful, yet erotic move set. Jackson's charisma, confidence as a plus-size model/wrestler and her social media presence has earned her a reputation as a New York-based indie wrestler to keep an eye on. BCW was also the former stomping grounds of Private Party, who are now dazzling wrestling fans as a tag team on the newly formed All Elite Wrestling; considered to be rivals of WWE.

The wrestling scene in New York City still has a long way to go, as far as recognition to a worldwide audience, however, with the long stream of talent that have either performed in New York City or have been affiliated with NYC promotions – it is on its way to becoming a city known for this sport. As the smaller wrestling promotions continue to churn out talent that go on to become bigger names in other major promotions, the Big Apple wrestling scene shows to be one that will strive to become better. Whether it is a show in a local high school gym, church basement or a viral video of fans dressed as old 90s wrestlers having their own version of the Royal Rumble on the subway (YouTube it), independent wrestling has become a popular subculture in the city that never sleeps.

Ami Moregore – Becoming a Ringside Photographer

Just a Jersey girl that has little regard for self-preservation taking photos of emotional events in combat sports or at concerts. Track her latest work at https://twitter.com/happypeep.

June 22nd, 2019. A 6 foot pane of glass explodes. It was a pretty sheet of glass with a frosted design on it. The cause was a man, Kenny Broadway, swung from both his ankles and chains wrapped around his throat being thrown into it courtesy of The Rep's Dave McCall and Nate Carter. This is happening in Tournament of Death (a non-tournament match but still during the "Death Match Woodstock" known as ToD). My eyes were already blurry from allergies but I managed to blink out any pieces of glass that managed to get past my glasses that afternoon. I have superficial cuts and scrapes on me from not just this but other ultraviolent stipulations happening today. My knee pads are covered in fragments of glass and thumbtacks. I'm not a wrestler. I'm just the ringside photographer and I caught everything and I'm absolutely in the zone.

Pro wrestling is such a spectacle and experience that it was hard to not want to take photos at any event. I rediscovered my love for pro wrestling in 2012, specifically local independent shows and was happy buying cheap tickets to get close to the action but finding it very difficult to stay in my seat for matches. My poor neighbors suffered from my pivoting in my seat tracking the action in my viewfinder. In Deer Park New York, I simply asked the staffers at the ticket desk if they minded me not staying in my seat and just taking photos from behind the chairs in the New York Wrestling Connection (NYWC)'s Sportatorium building. They were fine with it and I was happy to move around in the backrow, snapping shots where I could. Some wrestlers remembered me and would do silly poses when they locked eyes with me. I'd wave them off to focus on their actions in the ring.

NYWC became important to me with how friendly staff was to me. I came back for an all women's show entitled "We Can Do It" in Late February 2015 and checked again if my behavior was still ok. I didn't realize I was speaking with the owners. Shane spoke up and said I was welcome to go past the guard rail and take pictures if I wanted ringside. Thoughts flooded into my head. Did I feel ready for that? Also I had just paid face value for a ticket. Something didn't feel right with simultaneously working and paying to be there. I thanked him for his offer but suggested another time. After that event, veteran wrestler Marti Belle, contacted me directly and complemented my photos. I was saddened to learn that this show wasn't recorded, despite the video crew being there.

I have a background in fine arts with most of a BFA completed (color theory, as my professors taught it, was hard!). I'm old enough to have developed my own film and prints before digital photography rendered that obsolete but I wasn't sure if I was ready. The next event I went to was Inter Species Wrestling. They allowed, practically demanded, the entire audience to surround the ring. I thought this was as good a chance as any to shoot ringside and see if I had what it took. The owner endorsed photos I had shot and declared them beautiful. That elevated my confidence and I returned to NYWC for their next all women's show in May 2015. The owners saw me, didn't ask for money and directed me to go past the guard rail. I slipped my purse underneath the ring, considered best how not to block the view of others and went to work.

This all women's show, "She's a Wow" had many young up and comers. It was the first time I saw Deonna Purrazo, who went on to request a photo from that show to sell as a print. It was the second time I saw the young, and now indie darling, Willow Nightingale. My work was good enough that I stayed with NYWC for the next three years, happily watching their students join the main roster as well as seeing international and TV stars in action. NYWC has strong roots with wrestling. It's where the likes of Trent Barreta, Bull James, Mike Mondo,

Tony Nese and many others came from. The ring I learned to shoot around is a former ECW ring. It also has many connections with nearby wrestling companies. At the time it had ties with the owner of WSU, Women Superstars Uncensored, the biggest as well as closest company to me by proximity with a dedication to women and regularly streamed live pay-per-views. It was my goal to shoot ringside for that company, primarily because **I wanted to support women in wrestling**, and I regularly bought tickets for their shows. After overcoming some of my fear, I also started attending the more violent parent company CZW's shows as well.

The New Jersey based WSU has a long past that can be independently researched. I wasn't there for the history, I was there for its contemporary roster. I was thrilled to see wrestlers like the ground breaking LuFisto, Athena (now WWE's Ember Moon), Mickie Knuckles, Hania, Solo Darling, Veda Scott, Su Yung, Angie Skye, and more. It was the only regular running nearby women's only company and they delivered with a mix of styles

My method to get to WSU took some persistence. I had picked up a few freelance opportunities at a couple other small shows and built up a small portfolio. I asked the WSU and CZW owner, DJ Hyde, if he had room for another photographer whenever I saw him at NYWC shows. I didn't get a direct answer the first few times. CZW's student show was getting ready to have a major show December 2015, the Dojo Wars Mega Event. I asked their, then head trainer Drew Gulak, if I could shoot that show since he was in charge. He was ok with that. It was a way to get my foot in the door. By this point I had become friendly with the CZW/WSU senior photographer Lyle C. Williams. Hyde had been clear that before I shot any of his shows, I'd need the permission of Lyle. I had Lyle's BLESSING not just permission. At NYWC, I was frequently lone photographer aside from their video director who doubled as roaming video operator. Lyle guided me to understanding the relationship between photographing a show while remaining unobtrusive to the audience and video operators. He was in his 50s, somewhat tall, with bad knees, a small but serious list of health related problems and he would don his knee pads, just like me, and remain low to the ground so the audience could see. It took a few more months of asking permission but I finally was shooting for CZW in August 2016 and WSU the following September.

Many of my favorite established wrestlers had left WSU by this point but I was always fascinated by the cycle of newcomers willing to risk life and limb for the entertainment of people who bought a ticket. At previous venues, I was fairly at ease, but once I started dealing with this company, I found myself struggling with impostor syndrome, questioning why I was allowed to work and waiting for a tap on the shoulder to tell me I didn't belong ringside. And then after the show, sharing photos and being thanked profusely by amazing athletes for capturing a cool move they did would alleviate the feeling... until the next show.

New York state has considerably more restrictions on what is allowed in wrestling. I was present ringside for a Brooklyn Tier1 Wrestling show in which the State Athletic Commission representative seemed to have forgotten there was no rule against intergender wrestling and nearly ended a show prematurely. To my knowledge, it's currently illegal to use tables and chairs in New York State as of 2016. I say this as a preface because New Jersey, the home state for CZW, GCW, H2O, and many other companies, simply is the wild west in terms of how unregulated it is. I wanted WSU but the world of death matches with CZW was a package deal. The adrenaline I feel from hearing the oddly loud crack of fluorescent light tubes followed by the shrapnel spray of its glass amazes me still. Audiences should be wary since the spread of the shards can go far depending on the momentum. At the first Cage of Death I photographed, I joked to people I knew in the front row that I would be their "meat shield" after we beheld glass panes being positioned in the corners prior to the start of the main event. 90% of my best photos come from recognizing wrestling patterns. I was expecting a tease for the glass, not to get an explosion of glass in my face and down my blouse in the first 10 seconds of the match. At an outdoor death match tournament years later, a student offered to wipe blood off my bare shoulders. I was convinced it wasn't mine until the rough damp towel stung my open bleeding wounds.

I still love supporting all women in wrestling. Any chance wrestling helps show that they're able to do the same work any man can do warms my heart. I think women and POC are under represented in death matches and deserve more opportunities. I want to see more women photographers at these shows as well. As a queer, latinx woman, I don't want to be the sole minority involved at events, I know I'm not alone but there's room for more if you're willing to work.

The Ringside Photography of Ami Moregore

photo: Ami Moregore Twitter: @Happypeep

11 Feb 2017: Penelope Ford with a weed whacker in CZW Voorhees, NJ

photo: Ami Moregore Twitter: @Happypeep

10 Sept 2016: Lio Rush vs Joey Janela CZW Voorhees, NJ. CZW Wired title match

photo: Ami Moregore Twitter: @Happypeep

30 May 2015: Deonna Purrazzo making her entrance to the NYWC She's a Wow event - Deer Park, NY

photo: Ami Moregore Twitter: @Hoppypeep

30 May 2015: Deonna Purrazzo vs Brittany Blake NYWC She's a Wow - Deer Park, NY

10 Sept 2016: Joey Janela CZW Voorhees, NJ - CZW Wired title match

28 Nov 2015: Sonny Kiss moonsaults onto JGeorge Estrella - Tier1 Wrestling Showcase at NYWC - Deer Park, NY

photo: Ami Moregore Twitter: @Happypeep

6 Feb 2016: Deonna Purrazzo vs Christina Von Eerie Fiesta Pro (Jeff Jarrett's Global Force Wrestling Women's title was defended) - Deer Park, NY

photo: Ami Moregone Twitter: @Happypeep

5 August 2017: Lio Rush vs Joey Janela CZW Voorhees, NJ

30 May 2015: Deonna Purrazzo vs Brittany Blake NYWC She's a Wow - Deer Park, NY

Warning – the following photographs are from CZW (Combat Zone Wrestling), known for a brand of hardcore wrestling dubbed 'ultraviolence'. As such, those that object to blood and gore may want to skip past the next two pages.

photo: Ani Moregore Twitter @Happypeep

4 April 219: Casanova Valentine vs Chainsaw Tony Myers aka FMW's Leatherface 3 in a No Ring Death Match - Murder Mania night one Brooklyn New York

photo: AmiMoregore Twitter: @Happypeep

5 August 2017: Atsushi Onita vs Matt Tremont CZW Voorhees NJ -
Onita's first American appearance in over a decade

Allyssa Capri - Yelling Into the Void:
The Invisibility of Marginalized Identities in Wrestling Fandom and Media

Allyssa Capri is a Chicago-based pop culture writer. Her writing examines popular media as it relates to race, gender, and other social issues. She can be found at twitter.com/AllyssaCapri.

If you're reading this, chances are good that you are a wrestling fan. Let me be the first to tell you that if that is the case, I pity you. Fans of professional wrestling often half-jokingly say that the people who hate wrestling the most are wrestling fans. It's hard to argue anything to the contrary, really.

Constantly being let down, always watching the Chosen Guys or Girls get pushed when we don't want them to, storylines so dramatic and unbelievable that they would make a daytime soap writer blush. Man oh man, do we *hate* wrestling.

Yes, it is often exhausting and downright hard to be a wrestling fan. But, it is even harder for those of us with marginalized identities to choose to love wrestling in spite of the insidious oppression that plagues the industry. Endeavoring to love wrestling when you are all but invisible on screen is part confusing, part frustrating, and part heartbreaking. As a young black girl watching wrestling in the '90s and early aughts, I didn't have the language yet to express that these were the things that I felt.

You see, I am a black woman, but I have albinism, which means that I have little to no pigment in my skin. So, aesthetically, I share skin color with Caucasian people — but that's about it. My hair and broad facial features were and always have been tells to those looking for bits of blackness in me. But, because of my unique identity as a black girl,

181

especially with mostly white peers, I tended to gravitate toward the odd or eccentric characters in the ring; the ones who stuck out in a crowd, or the ones that looked how I wished I did (namely, those with darker skin). My favorite female wrestler as a child was Lita. I loved her tattoos, baggy pants, and deep red hair. I gravitated toward the way she moved in the ring and carried herself as a badass and confident woman, although she was disruptive by society's standards. And most importantly, she was edgier than the blonde, bubblegum faces that littered the division at the time. I saw myself in her alternative style, as someone who felt alternative to just about everything around me.

My other all-time fave was The Rock. I loved his charisma and the way he spoke — with the attitude and wit of the folks in my family, as well as the swagger that only a black man could have. Because my earliest favorite wrestler was a half-black man, I always found myself rooting for other black stars as they came up through the ranks in WWE. Although she was a heel, I distinctly remember liking the black female wrestler Jazz and her manager Teddy Long. At one point, her catchphrase was "The bitch is back, and the bitch is BLACK!" In my eyes, all I saw was a black woman trying to rise above the white women who were so often favored (and still are, although more covertly) as the stars of the division. I picked up on that from a young age. I liked the MVPs, the Shelton Benjamins, the Laylas. When black female wrestlers became sparse, I rooted for other women of color, like Victoria, Melina, and Gail Kim. It's just always how it was: I felt compelled to root for the unspoken underdogs, the black and brown bodies that padded the divisions away from the main event.

Once I came of age and went to college, I learned the language I'd been searching for to describe what I'd felt all those years before. Although I stopped watching wrestling in my college years, when I eventually came back to the fandom, I had a new pair of eyes through which to see the state of women's wrestling.

I came back to the wrestling fandom shortly after the #GiveDivasAChance hashtag had taken the internet by storm. Hearing that female fans had had enough of the bullshit sexism that plagued the women's division for so long, I decided one night in January 2016 to turn on Monday Night Raw. When I clicked on the show, the first person I saw was Sasha Banks. Like myself, she was fair-skinned, but had features that made me question her racial identity. (I would later discover, of course, that she is half black.) She had neon pink hair. She was on WWE TV. I'd never seen anyone like her before. And I decided then and there that I wanted more of her, and women like her, in my women's wrestling.

I've witnessed how wrestling promotions are diversifying their women's rosters, welcoming women of color of light and dark complexions, more queer folks, and women who didn't speak fluent English. Never in my wildest dreams as a child would I have believed I'd see more than three black women on a women's roster at one point in time. But it's happening now. *Regularly*. Who would have ever dreamed that we could watch a trans woman wrestle in her identity, in the women's division! By no means do I want to minimize just how far women's wrestling has come, in this decade alone.

All of the positive gains that women's wrestling has made in the last 10 years makes it more disheartening for me to take a critical look at the fine print of these so-called glass-ceiling breaking moments. I pause when I remember that Asuka's big win at the first-ever women's Royal Rumble in WWE is forever marred by a white woman's interruption (a white woman who is transphobic at that). I get angry when I remember that Asuka bowed down to the Queen Charlotte Flair — another favored white woman – at WrestleMania that same year, losing her coveted streak in the process. I shake my head when I remember that Naomi was on the active WWE roster for nearly a decade before she won her first championship, about a decade longer than many of her white peers had to wait before achieving the same. I want to smash my keyboard when I remember that Sasha Banks could never successfully defend the women's title against Charlotte Flair, to the point that it became a degradation in-storyline to her credibility as a wrestler. (As we start 2020, Charlotte's longest single reign is nearly twice the amount of days as all of Sasha's combined reigns as women's champion.) I wonder how a wrestling company like All Elite Wrestling, who has positioned themselves as the progressive future of pro wrestling, can barely manage to let their women speak on TV, let alone allow them to have more than one match per weekly TV show.

I also have to grimace when I realize the racial shortcomings of the men's divisions, particularly in WWE, when I remember that Kofi Kingston was the first black WWE champion (note: *not* World Heavyweight Champion) in more than a decade. It's even worse when you realize just how rare it is to see a man of color seriously challenge for a top title in WWE. Not surprising, when you consider that WWE lacked the racial awareness to actually go through with creating a t-shirt for black NXT Superstar Jordan Myles that resembled blackface.

Other charismatic stars of color like Andrade Cien Almas and Shinsuke Nakamura are relegated to the mid-card, or lose "the big one" when it counts the most. Women of color are simply lost in the shuffle if they are visible at all on TV. As a woman, a person of color, and specifically a black person, I find myself being tugged in different directions by my awareness of the oppressions I face, and in turn the oppressions that face marginalized wrestlers. I find myself cheering at the announcement of the first-ever women's main event at WrestleMania, but bring myself back to reality when I notice that of course, three white women are the focal point. And here we get to the meat of why marginalized fans hurt most deeply.

Watching our sport, our art, our entertainment of choice is a little like having Stockholm syndrome. We love the industry that abuses us. That oppresses us. That tells us, to quote Chimamanda Ngozi Adichie, "You should aim to be successful, but not too successful, otherwise you will threaten the man." "The man" in this instance being the white man (or in the case of the women's division, the white woman). And after the dust has settled over the latest misstep, we believe naively that things will turn out better next time. We, of course, have our favorites, and yes they include white men and women. But that pain, that deep depression that builds in our bellies when we can't see our faves of color rise to the same heights as our white faves, stirs a great conflict within us.

I think Becky Lynch is fantastic. At the same time, I think Ember Moon is enigmatic and should be a main event player. I think Bayley, when given the chance, is a worthy champion that deserves to have more than 5 minute TV matches. I think Nyla Rose has potential if she was allowed time to do more with her character.

Yes, the wrestling world has changed fairly rapidly over the last few years. Even still, I believe that with these changes in attitude toward inclusion, the industry is evolving in other ways. Promotions are getting better at covertly oppressing their marginalized talent. They'll have a division of black and brown stars, but only let them challenge for a title after five white opponents have gotten their chances in first. If they let a wrestler of color win a title, they'll get lazy with the writing of those stars' feuds or have them lose in unremarkable fashion.

And us marginalized fans have picked up on this, but are we ever heard? Are our complaints the ones highlighted? No. We are only heard in our bitter corners of Tumblr and Twitter, making jokes and memes and long text posts about how unfair, albeit predictable, these tactics are.

We are trapped in these corners, hoping in vain that someone will come over to hear what we have to say. All the while, we hear the loud voices of straight, cisgender, white men over the loudspeakers. As a black woman hoping one day to enter the wrestling media world, I want to speak for the voiceless fans who have helped me to process the anger and hurt that I feel about the oppression that still exists in wrestling. I firmly believe that wrestling is on the cusp of becoming the inclusive, equitable, and joyful space we've always wanted it to be.

But the only voices strongly represented in wrestling media — outlets like Cultaholic, WhatCulture, Pro Wrestling Illustrated, and the Wrestling Observer Newsletter — are those of straight, cisgender, white males. The wrestling world for far too long has had to bow to the tastes and sensibilities of what this small demographic believes constitutes good storytelling and wrestling. To them, merely *having* the diversity in representation is enough. I say we move the needle.

Change — real change — takes time. This we all know. At the same time, the truest of changes happen on a molecular level. While I will always welcome more queer, non-white, and female stars in wrestling, we need those people behind the scenes as well. They need to be in the board rooms, in the big chairs, in the writers' rooms. Like the wrestling media world immediately outside of these promotions, it is clear that there is a hesitance to tell the stories of marginalized people in a nuanced way because there is an emotional distance that the powers-that-be have toward them. Put simply, they can't tell stories or speak a language that they don't understand. But, be it sexism, racism, homophobia, or just plain greed — these white men don't want to relinquish the pen. And whether they can see it or not now, it's hurting their products. And potentially jeopardizing the fandom of those of us hanging on to our love of wrestling by a thread.

But as I said, change comes from deep within, from the inside out. We are two decades into the millennium now. Representation is a start, but not the finish. Now that we have it, let's see what we can do with it. We should all be living to tell the stories that little black girls like me wished they saw growing up. We should strive to represent romance between two women without straight panic used as a plot device. We should shout and scream and holler and uplift the voices of those who have never been heard, in the hope that one day we can **all** be seen in the wrestling world.

Sonya Ballantyne - Luna-tic Girl

Sonya is a filmmaker, writer, and lifelong wrestling fan from Northern Manitoba. As a child, she dreamed of being Bret Hart. Her Twitter is twitter.com/Sonyaballantyne

The Indian reservation I grew up on had a gas station that everyone traveling on the Manitoba number 6 highway ended up stopping at. Indian reserves are tracts of land set aside by the government for use by Indigenous people. Usually the government picks the worst places it can find, which was why my home reserve was simultaneously the worst and best place in the world.

One time, I saw a large van parked at the gas station, obviously having some sort of trouble. My dad, always sociable and willing to lend a hand, offered his help to the men in the vehicle. As a Cree girl, I had seen many white folks on TV and in the town of Grand Rapids, across the river from my reserve, but I had never seen white people like the ones in that van. They were tall, much taller than my Dad, with hair the color of dirty straw. One of the men had eyes like a blue Mr. Freeze ice pop. I was 7 or 8 at the time, super shy with people I did not know, but loud and mouthy with people I did know, or about subjects I loved. This time, though, I hid behind my Dad's legs, preventing him from moving, and he wanted me to get out from under foot. When he found out these guys were wrestlers, he told them, "My girl wants to be a wrestler too!" My Dad looked down at me and said, "My girl, tell them what you want to be when you grow up!"

There's a baby picture of me with my father. I am drooling all over myself in my car seat, which my Dad has turned to face the camera. On the TV behind me is a Stampede wrestling match I was watching with my Grandpa. Everyone in my family loved professional wrestling and we would watch it together.

As a child, I went to my first wrestling show in Winnipeg, Manitoba, where the main event was Shawn Michaels vs Bret Hart, two of my favorite wrestlers of all time. I wanted to be the kid Bret gave his sunglasses to, and so I tried to jump the barricade to get to him when he entered. My dad held me back and told me we would leave if I tried to run like that again. I promised I wouldn't. That promise was forgotten seconds later when Shawn Michaels' music hit and I went for the barricade again. My dad grabbed my oversized Shawn Michaels t-shirt in his fist and tried to pull me back into my seat. I leaned forward with all my weight on the shirt and began to choke myself out.

WWF was popular amongst the kids at Grand Rapids , the tiny school I attended across the river from my reserve. Every Tuesday morning, we would gather to talk about what happened on Monday Night Raw. The Raw match where the Undertaker crucified Stone Cold was one for the record books, and we were all horrified that such a thing could be broadcast on television.

Once when I was five, my dad asked me what I wanted to be when I grew up. I said, "Daddy, I want to be either a writer, a marine biologist, or a pro wrestler!" My grandparents had been fishermen, my mum cleaned hotel rooms, and my dad worked a series of odd jobs. No one had ever finished high school or gone to university. When I told my dad my plans, he knew that his daughter becoming a writer or a marine biologist was just as likely as becoming a pro wrestler, so he wished me luck in becoming a future WWF champion.

As a nerdy weirdo with a smart remark for everything, growing up was lonely. I learned to read when I was four, adoring books like The Hobbit, while my cinephile mum developed my interest in movies. The amount of movies and TV I watched matched the amount of books I read, and both lent themselves to dreams about what I would do when I grew up. I dreamed about visiting mythical lands like Middle Earth, Themiscyra, and Calgary, where I would train with Bret Hart, so I could one day be better than The Best There Is, The Best There Was, and The Best There Ever Will Be.

If only I was not a girl.

When I told my teachers I wanted to be a wrestler they said that I could not because I was a girl. Some would add, "and there aren't any Native wrestlers". I would mention Tatanka, except that he never won. Plus I did not want to wear a headdress and buckskin. I wanted to wear black and pink and change my last name to Hart.

The fact was, there weren't many women on WWF who were as cool as the guys. The few that were, like Bull Nakano, or my favorite, Luna Vachon , rarely had matches on TV, or ended up managing guys like Bam Bam Bigelow. The kids at my school thought Luna was ugly, but I loved how she wasn't afraid of anything, and was actually scarier than most of the guys in the WWF. I tried to shave the sides of my head like Luna's, but my Mum wrestled me to the ground to take the electric razor out of my hands. If I couldn't be like Bret Hart, then obviously, I wanted to be like Luna.

Even Luna, with all her power, could not go far in the WWF. She would lose to women with blonde hair and tits like armor, even though they could not wrestle as well as her. I realized that with my dark hair and brown skin, I would never be able to be in the WWF because I did not look like the girls that won...

At the gas station, my younger self had shyly hid my face in my dad's thigh, his jeans smelling like John Player cigarettes. Those white men with the van were the tallest men I had ever seen, and I was terrified. Truthfully, I was terrified of everyone at that age, so I often found myself burying my face in my dad's leg to hide. I felt my dad lovingly touch the top of my head. He proudly told the guys, "My little girl wants to be a wrestler when she grows up." My dad told me how these guys would put on wrestling shows in reserves even further north than us. He pulled me away from his leg and crouched down next to me. I put my fingers in my mouth and tried to make myself smaller. My dad said, "These guys are wrestlers!" My eyes brightened and one of the guys, the one with the scary Mr. Freeze eyes, crouched down next to me and my dad. "What's your name?" The guy asked me. Through a mouthful of fingers, I mumbled, "Sonya" and said it louder when he asked me to repeat myself. Realizing I was distracted, my dad went to help fix the van. "I'm Adam!" The guy told me, with a smile bigger than I have ever seen. "Do you like wrestling?" I nodded and looked at my feet. "Who's your favourite wrestler?" Adam asked me. "Bret Hart," I said, before Adam could even finish asking. "Me too!" Adam beamed. "Do you want to be a wrestler?" I nodded and said, "But I can't." Adam wrinkled his brow; his eyes less scary now: looking like the color you would draw a sky during art class. "Why not?" He asked. "Because girls can't be wrestlers," I said, as though it were the most obvious thing in the world. "They can!" He countered, "What about Luna Vachon?" Hearing Luna's name from an actual wrestler made my mouth fall open and my hand fall out. I thought I was the only person who liked her. I stood agog for a moment before saying, more to myself than to Adam, "YEAH!" Adam wasn't so scary anymore, though I was still not so sure about the other guys my dad was helping. I asked Adam, "Do you know how to do a hurricanrana?" He laughed and said he didn't but we could figure it out.

Of the three jobs I told my Dad I was going to have, I ended up becoming a writer. I did not end up moving to Calgary, and I have only met Bret Hart once, at a comic book convention. But I always remembered meeting Adam. I've faced a lot of racism and sexism as a Native girl growing up in Canada, and I remember every horrible thing I've experienced. However, I also remember every positive experience I have ever had: Adam was probably one of the first men I ever met (besides my dad and grandfather) who supported what I wanted to do, no matter how far-fetched the idea seemed. He made me feel like I could be Luna Vachon, and stand beside the likes of Bret Hart one day.

Like all of the other people I randomly met with my dad at the gas station, I thought I'd never see Adam and his scary friends again. I was wrong. I was a little older when I saw a wrestler called Edge on Monday Night Raw, with the same Mr. Freeze eyes. My dad didn't remember Adam, but I did. And even though I never became a wrestler, I could still write about meeting Adam and the time he told me I could be a wrestler.

Jacqui Pratt, PhD - Separate but (Un)Equal: The Rhetorics of Representation in Gender-Segregated Professional Wrestling

Jacqui Pratt is a musician, filmmaker, writer, teacher, and analyst who holds a PhD in Rhetoric & Composition from the University of Washington in Seattle. You can find out about her latest work at twitter.com/cheappopisaband.

As a female fan, watching the WWE's "women's revolution" has been both inspiring and frustrating. Seeing so many powerful women—their stories and struggles—get main-event recognition as viable competitors makes me feel joy and anger and anticipation and pride: all of the amazing, wonderful sensations that come with watching great wrestling. There is currently no shortage of diverse, talented, awe-inspiring women for young girls to look up to and to see pieces of themselves amplified within these larger-than-life characters the same way young boys have been able to for the history of the artform. In short: there is no better time than the present to be a fan of women's wrestling.

However, aside from Chyna's monumental Intercontinental Championship victories, women are simply absent from the pantheon of champions, the best-of-the-best, in regard to the titles that have the most history, weight, value, and prestige for WWE. But this isn't just a WWE problem. Outside of a small (but growing) number of mostly independent wrestling promotions, women are generally not eligible to compete for many top-tier or otherwise prestigious titles solely because of their gender. I argue that as long as women continue to be barred from vying for the top-most titles of wrestling promotions, they'll never be portrayed as or considered equal competitors to their male counterparts.

Some might think, *well, there are women's championships, and those matches are main eventing PPVs, so…women are equal now!* While yes, women are currently experiencing unparalleled opportunity and status in the world of professional wrestling, in the majority of televised productions, women and men compete in separate divisions. Rhetorically speaking, gender-segregated wrestling may best be understood as a contemporary iteration of *separate but equal*: the false assertion of equality in a segregated environment. While on the surface these divisions may *appear* equal, a closer examination reveals how segregating wrestling by gender continues to promote inequality.

In what follows, I examine the current landscape of professional wrestling through this rhetorical lens of *separate but equal* to help illuminate the core issues of gender-segregated wrestling. To be clear: by gender-segregated wrestling, here, I'm referring to promotions that feature separate men's and women's divisions (not promotions that feature talent of only one gender like Shimmer or Pro-Wrestling EVE). As I'll explain, this *separate but equal* rhetoric breaks down when confronted with the historic inequality of women in professional wrestling, the reality of non-binary competitors who are neither male nor female (and, thus, without a home in segregated wrestling environments), and the reward structure of title opportunities and reigns for individual performers. By understanding how gender-segregated wrestling environments function to rhetorically preserve male superiority, we can better understand the urgent need for women to compete for and hold top-tier titles, for what's at stake here is nothing less than who is allowed recognition as a top performer in the business.

The Rhetoric of *Separate but Equal*

As I mentioned above, the problem with representation and equality for women in professional wrestling is perhaps best understood using rhetoric that originated in the American antebellum period and remained highly influential through the civil rights movement: *separate but equal*. For those who might not be familiar, under *separate but equal* doctrine, segregated experiences are justified by the superficial appearance of equality (that is, each group has access to a version of the opportunity or experience in question), though the actualization of those opportunities/experiences are tangibly inequitable. For example: while *technically* there were public schools available to both white and black children in the American south leading up to the civil rights movement, the actual experience of attending those segregated schools varied greatly, with white schools being given clear preferential treatment. While historically tied to racial segregation in the United States, I argue that applying the rhetorics of *separate but equal* to gender-segregated wrestling environments helps us better understand how barring women from competing against men for a given promotion's top title(s) is an inherent injustice that furthers the inequality of women (and others) in the business.

In order to do so, however, I need to first overview three vital United States court cases that helped shaped the rhetoric surrounding *separate but equal* and its legal deployment in the 19th and 20th centuries: Roberts v. City of Boston (1849), Plessy v. Ferguson (1896), and Brown v. Board of Education (1954). By taking a moment to parse its dense legal history, I aim to demonstrate how *separate but equal* rhetoric, in general, works to consolidate power and opportunity among one group of individuals while simultaneously concealing the unequal treatment of others.

To start, one of the earliest legal documentations of *separate but equal* doctrine is an 1849 court case, Sarah C. Roberts v. the City of Boston, which centered around "competing notions of what 'equality' should mean in American civic discourse."[114] During this case, Peleg Chandler, the defense attorney for Boston's school board, "took the then popular position that 'equality' simply meant the symmetrical treatment of various races…that only the total absence of schools for blacks could be an actionable cause for complaint."[115] It's important to note that this view of equality as symmetrical treatment/opportunity does not address the *quality* of one's experiences and the ways in which a person might be

---

[114] Hasian Jr, Marouf, and Geoffrey D. Klinger. "Sarah Roberts and the early history of the "separate but equal" doctrine: A study in rhetoric, law, and social change." *Communication Studies* 53, no. 3 (2002): 269-283.
[115] Ibid.

treated—only that the opportunity-in-question exists in some form at all. For Chandler, and by extension the Boston school board, since black children had the opportunity to attend publicly-funded schools, they were, in fact, receiving equal treatment; the question of how that education tangibly manifested and the social impact of such was irrelevant to the case. Charles Sumner and Robert Morris (Roberts' attorneys) insisted, however, that equality meant equality in the eyes of law, both politically and socially. They argued that Roberts passed a minimum of five other schools on her way to her mandatorily-attended, segregated school which "did not have the same funding, faculty, or other materials that were available in the white schools of Boston. In order to be fair, Sumner and Morris maintained, the Boston school board needed to intervene and provide identical, integrated facilities" for all students, regardless of personal distinctions such as race or class.[116] In the end, Chief Justice Lemuel Shaw sided with the Boston school board and Chandler's symmetrical understanding of equality, establishing a legal precedent for upholding *separate but equal* doctrine that "resulted in the maintenance and legal codification of inherently racist views and institutions" by validating segregation in taxpayer-funded schools.[117]

Even though Justice Shaw's decision in Roberts v. City of Boston was essentially nullified in 1855 (when Massachusetts state legislature passed a bill integrating public schools), it was invoked in Justice Henry Billings Brown's decision in what is widely considered to be the national origins of *separate but equal* doctrine: the 1896 case of Plessy v. Ferguson. The case originated in 1892, when Homer Plessy, one-eighth black, was arrested in violation of Louisiana's Separate Car Act after sitting in a white-designated railroad car instead of a non-white one. He argued and lost twice in lower courts that the Separate Car Act was unconstitutional before appealing to the U.S. Supreme Court, which upheld the constitutionality of racial segregation via the *separate but equal* doctrine. According to rhetoricians Celeste Condit and John Lucaites, the Supreme

---

[116] Ibid.
[117] Ibid.

Court's decision to allow legalized segregation represented a national compromise. The pair note that "from 1865 to 1895 the nation struggled to find a way to integrate in practice the broader usages of Equality consecrated by the Civil War and mandated by the reconstructed Constitution",[118] and while most agreed "that the claim 'all men are created equal' indicated that persons could not be reduced to property," there was "no consensus on the scope of that Equality."[119] In its decision, the Court determined that "the sharing of public accommodations was a social rather than a political or civil matter," empowering local bodies of government to decide the degree to which its public institutions would or would not be racially integrated.[120] Eager to preserve the status quo, "segregation allowed [white supremacists] to exclude blacks from contact with whites in the public sphere...legally precluding all possible contact between races except in those situations where the lines of power and merit reproduces the relationship of the white overseer and black servant" (132).[121] In other words, segregation became a way to consolidate and protect the power and social prestige of white individuals. Collectively, then, these legal decisions to uphold *separate but equal* doctrine, codified as national precedent in the wake of Plessy v. Ferguson, effectively prohibited black citizens from receiving social and cultural recognition as equals while still maintaining a veneer of equality.

The ramifications of Plessy v. Ferguson and *separate but equal* doctrine were felt for nearly 65 years until eventually overturned in the landmark civil rights U.S. Supreme Court case Brown v. Board of Education in 1954. The plaintiffs argued that "segregated public schools are not 'equal' and cannot be made 'equal,'" thus violating the constitutional rights of black students.[122] Further, they argued that this fundamental inequality had a lasting negative psychological impact: it made black children feel inferior

---

[118] Condit, Celeste Michelle, and John Louis Lucaites. *Crafting Equality: America's Anglo-African Word.* University of Chicago Press, 1993, 101.
[119] Ibid., 110.
[120] Ibid., 142.
[121] Ibid., 132.
[122] Brown v. Board of Education, 347 U.S. 483, 74 S. Ct. 686, 98 L. Ed. 873 (1954).

to white children in all walks of life. This psychological component proved vital in swaying the Court's decision, as Chief Justice Earl Warren acknowledged that a symmetrical understanding of equality (that is, equal opportunity) wasn't enough to decide the case, and "we must look instead to the effect of segregation itself on public education" to fully comprehend the issue.[123] He observed that "to separate [students] from others of similar age and qualifications solely because of their race generates a feeling of inferiority as to their status in the community that may affect their hearts and minds in a way unlikely ever to be undone."[124] This fact ultimately led to the Court's decision that "the doctrine of 'separate but equal' has no place" in public education and that "separate educational facilities are inherently unequal,"[125] a ruling that effectively put an end to the legal execution of *separate but equal* doctrine across all public venues in the United States, not just education, and firmly established that equality is as much a social and cultural issue as it is a political one.

By examining these three moments in legal history, it becomes apparent that a rhetoric of *separate but equal* carries with it an inherent socio-cultural inequality that cannot be addressed through any surface (i.e. visible or material) measure of equality alone. As established in Brown v. Board of Education, though on the surface it may appear that segregated groups are equal, no experience occurs in a vacuum; the mental, emotional, and social impact as well the particular historical context must also be considered. As I'll detail next section, given the fictionalized nature of professional wrestling as well as its deep history of sexism, the insidiousness of the *separate but equal* rhetoric surrounding men's and women's divisions in professional wrestling becomes apparent: male talent will always be able to protect their power, privilege, and prestige by barring female competitors from accessing the top-most status symbols and rewards in the business solely based on gender.

---

[123] Ibid.
[124] Ibid.
[125] Ibid.

Making a Case for the Fundamental Inequality of Gender-Segregated Wrestling

Currently, the predominant *separate but equal* rhetoric of gender equality in professional wrestling mirrors the symmetrical understanding of equality forwarded in Roberts v. City of Boston and Plessy v. Ferguson: equal opportunity constitutes equality, even if the opportunities themselves are different. From this perspective, since women *are* being featured as serious competitors and they *do* have championships for which they can fight, they do not have a valid claim of inequality. Much like the court rulings on *separate but equal* in the 19th century, this perspective does not recognize the socio-cultural equality women strive for in the world of professional wrestling; it only grants equal access to being there, to participating in *some* capacity. However, Brown v. Board of Education established that such an understanding of equality is fundamentally discriminatory, as segregated environments are inherently unequal. To riff a moment on Justice Warren's findings that I quoted earlier: separating wrestlers from others of similar qualifications solely because of their gender generates a feeling of inferiority as to their status in the community that may never be undone. Given the historic portrayal of women in professional wrestling, the fact that gendered divisions do not address the reality of non-binary performers, and the dual rhetorical significance of championship opportunities and reigns, I forward that any professional wrestling promotion that features both male and female talent and does not showcase viable intergender (i.e. integrated) competition for its top-tier championships maintains the inherently misogynistic structures embedded in the history of the business and continues to disenfranchise women seeking equal recognition for their skill and labor.

Historically speaking, professional wrestling has been built around the male experience: the ideation of what the male body should (and shouldn't) look like, how a man should (or shouldn't) act, and what he should (or shouldn't) covet. Or as wrestling scholar Sharon Mazer succinctly puts it: "what is presented, affirmed, and critiqued is nothing so much as the idea of masculinity itself."[126] Meanwhile, as I've written about elsewhere, "women's wrestling has been primarily understood as a side-show within the larger spectacle, a vehicle for emphasizing the (hetro)sexual construction of the masculine ego" because "up until *too* recently, women have most often been used as eye candy for male spectators, filler content to provide fans with opportunities for bathroom breaks, or merely as props within a larger (male-centered) narrative."[127] Given this "longstanding tradition of mistreatment, trivialization, and overt sexualization," female wrestlers are inherently "othered" simply because their bodies are not coded male.[128] In short, the *assumed normal* in professional wrestling is male; all else is to be qualified, coded, and branded as "other."

While this might sound like an abstract issue at first, its impact is embedded in the everyday rhetorics of professional wrestling. For example, we have women's divisions and women's titles identified as such without consistent, equal branding for men. That is, we don't announce men's matches as "the following men's division match is scheduled for one fall" or call someone the Men's Champion. Any match or championship without a qualifier is assumed to be male; it's the women who must be identified as something else. This extends beyond the event, as well. Take, for instance, the fact that Pro Wrestling Illustrated annually publishes their ranking of the top 500 wrestlers in the world (no gender qualification, yet features only men), and then publishes a separate list for their top 100 women. By segregating their rankings and ceding less space to female talent (100 individuals compared to the 500 on the "main" or unqualified list), they continue to propagate rhetoric that presents women as less than men under a guise of equal treatment (since they both have lists in any form). Taken

---

[126] Mazer, Sharon. *Professional Wrestling: Sport and Spectacle*. Performance Studies (Jackson, Miss.). Jackson: University Press of Mississippi, 1998, 5.
[127] Pratt, Jacqui, Rai, Candice, Bawarshi, Anis, and Harold, Christine. *Delivering Rhetorical Entanglements*, 2019, ProQuest Dissertations and Theses, 162.
[128] Ibid., 161.

together, these (and other) small but impactful rhetorical choices surrounding the presentation of and public conversation around gender in professional wrestling reify the inherent inequities of the current, dominant *separate but equal* rhetoric, ensuring that male-ness remains the assumed normal in the business.

Second, even if one were to *attempt* to resist, as best as possible, this deep history of "othering" female talent by providing equitable labeling, opportunities, representation, and rewards to both male and female talent, there is another inherent issue in segregating divisions by gender: What do we make of non-binary wrestlers? While trans performers who identify as male or female can compete in the division that matches their gender identity, a *separate but equal* structure inherently excludes non-binary performers. Where does a non-binary wrestler compete in gender-segregated divisions? Do they compete in a men's division for men's titles? If so, it's acknowledging a hierarchy among divisions where women are the ultimate "other" — i.e. any persons *other* than women may compete in the "default" (i.e. men's) division while women are relegated to their own separate space. Or, on the other hand, does a non-binary wrestler compete in a women's division for those titles? If so, this communicates the message that anyone who is not a man is "other" and belongs in a segregated space away from the primary action. Or, are non-binary wrestlers excluded from the action all together, victims of blatant gender discrimination? No matter which way it shakes out, addressing the reality of non-binary talent in gender-segregated environments renders visible the inherently unequal position of women in professional wrestling at best, and at worst, it excludes an entire group of individuals from participating in the first place.

Finally, while there are absolutely athletic elements involved, we have to understand that professional wrestling is ultimately a *performance art,* a fiction. Much like dancers, stunt performers, and drag artists, professional wrestlers use their bodies as the primary vehicle for expressing stories to an audience. While performers should possess some degree of athleticism to safely execute the required movements, any "sporting" element of the artform is in service to the fiction/narrative being created. In other words, wrestlers-as-people don't authentically fight; rather, their characters simulate a fight, create the illusion of one, in order to dramatize a conflict. Championship opportunities and reigns serve an important dual rhetorical function, then: they allow for a continual *fictional* story to be told (that is, they exist as a permanent narrative element) while simultaneously rewarding *actual* people for their exemplary work. In gender-segregated environments, women are barred from competing for the same titles as men. While women's divisions may have their own championships for which female talent can compete (satisfying the fictional function of titles), since the assumed normal in professional wrestling is male, women's championships, rhetorically speaking, are secondary to the unqualified top-tier championships for which only men are allowed to compete. That is, as a symbol of recognition and prestige for the actual wrestlers-as-people (the second rhetorical function of title opportunities and reigns), men's and women's championships are inherently unequal in status. Thus, the inequalities within *separate but equal* rhetoric overviewed above protect men's status as the predominant figures in the business by ensuring that only they compete for the most prestigious titles, leaving women out of the conversation entirely.

There is something tangibly at stake for women, then, in desegregating championship eligibility: who is allowed to be recognized as a top performer in the business. In the current *separate but equal* landscape that generally permeates professional wrestling, no matter how hard women work, no matter how much buzz they generate, no matter how often they outperform everyone else on a card and steal the show, they'll always matter less than men simply because they are not afforded the same rewards and prestige in segregated environments. Until women regularly compete for and hold *the same titles* that have been held by the likes of Stone Cold Steve Austin, Ric Flair, Eddie Guerrero, Harley Race, Shawn Michaels, Bret Hart, The Rock, and other *legends* of professional wrestling, they'll continually be excluded from the pantheon of champions, the proverbial Mount Rushmore of talent, simply because they are not given the opportunity to *truly* perform in the *same* spaces as men. And that is the heartbreaking existence of being a woman in professional wrestling: even if she's the best worker on the roster, if she's working for a company where wrestlers are divided and classified by gender, she can never be presented as the overall best *wrestler* simply because she's denied access the top-most markers of success.

Integrated Wrestling: Towards a New Assumed Normal

In a performance space where the assumed normal is male (coding women as "other") and the action itself is make-believe, dividing or classifying talent based on gender continues to relegate women to a subordinate position; it denies them the opportunity to insert themselves into the ongoing conversation concerning who is the best in the business (currently *and* historically). Further, this conversation will only continue to feature men so long as only men are allowed to compete for the highest honors. If wrestling promotions want to demonstrate their commitment to female talent, if they truly want to brand themselves as champions of women's equality, then the best option is to desegregate, in some capacity, in order to allow women to compete for their top prize(s).

Fortunately, there is now precedent for how to desegregate wrestling and build championship storylines that feature performers of all genders. Promotions like Chikara, 3-2-1 Battle!, Elite Canadian Championship Wrestling, and platforms like IndependentWrestling.tv have been at the forefront of progressive booking, featuring female or non-binary champions (mid-card or top-tier) in recent years. Be it out of necessity (small talent rosters) or political action (women can carry the company), these and other independent wrestling promotions are leading the way in modeling integrated competition. In these integrated environments, women fight other women and men fight other men, as traditionally done. Sometimes, though, women and men fight one another. Other times, men and women team up to fight other teams of various configurations. And occasionally, in any one of these hypothetical matchups, a championship is on the line. All types of contests and matchups are normalized in these environments, which not only raises the value of non-male talent, it also creates new storytelling possibilities that are impossible with male-only or female-only participants.

As I hope to have demonstrated, in order to push back against the *separate but equal* rhetoric that currently dominates professional wrestling and inherently presents women as secondary to men, women need access to the same symbolic accolades given to the best in the business. This is particularly pressing for championships and companies with history and/or prestige—the more storied or historic the title, the more urgent and vital it becomes for women to regularly compete for, win, and defend it. Only when the dominant rhetoric of *separate but equal* gives way to a new assumed normal in professional wrestling, an inclusive one where the best wrestlers compete for the top prizes regardless of gender, can women finally celebrate their deserved seat at the table.

Carole Strudwick – Wrestling and Me

Carole is a UK wrestling fan who is awful at predictions despite being old enough to have watched wrestling since the early 90s. Her Twitter is twitter.com/cazziicaz.

When thinking about wrestling and me there are many emotions I feel but the main one is excitement, and it is this childlike excitement that will continue to forever fuel my love for pro wrestling.

I have been a long time wrestling fan, some of my earliest memories are of my Dad, back at the beginning of the 90s, recording the late night WCW Worldwide shows on ITV, so I could watch them with him after I finished school.

This went on to become the replacement for Local British Wrestling on Saturday afternoon TV and Saturdays in our household were not complete if they did not consist of watching WCW, Baywatch, Gladiators and eating chicken kiev!

I got to see many of the greats wrestle on these shows, such as a young Scott Hall/Razor Ramon, Dustin Rhodes and Sting, however I was too young to appreciate them as I do now. What I did love, was being caught up in the stories, the feelings of inexplicable, child like hatred for the heels and the deep, passionate hero worship I had for the faces.

Having a brother who is four years younger than me, meant I also got to enjoy a number of years of what I happen to think is the best generation of wrestling, the Attitude Era. I could endlessly list my favourite matches of this period but that has been done to death in numerous articles and Twitter polls. I will confirm, that it did solidify my belief that Stone Cold Steve Austin is the greatest wrestler of all time.

However I digress, I fondly remembering my Dad bringing home WWF videos that his work colleagues recorded for us (no cable TV at home), the countless hours spent playing out the most epic matches with my brother and his figures on the WWF official ring complete with sound effect keyboard, and perhaps most affectionately, I remember when we finally got to watch our first Royal Rumble live on TV (1999). My brother and 9 of his mates, who were staying over, decided that they would conduct their own Royal Rumble, in our living room with disastrous consequences for my parents furniture!

The point of this piece however, was not to rehash my childhood through wrestling tinted glasses, it was to share my own evolution as a fan.

Whilst I enjoyed all things wrestling when I was at home, when I got to my teens, a time when being cool was all consuming and gender stereotypes felt very definitive, my need to fit in allowed me to use my brother as an excuse for me watching/being interested in wrestling.

As clichéd as it sounds, at school I longed to join in the guys conversations about wrestling as I would have enjoyed those as much as I enjoyed talking with my girlfriends about boybands and brit pop but peer pressure and lame gender stereotypes won out and by the time I got to my late teens early 20s wrestling had fallen from my radar completely.

Over the following years I would glance every so often at an article, or my Dad would mention some late night highlights he had seen and then over time with the increase in social media, it began to draw me back in.

Four years ago I was in the gym at work doing the usual New Year, New Me bollocks, when I saw Sky Sports advertising Rumble. Rumble has always been my favourite of the Big 4 WWE shows, so that evening I causally asked my husband if he would be interested in watching it. His answer was a resounding yes and led to an amusing conversation about how we had been married for almost five years and not once discussed wrestling. The rest as they say is history.

Since then, I have caught up with the years of WWE I missed, (god bless the network). We have watched all the subsequent WWE PPV's, every weekly episode of Raw and Smackdown the whole way through not just highlights, we have watched most episodes of NXT and even started watching AEW regularly. We have watched Rumble in a New York bar full of very vocal fans, we have been to 6 WWE live shows in the UK and been to two Manias! I'm hooked again!

On the downside, it wasn't only my love that had stayed the same, non wrestling fan opinion's hadn't evolved either. Even still now, on the occasions when I mention to people that I like wrestling I get the usual "you know it's fake? why would you watch something fake" and most surprisingly with society changing as much as it has, I was/am still being lumped into the gender stereotypes of "oh is it because your husband watches". Although there is nothing that satisfies me more than at that moment pointing out to these less informed folk that I'm the bigger fan and then watch them stumble around trying to think of what to say next.

Even taking that joy, these comments continue to annoy me to no end. In a society where reality TV dictates most water cooler conversations, I am questioned as to why I watch something fake?! Because the Kardashians/Towie/MIC are clearly representative of every day life??!! If that wasn't enough, people assume I can only watch wrestling because my husband does I mean please this is not the 1950s!

I may have been quick to agree to these thoughts back when I was teenager but now I have developed a better sense of self, I find myself saddened that I wasn't more independent and indifferent to how people viewed me and I feel frustrated that I felt the need to follow the drone mentality of others.

I watch the women superstars that wrestle today, most who are my age or younger and find myself wishing it was me. The time that I spent pretending I was Lita could have become a reality, had I just been a little more self-assured.

Unsurprisingly from conversations had and blogs I have read, it is not just me that has felt this weird embarrassment, almost closeted mentality about being a grown up and admitting to watching wrestling/being a fan.

I am also not the first and probably not the last girl to have it assumed, that she only watches it for a number of male orientated reasons, but a change has come and I am realising, along with other fans that we shouldn't give a shit about what people think!

I have been really lucky in that I met a great group of fans through the Watch Wrestling London group, who I have got to know over the last couple of years. They have provided endless hours of conversation and banter as well as solidifying my beliefs as to why wrestling and wrestling fans are such great fun and why I should not care. It has been an education too with them opening my eyes to more of the independent wrestling scene as well as continued WWE love.

I am a wrestling fan, I love wrestling, scripted or not, it sparks an excitement in me that makes me feel 8 years old again. As we get older and life is more responsible its important to hold on to moments or actions that let us suspend belief and feel like children again, it's a beautiful nostalgic feeling and a perfect foil of escapism.

And not only do I love wrestling, I love it as a female fan, not one that has been pushed into watching it by her husband, or a girl watching it for the "good-looking men" but as girl who loves the stories that are told, the athleticism of the men AND women that is shown and whose inner child still feels like she is watching super heroes!

I have recently had a baby, a girl and she is already fascinated by the wrestling, in fairness at 5 months it could just be the movement and all the lights but I like to think she has inherited her mumma's love for it and as she grows up I will continue to encourage her to adore it regardless of other people's opinions.

So bring on your criticisms and stereotypes, scoff all you want but you can keep your Kardashian's, Towie's, Jersey and Geordie Shores, I have the ladies and gentlemen of pro wrestling!

Nell Haynes - How Skirts Are Changing Bolivian Wrestling

In ornate skirts and bowler hats, Indigenous female fighters claim their place in the ring.

Nell Haynes is an assistant teaching professor in anthropology at Georgetown University. Her research addresses themes of gender and Indigeneity in Latin America. Haynes earned her Ph.D. in anthropology at American University, with a concentration in race, gender, and social justice. She is the author of Social Media in Northern Chile and a co-author of How the World Changed Social Media. Her Twitter is twitter.com/doctoraluchador

This article was originally published at The Conversation* and has been republished under Creative Commons.

Though wrestling is widely regarded as the world's oldest sport, women have only recently gained a foothold. And even then, they've done so while facing tremendous discrimination and resistance from organizers, other wrestlers, and fans.

This is certainly true in competitive Olympic forms of wrestling. But it's also been the case for more spectacular forms of wrestling entertainment, where women have long been relegated to the roles of managers or girlfriends. When they do actually wrestle, they're often sexualized.

Yet these women are nonetheless making advances. World Wrestling Entertainment's most recent WrestleMania featured the first ever women's main event. And in the world of Bolivian wrestling, women have also made big strides. In fact, many Bolivian female wrestlers now have achieved far more popularity than their male counterparts. As an anthropologist of gender in Latin America, I actually trained and performed alongside these wrestlers while conducting ethnographic research.

These women have not gained respect easily: They have met resistance and sexism at every turn. However, their stories not only pay tribute to Bolivia's past but may foretell a more egalitarian future in the world of wrestling.

WRESTLING'S MASCULINE PAST

Bolivian wrestling traces its roots to Mexican professional wrestling, called lucha libre, and professional wrestling in the U.S. before that. The scale and production level of Bolivian lucha libre are certainly not on par with World Wrestling Entertainment, but the conventions are the same. This form of wrestling is less about the competition and more about the theater. Just like in the U.S., promoters, wrestlers, and others with a stake in the business at times decide beforehand who will win the match in order to further developing storylines. To this end, referees don't always enforce the rules. The wrestlers aren't just grappling. They're performing as characters.

In the 1960s, Mexican wrestlers toured South America and, while there, trained a number of Bolivian men. Early wrestlers like Médico Loco, Mr. Atlas, and Diablo Rojo helped build the tradition in Bolivia, which waxed and waned in popularity for four decades. But beginning in 2001, Bolivian women started appearing in the ring.

THE FIGHTING CHOLITAS

These female wrestlers began calling themselves cholitas luchadoras, or fighting cholitas. They take their name from the chola of the Andes, women who have historically worked in markets—though not all of them do—and have earned reputations for being aggressive negotiators and strong advocates for workers' and women's rights. At the same time, they're romantically evoked as national icons.

The luchadoras use their popularity to highlight the roles that Indigenous women may play in society. The combination of this character type with the spectacular physicality of lucha libre has made them popular with both local and foreign audiences. Some represent morally corrupt characters: rudas, or the equivalent of heels in English. They'll sometimes shake a 2-liter soda bottle and spray its contents into the audience. Others will simply sneer and hurl insults at the crowd. On the other hand, the good ones—called técnicas—will stand with a microphone in the ring and declare their loyalty to "the people" and promise to fight for their honor.

Once the match begins, the luchadoras often incorporate humor, pulling each other's braids or even ripping off the spandex pants of a male opponent to reveal hot pink boxer briefs. At times, they pull audience members up to dance with them or lean in to kiss the cheek of a young man in the crowd.

COSTUMES AND CUMBIA MUSIC

But perhaps their most eye-catching quality is the pollera skirt, a knee-length garment made by extensive pleating of sparkling fabric and further puffed by multiple petticoats beneath. As they enter the ring to local cumbia music, they'll swirl these layered skirts. As they flip from the ropes or throw an opponent to the ground, the polleras will billow in the air.

After a few years of wrestling, international journalists began to take notice. Outlets like National Geographic, the BBC, and The New York Times have published articles about the luchadoras. They even appeared as a "challenge" for competitors on The Amazing Race. Each of the stories plays up the novelty of women wrestling in these "traditional" skirts. And it doesn't hurt that the colorful pollera makes for a good cover photo.

But much of the media coverage fails to acknowledge the continued struggles the women face. They often find themselves demeaned by other

Bolivian wrestlers and spectators, who sneer at their gender, race, and performance styles.

"ALL SHOW, NO ABILITY"

As I wrestled alongside both men and women in La Paz, I heard trainers, current wrestlers, and even the retired luchadores of the country disparage the women for relying too heavily on the chola character — which they derided as a "gimmick" — rather than on their craft as wrestlers. Many of the men involved in wrestling have said that the women have degraded the skill level of the sport. Others called them payasas — clowns — or said that they were "all show, no ability," even as they urged male wrestlers to incorporate more elements of spectacle into their performance. The cholitas luchadoras have also been criticized by a number of Bolivians as a kind of racist performance. They suggest the characters are offensive to the image of the chola, Bolivia's Indigenous women, and Bolivians as a whole.

While some of these critiques may be valid, at times they are leveled by the same promoters who fill their events with male luchadores whose gimmicky personas often involve little technical ability. These men perform as stiff mummies who simply bulldoze their way across the ring or clowns who spend more time popping balloons than grappling with opponents. The luchadoras, many of whom identify as Indigenous, counter that they are using their popularity as a springboard for highlighting the roles that Indigenous women may play in society. They say they are attempting to act as role models, providing young Indigenous women with positive representations in the public sphere.

So while the luchadoras are bringing progress, critiques of them show that the more popular they become, the more backlash they have to contend with. But women's acceptance in sports is not only an issue in Bolivia. Even in the United States, women fight to be taken seriously in areas related to sports and entertainment. By understanding how these stories are linked, observers can understand the widespread difficulties women face when navigating power structures in sports that continue to be largely made up of men.

Originally published at https://theconversation.com/how-indigenous-women-revolutionized-bolivian-wrestling-115412

Kiana Parvizi - The Four Horsewomen of WWE

Kiana is an avid WWE and Wrestling fan, and a MAJOR women's wrestling and Becky Lynch fan who podcasts as The Rope Talk Wrestling Podcast. Her main Twitter account is twitter.com/wwethemanbecky

The Four Horsewomen of WWE. I am sure you have heard of them and their incredible achievements. But how did WWE's women go from Bra and Panty matches to main-eventing the Superbowl of Wrestling: WrestleMania?

Let us start at the beginning. October 23, 2000, the Attitude Era. A Monday Night RAW featuring two future legends, Trish Stratus and Lita. That match was the very first Bra and Panty match in WWE, but definitely not the last. The crowd was wide-awake, enjoying every minute of it, and there didn't seem to be any hesitation or uncertainty between the competitors. How do we go from wearing the bare minimum of clothing during a match to women main-eventing WrestleMania? Many fans only credit the Four Horsewomen, but there is much more to the story than that.

Every single woman on the WWE roster, both RAW and Smackdown Live contributed to the current women's division. Women like Paige, who became the youngest female to win the Divas Championship. She was a mere 21 years old. How about AJ Lee, recipient of the Slammy Diva of the Year in 2012 and 2014. Her character shed a light on mental illness like had never been done before in WWE. Still not convinced? Lita became a 4- time champion, Trish Stratus became a 7-time champion, and of course, we could never forget Chyna, a true trailblazer. Holding the Intercontinental Championship twice and the WWF Women's Championship changed the wrestling world, to say the least. She was the first woman to actually wrestle a man (also known as an intergender match) on WWE TV. Each of these accomplishments earned her a rightful place in the WWE Hall of Fame. Of course, there are many more women who should be credited for the success of the current women's division, but you get the idea.

Now that we have covered the roots of the current women's division, let us go back to the Four Horsewomen. Sasha Banks, Bayley, Charlotte Flair, and Becky Lynch. When you think of these women, you probably think, Four Horsewomen, a name derived from the Four Horsemen, a legendary faction built around Ric Flair, Charlotte's father, in the eighties and nineties. That is because these women are known for their massive accomplishments. They are recognized for breaking down barriers and being part of so many "firsts" in the company. Main-eventing WrestleMania. Check. Becoming the first-ever Women's Grand Slam Champion. Check. Holding both the RAW and Smackdown Women's Championships at the same time. Check. Headlining a major show with a violent Hell in the Cell match. Check. Moreover, these are only a few of them. In other words, the Four Horsewomen define what it means to be legendary. Impactful. Memorable. Remarkable. However, they could not have made this much impact without the foundation that the women before them laid down. The Four Horsewomen are able to achieve these extraordinary goals because the women before them (i.e. Lita, Trish Stratus, Torrie Wilson, Paige, AJ Lee, etc.,) stacked the building blocks, and now that women have a voice in all of the sports industry the only thing left to do is add the finishing touches to the groundwork already left for them. That is exactly what they did, it is the constant work and long hours put into the company that earned every woman on the rosters their respect and admiration today. It is because of the hard work and dedication that women have achieved lengths that nobody thought was possible a couple of years ago. Speaking of, let us look at just how far women's wrestling has come because of the Four Horsewomen and the women that came before them.

You cannot deny how far Women's Wrestling has come in recent years, especially when it comes to WWE. July 23, 2018. Monday Night RAW. Stephanie McMahon, chief brand officer of WWE, announced Evolution. The first-ever all women's Pay-Per-View event in the history of WWE. Wow. Not only could you hear the crowd's exuberance and energy, but also you could feel it. Whether you were physically in the arena (lucky!) or watching at home, that moment will forever go down in the history books, and for good reason. Everything the women in the past had worked towards, everything the women in the present worked for, it all came together. As if the pieces of a puzzle were finally put into place, everything just felt right. No, it felt perfect. To think that Bra and Panty matches were real does not feel true considering how far the women have come now. Dwayne Johnson, better known as The Rock once said, "Success in anything will always come down to this: Focus & Effort, and we control both of them." The women in WWE focused on what they wanted to achieve, put in the hard work and effort and reached them.

Emily and Dann Read – The History of Pro Wrestling EVE

Co-owners of Pro Wrestling EVE, the ground-breaking feminist-punk-rock wrestling promotion founded in 2006 that has continually played a major part in the popularity and increased exposure of the female professional wrestling scene. Follow Emily on twitter.com/EmilyReadEVE, Dann on twitter.com/DannRead and the main EVE account on twitter.com/prowrestlingeve

Interview conducted by Jason Norris on 15 December 2019, the day after their show LET'S GET SHITFACED & SCREAM INTO THE VOID: A CHRISTMAS WRESTLING SPECTACULAR (a reaction to the UK General Election), and in the weeks before the 3rd annual Wrestle Queendom

Jason: What is Pro Wrestling EVE in your eyes as its founders?

Emily: We are a DIY punk company and that dictates so much of who we are and how we function. If you know much about the riot girl movement (*a subcultural movement that combines feminist consciousness and punk style and politics*) I think that really encompasses how we function and who we are. And we are all about providing a platform for three dimensional and diverse characters in wrestling.

Jason: And in your eyes, why does EVE matter? Why are you putting so much into it?

Emily: One women's match on a show is very common, and it does not show off what women can do, and that's when you end up with people saying, 'I don't like women's style' and 'women aren't very good wrestlers'. Well that's because you haven't actually seen highly skilled women

218

wrestle on a regular basis. And on top of that, a lot of the women will struggle to get to that high level because how can they learn with such limited opportunities, and how can they become veteran level wrestlers if they are doing one five minute match a week.

Dann: And there's deeper aspects of that as well. its still a regular thing that will happen, someone will say 'just because I don't like women's wrestling that doesn't mean I'm sexist'. If the only reason that you don't like women's wrestling, if you don't like anything to do with women's wrestling then that is sexist. But if you were to say, I haven't found or I haven't watched any women's wrestling that I've liked, that's not the same thing because that's saying I watch it, but I haven't found anyone that I like. You are going to be watching fundamentally so little in comparison to guys and if you go to live shows, there are so many promoters that don't treat the women with the same respect. They won't want to spend the money on the women that they spend on the guys. And because the women talent are more spread around the UK because there's less of them you may have to spend more on a person's travel, maybe need a hotel and you would have to spend perhaps more than you like to so these promoters won't do it. Maybe they'll just book two local trainee girls and the match won't be very good and it's the only women's match on the show. A number of people will when go away saying women's wrestling isn't very good because they'll be comparing it to the rest of the card and they'll have some amazing male talent on the show. With women, one of the biggest things is that promoters and trainers don't hold women to do same standard that they hold the men to.

Emily:	A lot of fans don't expect the same standards from the women as well, and they also don't realize that can be damaging.
Dann:	A lot of that is because some of those fans will enjoy talking to those women. And to some it will be because they find those women hot and it's them interacting with hot women, you know? And that's not all of the fans, but that's just how it is for some. You know, they'll be ignorant enough to say it was a great match and it was the shits. There is subjectivity, but there's no way that they would have watched that if it was two guys and said the same thing. Sometimes, you know, shit is clearly shit. Maybe they just really like bad wrestling, there's always an excuse. A lot of the time it's just a case of they enjoy interacting with the wrestlers on social media or they find the person attractive.

But trainers also, a lot of trainers don't train the women or don't give them the same respect because they feel 'that that's not your job'. Some of trainers will still have the idea that the women's job is to be there for the dads, 'Your job is there to look good'. Some training school's have only got one woman, so they'll say 'you'll be the flyer' *(in wrestling you tend to have a base, the larger wrestler, and flyer they work off of to create movement from)*. As a flier its felt you don't need to learn how to take a load of these moves and how to base for the moves because you'll be the one doing the flying every time, not being the base, where the actual work is needed. But what happens when that person gets a booking elsewhere against another woman and they don't know how to take each other's moves because they've never been taught? They've only been taught that the guy's going to lift them up. The satellite DDT, how many times in intergender matches have you seen where the woman doing a satellite DDT or a head scissors *(both moves that involve the flier spinning around the body of the base and flipping them to the ground)*. These are the flying spots most women are taught.

The person that's taking the moves, they are one that's actually doing all the work, but there are so many women who aren't taught how to actually base and take that move because they're being taught at the training school you'll never need to learn that because you're the smallest one here. They aren't training the woman to be a wrestler for the rest of their careers. Your job as a good trainer is to train people so that they could go out and be a star around the world and make a career out of it.

Jason: Lets touch on training. EVE has its own training school called EVE Academy and it's an all female class for all who identify as women. That's pretty rare. I'm aware of WOW (Women of Wrestling) in the US having an all women's school. You have one as well and its rare as most of the time women are training in intergender training, that's the standard way.

Emily: I was actually going to say one of the other important things about EVE is showing strong women and showing diverse women, showing these loud women who aren't afraid to take up space. It's important for men to see that and to start seeing women differently. But it's also incredibly important for women to see that it's not something we see in the media. Its not something we are shown we are allowed to be, we tend to be shown that we should be timid and quiet and demur. Those are the kinds of things that are in general encouraged towards women. So our main focus when we started EVE Academy is teaching women how to stand, how to be loud, how to make noise in wrestling when you're working, because you have to make noise. When you throw a clothesline you should be making noise, when you're taking a move often you're having to make a loud noise.

With women when they start training with us, a large majority of them can't make a loud noise. They can't, their body like their brain will stop them from making it the noise, like screaming, showing pain or anger. A lot of expressions, if it's seen as maybe it would be an ugly expression or a non-sexy expression is a struggle to do.

Dann: But when you look at Joshi from Japan you'll see that.

Emily: The women there are really good. They make noise, they do the facial expressions but in western wrestling they don't so much. If you look through society, women being raped and sexually assaulted, you'll have people say, 'well why didn't they shout out?' and I think that's really something to look at. They didn't shout out because a lot of women have been conditioned to not make noise to the point that even in that situation they cannot make noise. And in meetings they might not be taken seriously because they're not able to stand and hold themselves in a way that says they can take charge and that they should be listened to.

It's a real sad thing through society and people don't notice that women have been conditioned to be like that from a very young age. So it does mean that making noise is important to focus on in training, and it's actually made us extremely popular with people who don't actually want to be wrestlers. They want to come and do keep fit and work on their confidence and its been amazing. They see wrestling as a hobby, Like you'd go to a dance class, but you don't want to be a professional dancer. So we do have a lot of students who love it for that reason and that's something we're able to focus on. The isn't like men who are more naturally rowdy or who do like play-fighting and things. You don't really need to focus on it with men when they have that come to them more naturally.

We also provide a safe environment. There can be a lot of groping from men, not accidental, but deliberate, when they're training with women and women know when they come to an all women's class, they're not going to have that issue. And there are just certain things that women will have to focus on and that men wouldn't. One of the things is a leapfrog and doing certain jumps, women have been conditioned to keep our legs together, which means a lot of moves the women can struggle with. A lot of women will struggle to do things if they need to have their legs wide for it because we're so conditioned to keep our legs together. You actually have to work on how to hold your legs for that and it's something where when you first start to do it, you feel really vulnerable doing this movement that you haven't done for 20 years. You've kept your legs together as much as you can for 20 years unless you're having sex, and so now suddenly you're in a public place and people are going to be watching you. And if you imagine you've got a load of guys around as well, and suddenly you have to have your legs open. Oh my God, oh that's terrifying. There was a lot of things with women that you would focus on that men wouldn't have to think about, just like there are a lot of things that men would have to focus on, but it's just not relevant to women, it's not stuff the women have needed to work on.

Women are a lot better at when given the chance having characters and depth. I find the women are really creative and more naturally creative in that area. They also seem to be more naturals at working together and supporting each other and have that camaraderie from the beginning. Whereas men seem to naturally have more of a competitive side, wanting to be the one that's the best so they might have to be encouraged in that area because with wrestling you have to work together. So it's strange, but I think it's really important to just really have an area where you can feel safe and you can flourish and you can focus on the areas that you need to focus on. So I think its a better rounded training, and we can focus in the areas that women typically, obviously everyone's different but is areas that women typically struggle more.

Dann: There's a couple of physical things as well. In terms of bumping safely, women have to bump slightly different to the guys as well and guys don't know about that. You have to think about those front falling bumps because some of those women have larger chests.

Emily: And with back falling bumps if you have a uterus and you bump the way the men are taught to land on their back

224

you can build up scar tissue in the uterus. It would mean that then the women will struggle if they want to have children that they can really struggle with fidelity and it'll take a year or more to really get the uterus back to where it used to be, or you could do permanent damage as well. It's not that women can't take bumps, it's just they need to land and take them differently. On certain things, guys, if they don't want to crush their nuts, there's going to be ways that they would train to move as well.

Dann: The majority of trainers are men, so they think about it from their side and don't know about this difference for women.

Emily: Also with certain moves for women just knowing the fact that a little bit of wee can come out, how woman are built differently where it wouldn't happen with a guy. It's nice to have a woman be there and warn, 'wee might come out, wear a pad'. It's not embarrassing, it's just that if someone jumps and lands on your bladder as a woman, a bit of wee could come out, that's standard, standard stuff that can happen to a woman's body. It's not embarrassing. Doesn't mean you've got weak pelvic floor muscles, but it doesn't happen to guys. Then guys could get like a semi in certain situations, we've seen that! Women don't have to worry about when that happens, but it's just a biological thing.

Dann: The other thing specific to the EVE academy and our events is the rare fact that EVE does not just attract wrestling fans. The majority of our live audience are not wrestling fans and a number of them are just EVE fans and what I mean by that is the amount of things that we've been able to just get out in mainstream media as opposed

225

to wrestling media. And that means a number of people, the women that come to the EVE shows, some of them may then come to Eve Academy. And so we have a number of women in Eve Academy who don't watch any other wrestling and they've never watched wrestling and they have no interest in watching.

Dann: The two main trainers of Eve Academy are Greg Burridge and Rhea O'Reilly. Nina Samuels also takes a lot of the sessions, and Cara Noir steps in as well. With it being all women, Greg struggled a little bit with this at first, which he found fascinating because Greg has been teaching people for 15 years, and he teaches people every day. What he found hard, surprisingly, and a bit of a challenge straight away is he'd be like 'so you know, when Roman Reigns does this', or when 'John Cena does this', only a few of in the class will say yes, but a load would ask 'Who's John Cena?'. He has to find a different way of doing it and explaining it because they haven't got a clue. They only know what they see when they come to EVE shows.

Jason: EVE have done really well getting more mainstream press coverage. I've seen EVE in Stylist, Timeout and The Evening Standard to name a few. Lots of press coverage and event listings or just genuine news stories that I'd imagine has really brought people in that would not know about wrestling.

Dann: The Telegraph were down at yesterday's show. We did BBC breakfast and The One Show and all these other things this year.

Emily: We've changed how we reach out to people. What we do with EVE, I believe very strongly in not just for providing a really good night out and a good show and doing storylines that can be completed in one night and enjoyable for one night, but also we look long term. The impact it can have on women's lives, seeing these strong women, seeing these loud women and seeing these diverse women. It's something I believe so strongly in and that having a safe community to watch any event as well. People should know that and to be interested and know that this form of entertainment is out there and know that these types of events are out there and I want people to understand the love of wrestling, which I have had since I was like six or seven. I've loved wrestling and I always wanted to be able to invite people into our world and be like, you've got movies and you've got theatre, there's also wrestling and it's wicked.

So much the way I wanted to show people what we are was just me deciding to embrace it and do that. Show people that they can see these strong women and show people that they can see this really unique and beautiful type of entertainment, bring them into something new. And I think what kind of added to that and how we reached out to mainstream media more, the media obviously liked the product we have, they liked how different it was, liked seeing these strong fierce, women that they weren't seeing elsewhere. The other point that helped with that is the wrestling press were not interested in covering us, and most of them still aren't. So it was pretty early I just thought, well I'll focus on the general media.

Dann: You know, the fact of the matter is as well, you have to analyze and just be honest. How many full time, and by full time I mean that they run a show on average twice a month, how many women's wrestling promotions are there in the western world? There's one and it's us so why is that? You've got all these other indie companies and they're able to run a number of shows around the year, but no other all women's promotion in the UK, the US or in the entire western world is doing it. Why are we the company that runs more shows than anyone else? And by a long way, and the simple fact of the matter is wrestling fans for the most part do not go to all women's shows and this is just how it is and that will probably piss some people off. But we've got the facts to back it up and they don't, we realized early that the wrestling world did not want us but that we were going to do it anyway. Wrestling fans, most wrestling fans, will not support an all women's product. And the fact of the matter is that's the reason why we're the only one who runs as frequently as we do and we have people who love EVE.

We don't just target wrestling fans, but it doesn't mean that we're not for wrestling fans. It's not just that Cheryl and Carol are not coming to Eve on a Saturday night because Meiko Satomura *(25 year veteran from Japan)* is going to be there, they don't know who that is. We have these people on the shows because we believe in delivering a quality product and we believe in helping the talent on the scene grow and get better and being able to share a ring with veterans and being in a locker room with them and learning helps that. That's the bottom line, a

228

wrestling promotion that relies solely on wrestling fans will not be able to run frequently and do well from it.

Jason: You talked about the women that have come through the company and what you've done. I had to look some of the former EVE champions that you've had. EVE has been around for 10 years, and these champions have gone onto work for the major companies. Paige with the first ever EVE champion. There's the Alpha Female Jazzy Albert now on NXT UK. Then Nikki Cross, who was known as Nikki Storm and was a multiple time EVE champion. Nina Samuels, Piper/Viper Nixon and Kay Lee Ray, who went on to become the UK NXT champion just after leaving EVE and was at NXT War Games. There were some big names everyone now knows from NXT, NXT UK and AEW that went through your doors.

Dann: It was always based on the fact that we recognize talent, we recognize how hard that they were working and we also recognize that they weren't being really given opportunities to be able to do more than just be the girls match. There is again, it goes back to like on the training side. Imagine you're an actor and you'll go into acting class and they teach you in an acting class how to be an extra. Okay, that's cool, but I'd quite like to learn everything about acting so that I can be the star and have a bigger career. And they'll go, okay, well we're not going to teach you that. We're going to teach you a couple of things, but we're not going to teach you everything'. They will teach you the mistress or secretary role at best but not really round you out. That's the equivalent of what's goes on at wrestling schools because if you're only putting women in a certain position on the show, how are they going to learn how to work a main event style match? There are differences in working a match and a structure that's a second match on the card as opposed to work in a match and structure that's the main event. How is anyone going to learn?

Emily: We give them that platform to learn the roles, so a lot of the women do go on to do these things because they know how to be main eventers. It's about confidence, the ability to do that and the skillset.

Dann: Now, does that mean that it all goes right from the start? Of course not because nobody else is doing it. We have to fuck up on shows. We have to provide people with an opportunity to fuck up. Because nobody else is really doing that.

Emily: Rhia O'Reilly *(current EVE champion)* is a great example of that. We just kept putting the microphone in her hand and she hated it and she'd cut some early promos where she was almost shaking and was so nervous, some where Dann's holding the microphone and feeding her the lines. Now we've got someone who's one of the best talkers out there.

Dann: Now you can just hand her a microphone and say, 'Something has happened, we need to sort this so fill time for a few minutes', and off she'll go.

Emily: And she'll have the audience. The audience will be there. There'll be with her, they'll be listening.

Dann:	That's a rarity because mostly when I speak to talent and ask how many promos they'll done the majority of the time the answer I get is none. Their job isn't to be a part of these long term stories on other shows. Their job is to go out there and have 'the women's match'. Where is the opportunity to develop that character and find more and learn how to talk? Because there's an art to doing that. It's not as simple as going out there, there are words to not use, there are structures to use, sentences to get out. It's not as simple as just take a microphone and off you go, you're dealing with butterflies in the stomach for the first time they're talking, and the tenth time or even the hundredth time, you've got to keep going. I'm a big believer in having people learn commentary as well because that is an art and also helps you as a wrestler. Learn how to do commentary, be given an opportunity to go out there and do things because you need to have an opportunity to fail and people aren't really getting that for the most part.
	You wouldn't suddenly tell a junior doctor you're going to perform this surgery. 'What? I'm not going to learn it?' Well, no one else has given you an opportunity to learn, so we're just going to get you to do it and see how it goes. That's effectively how it is in wrestling. They're not being given the opportunity in many places to do it. So there's randomly this surgery that is for you.
Emily:	With Nina Samuels, although she was always confident speaking, her hands used to be shaking so badly to start with because she had never been taught, no one had done it. Some women haven't had the chance to practice on smaller shows or just a simple thing where they're talking.

You're just throwing them out there, and a lot of what Dann does with EVE is talking to the women, making sure they understand what they're doing and speaking to them and discussing with them about who they would like to be as a character. Given that push through the door and preparing, off you go, you can do it.

We started calling Nina the superstar, Dann was saying 'The Superstar Nina Samuels' because it was just the Nina character, she's a superstar. She is another one now that we can just hand the mic, say is this is what its about an off she'll go.

Dann: Just before she went out last night she took me to one side, did her promo to me, I added one bit. I needed to add one bit, one line everything else was her, all she had from me is to what were we're doing and where we are going. I always work with talent, I'm big on encouraging them. I used to say the same thing about Tom Dawkins when he started the Cara Noir character at the start (*The Black Swan' of British wrestling has his unique brand of in-ring insanity, and one of the hottest acts in the UK*). People needed to stop trying to make him what they thought he was and work with him. Listen to who he says the character is and work with him. Get the talent's ideas on programs and stories and understand what they have. And it's the same with any talent, because ultimately they need to learn a number of these things, who they are themselves and then you work with them on what the version of that specific character is when they perform.

Emily: The biggest thing, the most consistent thing he does because Dann does the stories and booking, he'll hate me

232

saying, but he's credibly skilled at it. And this is not me as his wife, the number of people who tell me within the industry who are well respected that he's good. But moving on from that, the thing I have heard the wrestlers we are working with say the most consistently is Dann will ask them for more information. He'll ask 'what's your character?' and they'll say 'I'm the good guy,' or 'I'm peppy' which is not a character, or they go 'can I get back to you and have a think?' because they will say no one has asked before, but they're pleased someone has.

Dann: Its about the moves as well. 'You shouldn't do this move you're using'. What if you don't know the character? How do you know what moves you should and shouldn't do? Because the moves are a physical catchphrase of the character and everything's linked together.

You'll say to them, why does your character cheat? Why, why are they doing to cheat? Because they want to? Or does your character cheat because they have to? You know, there's differences in those things. What's your look, what's your gear like? Okay, so you're wearing ripped jeans and a ripped shirt. Wonderful. Why are you now doing all this technical wrestling then? It makes no sense for you to come in wearing ripped jeans and a ripped shirt and some Doc Martin boots and now you're doing a tribute to Johnny Saint (a British technician legend, now managing NXT UK and the former 'Man of a Thousand Holds'). What are you telling the audience? It makes no sense. And that's just a basic way, obviously it goes on more, but it's just easier if I just use the most obvious and basic way of explaining.

Dann:　　　　The most common thing when I asked that question, I do get back that nobody's ever asked me that before. This also comes back again to a lot of the training problems because that means trainers are not working with the wrestlers on it. It is one of the hardest things to find. When I first worked with Charlie Morgan I was at a show that she was at which had an EVE guest match, because there was a lot of shows when we first started as guests. Most shows didn't have a women's match on, so we actually started buying time on other people's shows in exchange for the footage because we actually started doing on demand streaming back in 2011. It just was individual matches rather than a subscription streaming service. So we would buy spots on other people's shows, in exchange for the footage we'd provide them with an Eve match. And there was one match on a Southside show in 2012. I can't remember who the original person was, but it was Alpha Female Jazzy Albert versus someone. And that person at the last minute wasn't able to do it. We were referred to a girl that lived nearby called Penelope. Of course she went on to become Charlie Morgan later on. And so this is the first time I met her and I spoke to her after the match when she asked for feedback. I just said, 'look, I really don't get it, what is a Penelope?' and she didn't really have an answer. At the time she was put on her back foot and she'd got a bit defensive but she subconsciously knew that this didn't make sense and she didn't like doing that character. But she had just been told this is your name and now you're going to go out and wrestle. You're just someone doing moves, it doesn't make sense. And that's part of the reason why Charlie Morgan then became so good is because she thought about who she wanted to be. What represents elements of who I am in real life and that I can then turn into this character and go from there. It's always heartbreaking as well as very frustrating when you're hearing no one's working with the wrestlers, no one's talking to them about these ideas because again, their job is to be the women's match as opposed to anything else.

Jason: I want to talk about the growth of the company. Did you start with all male fans before you grew the female audience? What has been the impact of things like Glow and the Mae Young Classic and the WWE horsewomen on awareness of what you guys do?

Dann: We've never ever heard anyone mention the WWE horsewoman before ever about having any impact on going to wrestling. No wrestling product or show or promotion has had any impact on anything to do with women's wrestling, at least on our side, ever. The only thing that has had an impact and it had a massive impact was when the Glow drama series launched on Netflix.

We didn't really have male fans to start. We ran shows in Sudbury in Ipswich, which was the town we lived in, and we were actually just getting families. You'd get a few hardcore dedicated wrestling fans, but they're the hardcore dedicated wrestling fans, but they weren't the majority of the audience at all.

We had family shows because when we would try to run an all women's shows and we used to get people trying to shut the shows down because they'd say that we were no different than porn. So we would get the general public seeing the posters and they just complained to the council.

That's what would happen all the time when we were doing all female shows, but not under the EVE brand yet. So when we relaunched a EVE we made the decision that we were going to have a big sticker, a big star on the side of the poster that read 'kids go free'. That was our way of basically saying this is not a porn show. This is a wrestling show that just happens to have an all women cast. And that also encouraged people because this is when a recession has kicked in, when austerity was being brought in. So money was difficult for a lot of people. This is at the start of food banks starting to occur. We were a cheap night out for families. So we were worth the risk. And again, because of our belief in having a quality product, we still made a point and bringing that quality in teaching, in training the woman up, we still made a point of bringing talent from overseas. But it was a family audience.

They didn't know who these people were. You could have called it All Star Wrestling Women's shows in terms of who the audience was. But it's just that the product was more of your kind of wrestling product that the independent hardcore fans would like but that everyone could get into it. Moms, daughters, sons, grandparents, everyone got into it. We actually drew well, there was one of the shows that we did in Sudbury. It was The Wrestle Fever, our second internet pay per view and it was a 300 sellout, turning people away and we didn't expect that attendance, when we started we were drawing a 100, we didn't expect 300 people, but we built that up. I just remember we were literally just trying to find more seats. I remember sending people down into the foyer and bringing up the couch that was in the waiting area, it was just crazy. Then it just became standing room only. That wasn't in a city, it's in a tiny town that no one knows unless you've gone through it. It's on your way to somewhere else. So that was what our audience was and at the start and that was actually really cool. We love doing the 18 plus shows where we have the attitude that we have, but we really enjoy doing those family shows still as well. You see the difference that you're making to kids, seeing the looks on young lads faces because they're seeing women portrayed in the same way as they're seeing men, and you're seeing the looks on young girl's faces because they're seeing opportunities for them, they seen representation of them because so many superheroes on TV tend to be all male, and so many heroes on TV, tend to be male, and now that's not the case. Stuff like that really, really means a lot to us, especially like you'll often get like the parents then email us or Instagram us afterwards and tell us about how much of an impact we've had on their kids and how they've gone home and started dressing up and created their own wrestling character.

Emily: Mermaid Princess Sparkle is my favourite, she made herself little outfit, she had a cape. There was a character in there. I love her.

Dann: I'd like her to go to some wrestling schools and help train and teach the trainers on how to create some characters. So that's how it was when we started out.

Jason: How does it work for you guys now as a business? From the outside, I think the main way this works is the streaming service and the interest around the world in

237

finding good women's wrestling and paying to stream. Is that like such a big thing or is it still more about the live shows for you?

Dann: The on-demand service is extremely important to us. That's another reason for bringing in some of these big names from other countries. Every wrestling show is a self contained story, but obviously also part of a longer story arc, and that's where the on-demand also comes in. They're one and the same, they work together, and streaming allows people around the world to be able to follow it.

The US and outside of the UK does have a horrible habit of ignoring what's going on in the UK though. Because of the likes of Progress and to a lesser extent Rev-Pro that's not quite the same as it once was, but it certainly is with regards to the women talent.

Jason: I see on social media when you end up going down and finding the right groups of people, there is still a very passionate audience. It's finding that audience, but I agree, when you go on the news sites, they're not talking about EVE unless it's the specialists like Bell to Belles, it's very rare to find it.

Dann: Exactly. They act like the UK doesn't exist yet there'll be promotions who run 4 or 6 times a year in the US that will get a ton of coverage, some of whom draw 30 people in the audience. There we are doing what we're doing and using the talent, we brought the legendary Manami Toyota over and no one did anything to cover it. We were the first people to bring Meiko Satomura over semi-regularly, no one covered that. Emi Sakura, Awesome Kong and others have been coming over here for us since 2011. There's a lot of ignoring of what's going on outside the US. Not everyone's like that because some of our most dedicated fans are in the US and but certainly among the wrestling media.

Jason: I noticed you got some attention for the first Wrestle Queendom because it was such a landmark event (biggest all women's show in Europe ever). Not what it deserved, but coverage was actually happening.

Dann: Yeah, Mike Sempervive was a big help in that. A number of people actually at the Wresting Observite website were a big help in that as well. There are numerous journalists who follow us who send stuff into the bigger websites, it's just that the sites omit a lot of stuff to do with us. They'll put something up that some other promotion is doing, but they'll leave out what we're doing. I remember when Pro Wrestling Illustrated first started doing the top 50 women wrestlers of the year. I messaged them and I asked if they wanted to look at any of the EVE footage? They said they were not interested in wrestlers unless they compete in the US. So no EVE, no Stardom (World Wonder Ring Stardom is Japanese joshi puroresu, a women's professional wrestling promotion), missing a lot out for the world. They would only include wrestlers from these promotions if they had travelled to the US even if they weren't regulars. Their whole view was, 'if the women don't wrestle in America, no one cares'.

Jason: Wrestle Queendom was the big show in 2018, Europe's biggest ever all women's show. You brought in legends for

239

that one, including Aja Kong from Japan. For Wrestle Queendom 2 in 2019 you had a Jordynne Grace from the US and some of the top talent in Japan again. Wrestle Queendom 3 happens in January 2020 with top women from Stardom.

Dann: Jordeyn Grace was a regular for EVE back in 2018, so like she kept started coming over. She came out, she was coming over like like every other month. Aja Kong was the only person we had not worked with before for the first Wrestle Queendom, all the other 'imports' from the shows have been regulars for EVE.

Emily: Here's the funny thing, like what we did just now, we do so often. People will be point out that Emi Sakura is on the show but for us its just Emi, she's not a featured import, she has been part of EVE for 8 years.

Jason: When it comes to putting together the Queendom show, what's influencing who you bring in for these shows? It sounds like there's the hardcore fans that want to see these 'imports' coming over, but then you've got your EVE fans who are going to be there because they know it's going to be a great show.

Dann: Imports don't really sell a lot of tickets. I know people don't always struggle with that, but they don't. That's not the reason why we bring them over. There'll be some people who bought a ticket for them, but that's a very small number of people. It doesn't mean we don't appreciate them because of course we do, we want you to buy the ticket and come and enjoy. Part of the thing is it's about us offering the fans the opportunity to come and see people that they wouldn't normally get to see as well.

Emily: Also that person maybe only really follows Joshi wrestling and I love that they'll come to EVE for that wrestler that they're watching and excited to see and then they'll see the other performers. The number of times I hear 'I came there to see this wrestler, but oh my God, these EVE regulars are good',.

Dann: Well I think Wrestle Queendom 2 is a prime example of that, where there was a number of people that watched because of Stardom, but the best match of the night was Laura Di Matteo versus Jordynne Grace. No disrespect to anyone else on the show, but it really stole the show and then some, and that's a show that had Kay Lee Ray versus Viper Niven in the main event, knocking it out the park.

Emily: I love introducing wrestling fans to wrestlers that they might not know or be as aware of.

Dann: The first Wrestle Queendom was a moment and then there was this idea from wrestling fans that 'you've done it now, so you don't need to keep doing it, you don't need to keep going on.' Now with Wrestle Queendom 3, there'll be some people that say it feels like it's normal. Yeah, because its the third one!

Wrestle Queendom 3 is the day before WWE's NXT UK Takeover and six days before their TV tapings. WWE Have a rule that no talent are allowed to work for other shows within the seven days of there being an NXT event. However Jinny, Nina Samuels and one other person I can't

241

reveal yet are contracted to WWE and will appear at Wrestle Queendom. Now think about that and think about how much that therefore must mean to the talent. They've put their necks on the line to say they want to do this. This means a lot to us. I just think that there's always going to be a sector of wrestling fans that don't understand the difference of what it's like for the women in the wrestling scene as opposed to what all these other wrestling shows are doing. Wrestle Queendom is special for us. The fact that it's regular big show every year now is what makes it special because no one else is putting on a big annual show. Still no Evolution 2 from WWE. A number of promotions have stated we're going to do an all women's show and then it maybe doesn't go quite to plan or they're just feel 'right, we've done one now.'.

Where's your follow up, what are you doing? Again, it comes down to the opportunities and it means a lot to us. We're extremely grateful to WWE for allowing it and for understanding how much doing this show means, to everyone. So Nina Samuels versus Jinny is happening and I'm extremely excited about that match. It's the first time they've ever told this story with these versions of the characters.

Jason: What is next for Eve now? Wrestle Queen is now an annual event. What's next on the radar? What's going on in 2020?

Dann: Its a normal thing, but Queendom is still our WrestleMania so I'm still looking forward to that and I'm really excited about the new venue we are using. Then in 2020 we've obviously got 10 year anniversary.

We've also got Eve 100 at the end of next year as well. 2020 is a really important year. We've got three major shows plus the She-1 tournament weekend. Everyone needs to do She-1, its a hard tournament of wrestling in blocks of 4 and we get guests, such as Jazz this year. Its our version of New Japan's G1 but over one weekend.

Emily:　　　　We have all out regular monthly events going on in 2020, the first Saturday of every month at Resistance Gallery, and other plans under way for more shows. Really we will try and keep our shows well balanced, with a complete wrestling show every time for our audience. Once Wrestle Queendom is over we'll move onto the next big show to celebrate 10 years of EVE in May.

Joseph Telegen - This Ain't No Bra and Panties Match, Little Boys: An Accomplished Novice Takes on Joshi

PhD in English from the University of Washington who writes about subjects ranging from Israel/Palestine to Buffy the Vampire Slayer; also wrestling. Every. Day. On Twitter at twitter.com/JTelegensAgency

Dear Boys (From a Man Who Is Tired of your shit):

Stop sending women wrestlers DMs of your dick on Twitter. Stop proposing marriage to said women (shoutout to my favorite Luchadora, La Avispa Dorada, who gets that stuff regularly and even wrote a blog entry about it on her "Jump Higher!" website. It's called "Guide to Not Being a Creep: Avispa's Adventures In Social Media." Google it). Stop arguing that calling said women "hot" is a compliment when they've just put on five-star matches in which they and their partners put their bodies on the line in an act of cooperative violence for your enjoyment (I mean it's OK if you praise their hard-earned-at-the-gym appearance during a lengthy conversation in which you spend 99% of your time talking about the match, but you know damn well you're just looking at their asses and that's it; I've seen your Twitter feed). Social media has become an essential aspect of pro wrestling, right along with the in-ring product, the microphone work; now women have to put themselves over online (Becky Lynch take a bow). So stop using your own fanboy social media as a means of acting out your inevitably-unrealized attempts to hook up with female athletes.

You know what? While we're at it, don't call yourselves feminists even if you aren't just panting over T and A. Don't even call yourself allies. Relearn how to watch women's wrestling before you say another damn word about it. Watch horizontally. Nomadically. And start with Joshi, for fuck's sake. Prime Akira Hokuto would've beaten the shit out of HHH in a shoot-fight in their respective primes and we both know it. If you haven't yet, go watch her match with Shinobu Kandori (2 April 1993, AJW Dreamslam) and thank me after and keep watching more and more Joshi. Joshi, if I must take the time to define it, is not so much a "style" of wrestling, as a descriptor of Japanese women's wrestling on the whole. Tendencies exist, principally a realistic, "strong-style" approach where the strikes are designed to not only look, but actually are, as "stiff" as possible. Don't you dare, however, try to say "Joshi __." You'll sound like a jack-booted Western bro/facist.

Anyway, back to horizontal learning. The concept of the horizontal acquisition of knowledge comes, regrettably, from two men, Gilles Deleuze and Felix Guattari. Their Anti-Oedipus and A Thousand Plateaus have been explicated far better than I can do it (even though they've featured prominently in the dissertation I'm just about to finish after I'm done teaching you pigs how to watch women's wrestling), but let me break it down for you so you can go watch Akira Hokuto like a Sasha Banks-quality boss.

Horizontal Learning: Here's where you learn about a subject (say wrestling and more specifically the rich and violent and beautiful history of Joshi) through an active rejection of the Western tradition of learning, starting with Plato's construction of objective truth and including a rejection of the "reductive glee" of Freud and Marx. To follow Deleuze and Guattari's observatory approach to the world, don't start with the classics as dictated to you by the "ponderous academic apparatus" of the Dave Meltzers of the world (Ric Flair and Shawn Michaels ought not to be the unquestioned GOATs, sorry Ric I love you); move in all directions to find your wrestling gods. Lucha, The Territory Era, Minis (call them midgets and they'll kick your ass), Japan (and when I say Japan, I am not just talking about the 5-star Meltzered matches though those are really fucking good).

When Deleuze and Guattari call for an approach to learning that is an "antigenealogy," that means a refusal of a hierarchy of learning that starts on the shoulders of giants (let's say Lou Thesz for the first giant you'll acknowledge and like it, damnit because that's the history of this business, then Bruno Sammartino, then basically Hogan and HHH [the latter of whom's first famous storyline involved marrying a woman out of daterape and don't even get me started on what Hogan said about his daughter's black boyfriend that time]). We can do better, and again, we start by looking where others haven't bothered.

Joshi women beat the shit out of each other. For example, let's start with Akira's match with Aja Kong, 20 October 1994 at the legendary Big Egg Wrestling Universe show in front of 32,000 people. Kong is the covertly gorgeous, massive (here I'm speaking both in stature and legacy) legend of Joshi whose basic job was to beat the living crap out of the gorgeous Joshi baby faces and look like she was having a lot of fun doing it (she was so good at this last part that the fans couldn't help but love her even as a Monster Heel). Akira could do it it all. She could fly like the glamorous Manami Toyota, grapple like an Inoue sister, and just run over to a mic, scream "Akira!" into it, and convince you she was the monster even against Aja, who still works in AEW as this fledgling new superpower strives to knock Vince McMahon off his monopolistic throne.

By the way, AEW, one thing? Give Joshi it's own show, opposite "SmackDown" (what a stupidly outdated show name), on Friday nights. You have the talent in the remarkably gifted and equally tiny Riho, your current women's champion. The women of AEW who don't borrow from the rich tapestry of stylistics that constitute Japanese women's wrestling are plenty capable of holding their own on AEW's flagship Dynamite. Joshi is its own, ineffable presence and deserves to be presented independently.

That's in keeping with the nature of Joshi promotions in Japan, by the way. The women run the companies and don't even perform, in general, with the estimable male promotions of the country (I will leave it up to you to decide whether that last part is a good thing or not after you've spent hours watching Joshi and with your hand decidedly not down your pants. You make me sick).

Oops, I forgot about Akira H vs. Aja Kong: We first hear a promo from the terrifying Kong. Facepaint like Ziggy Stardust, almost lazy seeming in her expressions of confidence. I assume. Look, the promo's in Japanese, and understanding Joshi, like understanding all great art, is largely beside the point. When you listen to free jazz, do you try to grasp every last nonsequitur instrumental blast? Hell, I'll set the bar lower, are you really one of those people who needs to read a No Fear Shakespeare version of Hamlet or can you allow yourself to just derive (more French theory, this is surrealist talk for a temporary embrace of madness in order to obtain true variant mentalities), to simply drift in and out of the Western consciousness from which you've been imprisoned by listening to Michael Cole tell you that HHH's the greatest wrestler of all-time so go watch his matches if you really want to see a legend. God I hate those guys. Stop asking yourself whether form of wrestling's the "best." Ask yourself, as do Deleuze and Guattari: "Does it work?" Joshi does. Akira Hokuto does.

Here she is. She's in full-on Samurai gear, with a magnificently ridiculous red wig and a damned sword (albeit decorative). The Dangerous Queen. She doesn't crack a smile as she cuts her promo (again, I have no idea exactly what she's saying, but haven't you sussed out by now that that's not the point)? Black lips. She scoffs at the interviewer's question. How dare that little diminutive man in the suit suggest she can't beat Aja Kong? And now she's in the ring. The wig is off, revealing splendid streaked punk-rock hair below (ah, excess, thy name is Joshi) and she's on the mic again. "Aja!" She begins. We're about to have ourselves a moment. This ain't no bra and panties match, little boys.

Aja waits in the corner, undaunted (go ahead, you try to daunt Aja Kong). The 3WA World Title's around her waist, and no, I neither know nor care much about Joshi title lineage. The strap's on the line and you'd better buckle in. Bull Nakano's on commentary! A third Joshi legend, with animalistic facial makeup. Unlike Aja and Akira, Bull's a Gaijin (foreigner in Joshi/Japan wrestlespeak) and she's intently sizing up two of the other all-time greats of this very different universe. Aja spits something back, and the crowd applauds. This match is clearly going to be more about the genuine competition between two athletes than a particular story. Storytelling, Deleuze and Guattari would argue, diminishes the potential of a product like Joshi, "gleefully reducing" it to a set of limited outcomes. I do not want to know the backstory. I wish to travel nomadically, another "D and G" term, without a preassigned school of thought guiding my mentality. When Aja and Akira nod at each other I am fucking pumped. And you should be too. Here we go.

Aja charges at Akira full-throttle and she dodges, sending the beautiful behemoth over the top ropes. Instantly, Akira signals to the crowd and hits the top rope for a summersault-splash and takes out both Aja and her second. Back to the top for Akira, she performs the common Joshi trope of clapping prior to the big move to get the crowd Right-There-With-Her and missile dropkicks Aja in the middle of the ring. Aja Kong takes a bump with the best of them: Despite her nearly doubling the size of the average opponent she works with, you never doubt that the best among them could give her a match. That's humility and professionalism. Five seconds later, however, Aja's got Akira an inch from submission: "No No Nono!" The remarkable aspect of Joshi is that the voices of the performers cue you not only to the basic reality of the situation ("Akira's not submitting!") but to the broader point ("Akira would rather die than let Aja think she's even gained an advantage"). And the best part? This is, obviously, all an educated guess, as is my entire Joshi fandom. Like free jazz or, to a lesser extent, Shakespeare, I dive in the deep end and take my own precious pearls from the bottom without stripping Joshi of its particulars. Joshi's secrets aren't for me, after all. All I am is some white hetero dude who's good enough to keep my hand out of my pants when discussing wrestling and stop acting like that makes me a feminist.

Aja's matches-back to it-have a great logic to them. She taxes a body part with a submission hold, and then kicks the crap out of it. Akira's just as great a "seller" as Kong; one doubts it's hard to make Aja Kong's offense look like it hurts, but she's good at convincing you it kills.

Enough for now. I end the match in tears. So do they. Earn these reactions for yourself. Watch Joshi horizontally, like a nomad, and stop with your bullshit, boys.

Sonal Lad - Diversity in Wrestling Performers: a UK Perspective

Freelance Journalist, wrestling blogger and podcaster based in the UK with a love of Japanese and women's wrestling. Keep up with Sonal at twitter.com/Wrestling_chat

Every little girl dreams of being a princess, a superhero or in my case a badass international superspy. Wrestling is one of those professions where women can be a combination of all three. It is an industry where you can find a role model and see diversity, right?

Unlike a lot of wrestling fans across the world, my first interactions with wrestling came very late. I didn't start watching the sport until I was 19 years old. Apart from my great-uncle occasionally watching World of Sport, an iconic UK afternoon show that ran for 20 years and starred the likes of Big Daddy and a young William Regal, when my mother was little, neither of my parents really had any interest in it. We never had Sky Sports, the satellite service that tan all WWE programming, so it wasn't like I just flicked onto a channel and saw two giant men powerslamming each other in a small squared ring. I only really knew about the Rock because of his films and John Cena because some boy in my primary school class used to go around shouting, "You can't see me."

It was actually my sister who started watching it after we'd spend hours on E! watching Total Divas. A lot of people have a lot of hate for the show but, without it, I don't know where I would be. She started watching the product on YouTube and we bought her tickets to a live show in Manchester for her birthday. Unfortunately for my sister, she couldn't make it due to school commitments, but I went anyway, and my life changed. I became immersed in the theatrics, the athleticism and the attention to detail from these brightly dressed and sometimes flamboyant

250

characters (one of the first wrestlers on that show was Tyler Breeze). What stood out for me was the women. They were strong, beautiful and completely in control.

I eventually started watching wrestling full time at university, I was a lot more mature and was aware of the world around me. I was starting to see more variety in the women in mainstream media which made me so happy. I was even happier when I started watching Total Divas and wrestling when I saw the likes of Naomi and Alicia Fox, both from ethnic minorities.

Growing up in a British Indian household, I never felt anything but English. However, growing up and watching the television and listening to music, there seemed to be one thing in common: they didn't look anything like me. They all had pale skin, beautiful blonde hair and a model figure. When I started watching the sport full time, WWE seemed to provide everything I needed at the time to combat these issues.

How wrong I was.

Women's wrestling

With the women's Evolution seemed to be in full force, women of color were at the forefront. At the time, we had Team B.A.D with Sasha Banks, Naomi and Tamina who were not only women of color but all shapes and sizes as well as the Bella's who are of Hispanic descent.

I thought I'd found a sport where everyone was allowed to shine, and differences were celebrated to give little boys and girls someone to aspire to be like, someone who they could relate too.

As time went on, I saw these familiar faces fade to the background and a new crop of women wrestlers rise on the main roster. In basic terms, they were women who all had a few things in common: they could be called stereotypically beautiful in mainstream media and it's up to interpretations on what that means.

However, this doesn't have to be the case.

Within WWE, there is such an amazing array of women across the different brands from different ethnicities such as Asuka, Kairi Sane, Bianca Belair and Mia Yim, Sonya Deville the first openly LGBTQ+ female wrestler and Nikki Cross who has this more underground, grunge look to just name a few. For all the talent they have, many have struggled to make it to the upper card or to stay at the top of their divisions. Sonya Deville is being used as a 'sidekick' to her partner Mandy Rose who uses her sexuality in story lines that aren't benefitting Deville. For a long time, Asuka and Sane's Kabuki Warrior gimmick portrayed them worlds away from the badass wrestlers they are but has now finally been utilised in a positive way but after public outcry. This says a lot about the company itself. For a company who apparently publicly prides themselves on diversity, we're not seeing it at the forefront near enough.

Even the new company All Elite Wrestling, who pride themselves of diversity and using every woman properly, has fallen in a similar way to WWE. The biggest example is Nyla Rose. A huge signing for the company and initially a huge staple of the first PPVs. She was a pioneer for the industry and seemed to mark a change in the stigma within the industry with Transgender athletes. However, since losing the title match to Riho, she has barely been present on the weekly show despite the consistent showing on advertisements. It almost seems as if AEW have been using diversity as a statement of change but not following through with it, instead using it for publicity. For someone as dominant and talented as Rose, you would expect her to be on TV a lot more.

With all of these grumblings, the natural desire when expectations desire for the industry changed is to find somewhere to cater to those needs of seeing diversity promoted and welcomed not just used and abused.

This change came in the form of British wrestling and the world I was opened up to almost a year after my first exposure to wrestling. By this time, I had started getting bored with the product that had initially opened my eyes to a whole new world. I got pointed to the world of Progress and from there promotions such Defiant, Futureshock and the one and only Pro-Wrestling: EVE.

"When you look at the women's wrestling scene and the top 50 in the world, the diversity in look is tremendous. There are so many looks, body types and characters. Then you look at WWE and their division, where's the diverse characters? The wrestlers they show and rave about are what I say are commercially beautiful whereas women who maybe don't fit in that box won't be given credit by those people." – Emily Read, Pro-Wrestling: EVE

Apart from opening my eyes to a world of wrestling that wasn't only focused on entertainment, I was able to see women who I could relate too. It wasn't because the wrestlers I was watching came from the same country, spoke in the same way as me and used references in their promos that I could finally understand. None of that mattered. It was more that I was just amazed at how different they all were. The British scene prides itself of utilizing amazing female talent from across the world and from so many different walks of life. It showed that there was diversity in the industry, and it was celebrated in so many places.

You just had to look a bit harder to find them.

For many wrestling fans in the UK, Pro-Wrestling: EVE has been that pioneer and really given a voice to all women from all walks of life and it's something the company has always prided itself on. It is a company that not only prides itself on nurturing the future of women's wrestling, but a safe place for people of all ages to enjoy an industry that can sometimes be toxic.

With Emily and Dann Read at the center of the organization and their daughter a massive influence for creating EVE, it's no surprise that they have one of the most diverse roster's in the world and celebrate differences within every performer and fan. They are a company that celebrates women of every shape and size, something that a lot of companies could learn from.

From this company and across Britain, we are lucky to have an amazing diverse range of female wrestlers who are all so different from each other and reflect the diversity within the UK itself.

For me personally, one woman on the British scene really stood and made me see this diversity on an even bigger scale: Kanji Duku aka the Asian Sensation. On seeing her, the first thing that stood out for me was the Om on her wrestling gear, a sign that represents Hinduism. For her, it is a celebration of her culture and family's religion. For a Hindu like myself, this was refreshing and exciting. A woman embracing her religion not becoming it.

We then have Piper Niven aka Viper who is this curvaceous, strong and powerful woman coming out and owning the ring. She takes every bit of negativity she might get from people and uses it against her opponent combining beauty and strength in all the best ways possible.

Bea Priestley, although classed as Caucasian, was also a breath of fresh air in professional wrestling. With her jet-black hair, dark persona and almost villain-esque way about her, she was mesmerizing alongside the likes of Lana Austin, Rhia O'Reilly and Jamie Hayter who are all so different from those on WWE and each have those unique parts that make them special.

This is just a small number of the women dominating the British scene and you've already seen women of different colors, sizes and outlooks in life. I haven't even gone into those from across the world who epitomize diversity from Kris Wolff, Tessa Blanchard, Jordynne Grace, Meiko Satomura and so many more. Alongside promotion such as EVE. Impact, Stardom and so many more, we are seeing women

Gone is that perception from the past that a wrestler had to look like a 'supermodel' or whatever that is meant to be and have this grace and poise about them. Women don't have to be 'lady like' and can be strong, aggressive and dominant in a way that isn't frowned upon.

With the women's evolution well and truly underway across the world, we need to help combat the war on diversity within this evolution. This diversity doesn't just come in ethnicity, but in body shape, sexuality and personality. So, if other companies can do it, then why isn't it the norm in what can be called the biggest wrestling company in the world?

Male Wrestling

Maybe the issues within diversity women's wrestling is more a wider problem across wrestling in general. It almost seems unfair to look at this issue without looking at it from all perspectives, including in male wrestling. If men and women are equal, we should see that both sexes suffer from similar issues, just in different ways.

A lot of people probably look at the issues of diversity and automatically associate it with the female superstars. Whilst it's true that women in wrestling are subjected to more pressures and prejudice, it would be unfair to disregard all of the issues within the entire company whether male or female.

In the modern day, there seems to be as many unrealistic expectations for men and none is more true than in the cutthroat world of professional wrestling. Like the WWE women's division, WWE is full of so many men from all walks of life and representing different kind of men. We have tall men and short men, Caucasian, Asian, African American and Latino men, big men and small men. Each superstar brings their own personality and style to the ring.

However, sometimes their differences aren't celebrated either. Like female superstars, it sometimes seems that, especially in the larger companies, they are placed in a box with restrictions. In the same way that women superstars may be expected to be graceful, ladylike, slim and beautiful, male wrestlers are expected to me manly, strong, big and muscly. If you're from a different ethnicity, you're suddenly placed into this stereotype regardless of where you were brought up.

Take the Singh Brothers and Jinder Mahal. Three superstars very proud of their Indian heritage, but they suddenly became their religion. Rather than showing these three as superstars who are Indian, they became Indian superstars regardless of being raised in Canada. Their gimmicks became very one dimensional with the Bollywood dancing and the traditional outfits becoming them rather than aiding them. However, this doesn't just stay within WWE. Even Impact have had this tendency with their stable, the Desi Hit Squad. Although all members of the faction are strong athletes, their gimmick is centred around an Indian stereotype like the Singh Brothers and Jinder Mahal. Although coming out with traditional outfits might seem to celebrate culture, it's more evidence that this is all the company sees for them: a gimmick.

Recently, Olympic athlete and former tag champion Chad Gable has been ridiculed and had a storyline created surrounding his height, or lack of it. By calling himself Shorty-G, WWE tried to turn this negative storyline into one about embracing his height, but has it just added fuel to the fire? It's turned one of the most talented athletes in the company into a joke with a gimmick name and sports styled gym gear, worlds away from the American Alpha we knew.

Here, we have a company that has so much diversity, but is keeping them firmly inside a stereotype. So, in one sense we have those of diverse backgrounds being placed within boundaries, but should we be glad that they are getting any attention at all?

Like the case of Nyla Rose in All Elite Wrestling, Sonny Kiss was a huge signing for the company and was a real pioneer being openly gay. But where has Kiss been in the initial weeks of AEW Dynamite? With all that talent and charisma, Sonny should be on the main show every week showing the world true athleticism. Instead, Kiss has been relegated to small matches mainly on AEW Dark.

From my perspective, it all stems from what older executives believe people want to see and to some extent, audience's still traditional mentalities.

Whenever there's a woman's match with someone not typically 'beautiful,' people on Twitter are quick to make rude comments or to claim that it's all been done for the sake of diversity if someone doesn't fit the mold they've grown up watching throughout wrestling history.

Whenever stars, such as Shinsuke Nakamura, Asuka and Ariya Daivari, are cutting a promo in another language out comes the 'What' chants. How has Stone Cold Steve Austin iconic phrase become a sign of ignorance and underlying racism?

Why do we automatically assume that foreigners should be the heels? When Mustafa Ali was an alternate in the Cruiserweight classic, he immediately became a heel as he represented Pakistan from the fans.

It was the fans using their own initiative and taking upon themselves to show the world their reaction to diversity.

Is it any surprise that companies are deciding to stick with their views on what a 'superstar's is? Fans keep asking for change, but then fail to embrace it and give the executives no reason to try again. If we don't change our attitude then women will continue to be expected to look a certain way, men will be made to feel inferior for not fitting a specific set of requirements and foreigners will be portrayed as heels.

In short, we need to give children of all shapes, sizes, colors and creed someone to look up too and to think, "If they can do it, why can't I." We need to celebrate everybody in the industry and help those promotions who have this at their forefront and spread it to those who don't. Give little girls and boys across the world no reason to believe this one thing is the norm or that one thing is beautiful.

In a world that is so diverse, it should just be expected that this spreads across mainstream media and sports entertainment. It is up to the companies, the fans and the wrestlers to take a stand and show the world that change is needed on a much larger scale. How can we expect the new generation to be happy with themselves when they're not being shown this by those they look up too.

Every human being is special in their own way and the more different, the better.

Samuel Preston - The Current Stars of Intergender Wrestling

With twenty years dedicated to a love-hate relationship with wrestling, Sam is currently affiliated with Independent wrestling inspired website Rasslin' Blogs, and from his small town of Plymouth, Devon, continues to be inspired by the magic wrestling can produce. Hs is *twitter.com/BigBadaBruce.*

Intergender wrestling is a rare occurrence in the history of professional wrestling, having only really started occurring in the late 1970's to mid-1980's, but not really gaining prominence until the Attitude Era of the late 1990's and early 2000's. However, with the gradual changing of the guard from a more adult, raw interpretation of wrestling into a more family-friendly version, intergender wrestling was downplayed and eventually deemed a dirty disappointment from the history of wrestling. Until, that was, the introduction of women wrestlers over the last decade who prided themselves on their determination to battle male wrestlers, gaining reputations for toughness and ability, becoming equals for the wrestling world. These female wrestlers have gradually broken down the obstacles laid in front of them, even having a successful event called Lit Up organized by Beyond Wrestling with every match an intergender match, an unprecedented event in wrestling history. In this essay, I shall be highlighting some of the wrestlers who helped develop the history of intergender wrestling, before focusing on some of the biggest women wrestlers who have regularly participated in intergender wrestling over the last decade.

Andy Kaufman

When discussing the history of intergender wrestling and highlighting the biggest stars in the context of intergender wrestling, it would be

259

impossible to not give mention to the man who first popularized the match style, the entertainer and performance artist known as Andy Kaufman. Kaufman never viewed himself as the obvious archetype of a 'comedian'129, he prided himself as being a 'song and dance man'130, often more interested in antagonizing the audience as opposed to making them laugh. This preference and aspect of theatricality present in wrestling would fascinate the entertainer, leading to the integration of wrestling women during his onstage acts, even referring to himself as the Inter-Gender Wrestling Champion Of The World131, which would lead to an introduction by friend and wrestling reporter royalty, Bill Apter, to one of the creative and lead bookers of Memphis Wrestling (Mid-South Wrestling under the Continental Wrestling Association umbrella), Jerry 'The King' Lawler. The early-1980's would feature Kaufman to start appearing in Memphis Wrestling, wrestling on the undercard against women, which would lead to a feud with Lawler himself after Kaufman defeated a woman Lawler trained himself. Whilst the antics of Kaufman were of a less-serious and more comedic interpretation of intergender wrestling, even featuring Kaufman offering a prize of $1,000 to any woman who could successfully defeat him.132 However, despite the fact the ongoing story would feature Kaufman win every match against the women, it also helped normalize the idea of intergender wrestling, with the joke being Kaufman's arrogance, not the women themselves. Despite

129 Brennan, Sandra. "Full Biography". *The New York Times*.
130 Givens, Ron (December 23, 1999). "Andy Kaufman recalled as bizarre, gifted". New York Daily News; Reading Eagle.
131 Page 17, Rosenberg, Howard (December 21, 1979). "Corpus Christi Cosmetician Among Competitors: Woman-Wrestling Comic May Meet Match". *The Victoria Advocate*.
132 Page 56, "Ms. Peckham eyes rematch with Kaufman". *Bangor Daily News*. December 26, 1979.

this, intergender wrestling wouldn't gain much exposure for at least another decade, until a true trailblazer arrived in the wrestling business.

Chyna (Joanie Laurer)

In early 1997, Joanie Laurer would enter the World Wrestling Federation (now WWE), becoming an enforcer for then middle of the card heel Hunter Heart Helmsley (which would eventually be shortened to Triple-H) and regularly battling male wrestlers on Helmsley's behalf. Following skirmishes with wrestling personalities such as Mick Foley, Chyna would go on to feature in a 15-member Battle Royal to win the opportunity to be the Number Thirtieth entrant in the *1999 Royal Rumble*. To the shock of many, Chyna would win the Battle Royal for the right to enter the Royal Rumble at Number 30, becoming the first ever woman to feature in the Rumble. In a historical moment, Chyna would enter the Rumble, she did not win but did eliminate former (storyline) love interest Mark Henry, immortalizing herself in Royal Rumble history. This would lead to Chyna appearing in several matches at Pay-Per-Views against male wrestlers, culminating in her challenging for the prestigious WWF Intercontinental Championship against then-Champion Jeff Jarrett at *Unforgiven 1999* in an unsuccessful effort. At the time, this might have seemed like an attempt by WWF to placate Chyna fans by featuring her in a title match, but not wanting to take the chance of putting Chyna over. However, in a surprising turn of events, a rematch would occur at *No Mercy 1999*, with Chyna cleanly defeating Jarrett to become the first ever woman to become the Intercontinental Champion.

From there, Chyna would regularly feature in matches for the Intercontinental Championship against Chris Jericho, Hardcore Holly and Val Venis over the next year, before segueing into the Women's Division. Chyna would become synonymous for her work in intergender wrestling and as a feminist icon, refusing to bow to the expectation of gender normality as a woman.[133] Other women wrestlers who would be inspired by Chyna at the time would be wrestlers such as Jazz in ECW and WWE, Jacqueline Moore in WWE and TNA, Madusa in WCW and Lita of WWE fame, all fondly remembered over the next two decades. However, once the PG rating was brought to the WWE, intergender matches were all but extinguished in an attempt to avoid any possible allegations of positively enforcing male-on-female violence. The closest really allowed over the next fifteen plus years would be either comedy matches, or surprise appearances in the Men's *Royal Rumble,* such as Beth Phoenix in 2010 or Kharma (formerly known as Awesome Kong) in 2012.

Sexy Star (Dulce Maria Garcia Rivas) & Ivelisse

Whereas wrestling in the United States find the prospect of intergender matches an uncomfortable prospect, Mexican Lucha Libre have very much normalized the concept due to its regular occurrence in tag team matches. However, the possibility of male wrestlers taking on female wrestlers is avoided due to the inclusion of rules only allowing wrestlers to attack their own gender. This was negated in the 2014 released *Lucha Underground* series, which featured intergender wrestling on a regular basis (twenty-eight different matches featuring a female wrestler in a match with male wrestlers in just the first season, which had thirty-nine episodes). The two biggest representatives were Ivelisse and Sexy Star, with Ivelisse going on to become one member of the inaugural Trios Champion, alongside her frenemies Angelico and Son Of Havoc. The winning of the Championship itself would feature a legitimate leg injury by Ivelisse, but in a demonstration of the toughness of her character, she would finish the match on one foot and with both partners down, use a cane to batter The Crew (Cortez Castro, Mr Cisco and Bael) to level the

---

[133] Docking, Vanessa Vitiello (April 21, 2016). "Why I'll Miss Chyna, the Female Wrestler Who Broke All the Gender Rules"

playing field[134]. Ivelisse would go on to gain a Number One Contendership for the Lucha Underground Championship but would lose in an unsuccessful attempt against then-Champion Mil Muertes[135].

Sexy Star would appear in an intergender match on the very first episode, ironically battling Ivelisse's partner Son Of Havoc in a losing effort, but would feature over the first season in an ongoing feud with Chavo Guerrero Jr, of the infamous Guerrero family, as well as participating in the tournament for the Lucha Underground Trios Championship that would be won by Ivelisse's team. At the end of Season Two, Sexy Star would shock many by winning an Intergender Seven-Way Elimination match to gain the Gift Of The Gods Championship, officially making her the Number One Contender for the Lucha Underground Championship[136]. During Season Three, Sexy Star would feature in *Aztec Warfare III*[137], a twenty-person Intergender Elimination Match (either by pinfall or submission only), entering at Number Twelve and going on to win, becoming the first ever female Lucha Underground Champion, and the first and only woman to hold a World Heavyweight Championship in a major wrestling promotion. Unfortunately, Sexy Star's legacy would be damaged after she controversially legitimately, and intentionally, injured fellow wrestler Rosemary at a Lucha Libre Pay-Per-View, which would lead to calls for her to be blacklisted from the wrestling business, leaving the wrestling business for just short of two years. However, both Ivelisse and Sexy Star would become great representatives of intergender wrestling, both of their performances in *Lucha Underground* would help bring the product to a worldwide English-speaking audience.

---

[134] "Trios Champions", Episode 24, aired on April 22th 2015.
[135] "A Much Darker Place", Episode 40, aired on January 27th 2016.
[136] "Ultima Lucha Dos Part Two", Episode 64, aired on July 13th 2016.
[137] "Aztec Warfare III", Episode 76, aired on November 16th 2016.

Jordynne Grace

During the historical 2018 independent Pay-Per-View *All In,* which would go on to inspire All Elite Wrestling to come to fruition, the pre-show *Zero Hour* would feature an Over Budget Battle Royale, with the winner going on to face Ring Of Honor World Champion Jay Lethal later in the evening. During the Battle Royale, one of the more infamous moments would be a stand-off between 'The Machine' Brian Cage and Jordynne Grace, with Grace eliminating the much bigger man in a shocking moment. Unbeknownst to many, though, would be that Grace has regularly faced male wrestlers in her career, with her debut match featuring herself against a 120 pound man. Over the duration of her career, Grace has combined her enjoyment of weightlifting with her challenging of male wrestlers as an equal, often being the stronger of the two, bench pressing opponents in an impressive display of strength, culminating in her then-career highlight of overpowering man mountain Cage during the *All In* Pay-Per-View. Despite her young age of just twenty-three (as of December 2019), Grace has gained a reputation as not just a locker room leader for other women wrestlers but has inspired other females to participate in intergender wrestling over the last few years. Ironically, Grace herself has focused on the Knockouts Division of Impact Wrestling (their women's division) but has certainly laid a standard for intergender wrestling over the last few years.

Session Moth Martina

In a growing world of Independent organizations with strong localized following, one that has cemented itself as a highlight of Dublin, Ireland night outs is Over The Top (OTT) Wrestling, thriving with classic matches featuring Matt Riddle, Will Ospreay, Walter, David Starr and its hero, Jordan Devlin. However, a lesser known but no less appreciated highlight of OTT wrestling is Martina, a cult crowd favorite who was possibly inspired by Kaufman when she became the inaugural OTT Gender Neutral Wrestling Champion. Martina has admitted to having been the only female wrestling when training with OTT, which normalized the idea of wrestling men regularly, very suitable for the Irish-born Session Moth (an Irish term for students or twenty-somethings who are regarded as party animals, or up for fighting and drinking). Despite being the only female wrestler to have held the OTT Gender Neutral Wrestling Championship, Martina has laid a platform for other female wrestlers to challenge for the Championship, currently held (as of Christmas 2019) by *Ring Of Honor's* Mark Haskins, showing the level of recognition for the title. More importantly, Martina has become a permanent mainstay of British Wrestling, and was signed to *Ring Of Honor* in the latter half of 2019, turning down a WWE contract in the process.

Kimber Lee

Kimber Lee began her wrestling training at the Combat Zone Wrestling Academy, with her first match for CZW being an intergender match with Austin Uzzie, and would regularly appear in intergender matches over the next three years. This included victories over wrestlers such as Excalibur and Greg Excellent, with victories in other promotions over wrestlers such as David Starr and JT Dunn. This would lead to a run in Lucha Libre-inspired American promotion CHIKARA, a promotion entering its eighteenth year as of 2020, but didn't debut the CHIKARA Grand Championship (its main title) until 2011. Kimber Lee, then referred to as Princess Kimberlee, would spend the whole of 2015 as a true underdog, battling in a competition over the entire year that would contribute to her being built as a credible threat.

It would be at the end of this year, after the tremendous amount of time and work put into her character and investing the audience into her story, that she would finally cash in an opportunity for the Grand

Championship, defeating Hallowicked in an emotionally-charged moment that shocked and delighted the live audience. Kimber Lee would successfully defend the Championship for five months, but more importantly, might have laid the groundwork for the similar run currently being enjoyed by Impact Wrestling's star, Tessa Blanchard. Either way, it feels tremendously appropriate that Lee was inspired when younger by the trailblazer Chyna, and Lee deserves tremendous respect for being the first female wrestler to hold the leading Championship in a non-female orientated promotion.

Mercedes Martinez

Martinez has predominantly featured pushing the boundaries of women's wrestling in Women Superstars Uncensored (WSU), twice breaking the record for the longest women's match in history. The first was in 2009 with a 60-minute Iron Woman Match against former partner and bitter rival Angel Orsini (who herself had confrontations with Jerry Lynn in ECW) that went to a ten minute overtime Sudden Death before Martinez would retain her WSU Championship, only to break the record two years later in seventy-three minute title defense against Lexxus. Both matches would help contribute to WSU's reputation as one of the top women's wrestling companies in the United States, but Martinez's own reputation would gain extra attention when by popular demand (originally suggested by fans on Twitter), she met Independent mainstay David Starr. In October 2019, at Beyond Wrestling's Uncharted Territory, Martinez would meet Starr in a physically exhausting thirty-minute war, one where Martinez would be treated as an equal, with the crowd cheering her on wildly as she weathered every shot from Starr. In the end, despite Martinez losing, she would be given respect by independent legend Starr, with the match even being named as possibly one of the greatest intergender matches in the history of wrestling (big words granted, but I would not be in a rush to disagree). Martinez has gone on to feature for both WWE in the *Mae Young Classics,* and All Elite Wrestling, but her reputation as a shining light for women's wrestling over the last nineteen-plus years, and her tremendous performance in a match that truly epitomized the best of intergender performance, will be her true legacy in wrestling.

Candice LeRae

Whilst based in Pro Wrestling Guerrilla, LeRae would spend much of 2008 participating in intergender matches, including matches with wrestlers such as T.J. Perkins and Chuck Taylor, who would respectively go on to feature for WWE 205 Live and AEW. These matches would help set LeRae up for an opportunity in 2011, where she would win a Gauntlet to gain entry to a Number 1 Contenders Match against Joey Ryan, with the winner facing Claudio Castagnoli for the PWG World title. Whilst LeRae would lose this match, it would eventually lead to a partnership developing with Ryan, coming to fruition at the end of 2013 and leading into 2014, with two huge matches in LeRae's career occurring that year. First at *PWG Mystery Vortex II,* she would answer an open challenge issued by PWG World Champion Adam Cole, a match where even though LeRae was portrayed as overmatched, her gutsy and brave performance had the crowd emotionally hooked, cheering her on throughout. During the match, LeRae would suffer tremendous punishment, an integral part of her character in intergender matches, that would reach its zenith in July.

At *PWG Eleven,* LeRae would tag alongside her friend Joey Ryan and take on The Young Bucks for the PWG World Tag Team Championship in a Guerrilla Warfare match, a No Disqualification, No Count-Outs, Fall Counts Anywhere match that had gained infamy in PWG as a violent feud ender. These four wrestlers would take each other on in a bloody, painful match, with Candice especially taking an extreme amount of punishment, receiving a thrown chair to the face, a Tombstone on the outside floor, and a superkick to the face by The Young Bucks with a boot that had thumbtacks glued to it. Candice would bleed profusely, her face covered like a crimson mask, and yet she would battle back in a perfect babyface performance, gaining the victory with the use of thumbtacks. Candice would cement herself as not only one of the toughest women in wrestling, but a respectable badass, one whose career has now taken her to the glitzy lights of NXT alongside her husband, Johnny Gargano. But through the blood she shed in matches such as Guerrilla Warfare and her sheer determination to be seen as an equal in the ring, she has become a beloved favorite of the wrestling community, one who might even raise the possibility of a return to intergender wrestling in WWE. Some may view it unlikely, but Candice has made a career of surprising people around the world.

Tessa Blanchard

As a third-generation professional wrestler, Tessa comes from wrestling royalty, with her father the former Four Horseman member Tully Blanchard and her stepfather the former NWA Superstar Magnum T.A. both renowned as legends in the business. Tessa would join the business in 2014, joining Impact Wrestling in 2018, becoming Impact Knockouts Champion within just a few months. However, it was during Impact Wrestling's biggest Pay-Per-View of the year, *Slammiversary XVII* in 2019, that Tessa gained the biggest show of faith in her ability, as she faced hardcore maniac Sami Callihan in a losing effort in the main event. This match could quite possibly be the first ever intergender match to main event a professional wrestling Pay-Per-View, and would elevate Tessa into the main event picture, culminating in her gaining the Number One Contendership for the Impact World Championship. This will lead to

Tessa Blanchard challenging for the Impact World Championship in the main event of January 2020 pay-per-view *Hard To Kill*, giving Tessa the opportunity to match Sexy Star's achievement of becoming a World Champion in a major professional wrestling company. The decision to promote Tessa into the main event scene by Impact Wrestling is affirmation of Tessa's reputation as one of the toughest and best female wrestlers in the United States today, treated as an equal to the men's division and a leading light in the world of intergender wrestling.

Intergender wrestling was once treated like a dirty word, a match designed to often embarrass a weak male, or as an attempt to put over a male heel dominating a defenseless woman. But the days of inequality in such matchups has gradually rescinded since the turn of the 2000s, as the popularity of women's wrestling in Japan and lucha libre has begun to impact on English-speaking audiences, helping to eliminate the stigma of women's wrestling being viewed as a bathroom break, a stigma originally perpetuated by promotions such as WWE. Once the English-speaking audience had the concept of women's wrestling being able to be treated seriously normalized to them, the gradual incorporation of intergender wrestling was but the next step, one that has lead to the ever growing possibility of women wrestlers battling for the leading championship in every wrestling organization possible, already demonstrated in CHIKARA, Over The Top (OTT) Wrestling, Lucha Underground, Pro Wrestling Guerrilla and now one of the leading wrestling companies in the United States, Impact Wrestling. The possibility of intergender wrestling in companies such as WWE or All Elite Wrestling still seems less likely to become popularized, but the successful integration of legitimate women's wrestling continues in major promotions, with examples such as the superstars mentioned above continuing to set standards in Wrestling, whether wrestling men or women. Intergender wrestling is no longer a dirty word in wrestling, but a wonderful representation of the tremendous work and effort from an entire world division of wrestlers, one celebrated in the pages of this book and by fans around the world, women wrestlers now no longer weaker or derided, but at least equal, if not possibly better.

Sarah Elizabeth Cox - Grappling with History: The Search for Jack Wannop, champion wrestler of late-Victorian England

Sarah was born in Luton and now lives in Hither Green, south east London. She is the press officer for Goldsmiths, University of London by day, a postgraduate history student by night, and trains with the London School of Lucha Libre during the hours in-between. Sarah originally graduated in 2010 with a BA in Politics and an MA International Relations from the University of East Anglia, but after slogging her way through a first dissertation on the UN's failure to protect women and girls from sexual violence in conflict zones, decided to focus on something a bit more palatable the second time around: moustachioed Victorian men fighting in tights. She writes the blog grapplingwithhistory.com and you'll find her on Twitter at https://twitter.com/spookyjulie and https://twitter.com/wrestling1880s.

I hadn't thought about wrestling in seventeen years. As a teenager I idolized The Rock, wore my Edge t-shirt religiously, and in the years before social media, taught myself basic HTML just so I could build a fan website called The Church of Jeff Hardy. Chyna was a goddess, the most beautiful woman in the world, and there's a photo of me somewhere grinning like an idiot next to Rikishi in the Luton branch of Woolworths. My parents didn't have Sky, so regular fixes came through illicit video-tapings of pay-per-views, slipped to me by the younger brother of a friend every few weeks. WrestleMania 17 was the last I watched. Then wrestling stopped and life took over.

I started working as a press officer at Goldsmiths, University of London in December 2014, stayed for two years, went elsewhere for two (this always sounds like I was in prison when said out loud, but the reality was worse: another university a mile outside of Uxbridge), and came back at the end of 2018. Shortly after returning, I was catching up with Goldsmiths history via the blog of university legend Professor Tim Crook. He had written a piece which detailed the history of the Laurie Grove Baths in New Cross, south east London. Initially built as a public swimming and washing facility, the building, with pools drained, now serves as Goldsmiths art studios and a beautiful gallery.

The article referenced the venue as a location for British wrestling during its 1970s heyday, when televised bouts - by this time firmly in the category of sports entertainment rather than 'legitimate' competition - regularly attracted weekly audiences of up to 10 million. Sat in the pub, I logged on to the British Newspaper Archive and began to search for references to the Baths, New Cross, and wrestling, in the hope of finding a bit more information from the 1970s. Why? I honestly couldn't tell you. It was late and there was wine involved. Quite by accident (ok, it had been a while since I'd done any research and I'd forgotten to set the date search boundaries), I came across a lot of references to wrestling in the area across the 1880s and 1890s instead.

The same location names, chiefly a pub known at the time as The Glass House, regularly appeared as a venue for wrestling and boxing matches and training. And the same man came up over and over again, in dozens, hundreds, of copies of The Sporting Life and several local newspapers: Jack Wannop. Jack Wannop. Jack Wannop.

Beyond a few one-sentence references on wrestling websites to Wannop in the context of fighting high-profile and better-remembered opponents (chiefly, Evan 'The Strangler' Lewis - more on that later), and one mention on Wikipedia of a J.Wannop attempting to popularize catch-wrestling in England, there was little to be found about him via Google. I scoured academic papers on British wrestling history, books, blogs. Nothing. General histories of Victorian sport barely touched on wrestling at all during this period. How could Wannop's name appear on the pages of late-Victorian newspapers on both sides of the Atlantic more than a thousand times yet he seemingly left no legacy at all? How could a man described as 'The Most Popular Man in New Cross' have entirely disappeared?

So I've set out to write Wannop's biography, positioning him as a working-class celebrity, a figure of significant importance in New Cross, and a pioneer of British wrestling. His story is interwoven with what could be described as a micro-history of the people, places, and events on New Cross Road in the last two decades of the Victorian period. Joining Jack are a number of secondary characters: Deptford boxer and wrestler Tom 'Curly' Thompson, Brixton-based wrestling journalist, referee, and absolute eccentric Walter 'The Cross-Buttocker' Armstrong, Wannop's best pal, wrestler, MC, and match organizer Dais Patte, and Steve the Donkey (an actual donkey) among them. Through my research into Jack I've found myself on countless tangents: with the Caribbean-born boxers of Shoreditch, or the female fighters taking to music hall stages. And then there's the numerous unfortunate incidents involving bears.

Jack also had a career as a boxer. Many of the men he knew and fought have been remembered, among them Jem Smith the British champion - who fought Wannop to warm up for Peter Jackson - and George Godfrey, the black American heavyweight champion, who was denied a shot at the US title by legendary boxer John L. Sullivan on account of Godfrey's race and Sullivan's fear of being beaten. On the subject of Sullivan, we can place Wannop several times in the man's vicinity. When the Prince of Wales ordered up an illicit night of prize-fighting headlined by Sullivan during the Boston brawler's British sojourn, it was Wannop who was invited to provide the night's exhibition wrestling. When Sullivan found himself flat on his back, drunk on the floor of a Boston bar, it was Wannop who had thrown him there.

A cablegram from The Sporting Life's New York special correspondent, published on 10 May 1888 to update British readers on Jack Wannop V Evan Lewis three days prior, concluded: Wannop was nearly killed. The wrestling match at Chicago's Battery D Armoury for the first wrestling 'Championship of the World' had been hotly anticipated. A confident Wannop arrived in America in February, expecting to meet 'The Strangler' a few weeks later in the catch style – no hold barred – best of five falls with shoulders on the floor.

Jack's farewell benefits in New Cross were covered by the press, interviews conducted, and arrangements made. He was set to meet his brother 'Joe' on the other side of the pond – a man I believe might actually have been Christopher Wannop, who fled to America in 1884 after the arrest of Jack and two sex workers on a night out in Greenwich. That's another story for another time. Wannop's Big 'un, his 17-stone wrestling pupil George Brown, took over Jack's New Cross Boxing Club, and Jack and his backer, Harry Hoare, crossed the Atlantic in search of fame, glory and a big pile of cash. In April The Sporting Life made an ominous prediction:

During the past month an effort has been made to revive the interest in public wrestling, but the "fancy" seems to have tired of the sport, and now there is no money in exhibitions or gate-money ventures. Legitimate matches are the only things which pay…

The most important thing on the docket is the match between Jack Wannop, the Englishman, and Evan Lewis, the "Strangler". This contest will be for blood and money, and somebody will be hurt when the pair meet in the West next month.

Wannop was billed as the English Champion in this match for a thousand dollars a side, although it's interesting to note that shortly after the fight, while he was still off in America, George Steadman and George Brown fought at the New Cross Public Hall for the same English Championship. In the years before a regulatory body for the sport, title claims appeared to be somewhat of a free-for-all. In May 1888, for example, The Sporting Life answered an unknown question from a correspondent called Nick with a one line answer: "Wannop is not the champion wrestler of England."

This note sits above an answer to another unknown, but probably quite weird, question: "Jimmy Shaw's Jacko killed 200 rats in 1 ½ minutes, 37 seconds."

Lewis's brutal strangling method – probably a move similar to today's rear naked choke – was notorious but his signature hold was banned from the match on this occasion. Chicago's Mayor ordered him to be closely watched by the police, should he forget himself. An audience of 2,000 to 4,000 men, depending which reports you believe, gathered to watch. The expected $1,000 stake or side-bet was also withdrawn on the Mayor's orders, replaced with an agreement that the winner and his team would take 75 percent of ticket receipts and claim a new World Heavyweight Championship title, while the loser would go home with 25 percent of the profits.

Wannop went shirtless, wearing white tights and dark brown or black velvet trunks. At 190lb, he was the heavier man by 20lb and credited with greater strength, reports say. Seconded by Hoare, he was first to enter the ring, "a perfect picture of a typical English bulldog," observed the Galena Gazette. Lewis's manager Parson Davies then appeared in the ring, having received a challenge from Japanese wrestler Matsada Sorakichi, who sat at ringside. Sorakichi requested that the night's winner fight him the following week to take half the gross receipts of the house, providing Sorakichi was thrown within fifteen minutes. Hoare and Davies accepted on behalf of their men.

The match began at 8.47pm and it quickly became evident that Wannop was outclassed by the American professional. "Experts looked upon the match as a one-sided affair from the first", with Wannop looking visibly nervous from the bell. Both men went down early in the first bout, with Wannop on top, but Lewis quickly broke the hold and found his feet.

After several attempts to trip each other, Lewis caught Wannop in a grapevine lock with his right leg, before hoisting Wannop onto his shoulders and landing him squarely onto the mat. The bulldog rose but seemed dazed after the first fall. He was shocked, and evidently in distress.

A fifteen minute break was called, with Wannop disappearing 'backstage' to remove his traditional wrestling tights. Both men returned in trunks only.

The second bout opened with a series of headlocks, before Lewis forced the battered Brit under the ropes. Lewis went in for the grapevine lock again, but Wannop turned it on him into a hip-lock to immense cheers from the crowd. It didn't last. Wannop was forced down onto all fours by an aggressive Lewis, and was out for the count thanks to a hammer-lock and half-nelson which pushed his shoulders to the floor. By the third round he had blood pouring from his ear and knee. The third and last bout lasted just 58 seconds. After reaching for a number of different holds, Lewis, by a grapevine and shoulder-lock, lifted Wannop from the floor and slammed him down again, square onto the mat to end the match. "The big fellow's heart was broken," stated the Galena Gazette on 8 May 1888.

A mass of spectators broke through the ropes, hoisted the new World Champion onto their shoulders, and carried him around the hall to wild applause. Jack's big break, months in the making, was over in minutes, but rumour abounded of fix and scandal. In June, word was received in England from Wannop that he'd been too scared to win the match: he had deliberately lost because Lewis's Chicago "mob" had threatened a reprisal attack if their man went down. A poor excuse from a sore loser, perhaps? Sorry, Jack. Rumour also circulated at the time that Wannop had been drinking ahead of the contest – a pre-fight habit more typical of Sullivan.

It was in the American newspapers' best interests, of course, to support their countryman and if I may be permitted to do the same for mine, it was likely that Jack was simply outmatched and perhaps a little out of shape. At 33 (albeit pretending to be 29), he was the older of the two men by several years, had spent weeks waiting on unfamiliar turf for the postponed date with Lewis, and he was also prone to rheumatism. Upon his return to England the following year, Wannop went into more detail in an interview for The Sporting Life about what happened with Lewis. He had been lured to America by a man who turned out to be Lewis's uncle, to compete in a match designed purely to enhance the reputation of his nephew, Wannop claimed. He stayed in America for the rest of 1888 and on to 1889 but turned his hand to boxing instead, with some success and an awful lot of disappointment.

Back in New Cross, Wannop's story is a story where the pub is at the heart of the community, during the years when sporting culture expanded across all societal classes and prize-fighting rapidly began to move from dirty and illegal brawling toward wrestling's acceptance as an Olympic sport in 1896. It is a story where working-class men beat each other into submission for the sort of astronomical sums of money their pro-wrestling successors almost a century later could hardly have dreamed of.

Building Wannop's biography largely involves archived copies of sporting and local newspapers such as The Sporting Life, Sportsman, and Kentish Mercury. The Sporting Life is a fascinating and frequently hilarious read: the wrestlers' and boxers' Facebook of its day, I argue. A place for gossip and banter, match adverts and results, opinions, campaigns. They looked after your mail and answered public queries on who won what many years after the fact, held meetings, facilitated challenges. You want to meet a man for a fight later that day or tomorrow? You posted a message in The Sporting Life.

It is here we see early signs of the drama and over-the-top showmanship of wrestling from the 1950s onward: the grudges, nicknames, personalities and novelties appear long before your Big Daddies and Kendo Nagasakis. These guys are cutting beautiful promos, albeit published in print, rather than on YouTube.

Despite taking somewhat of a thrashing ('Wannop Walloped'!) on several occasions in America by some of the best-known American white and black champions, Wannop was so well-known and so well-liked at the time that on his return home to New Cross, The Sporting Life reported the names of every man who lined up to shake his hand.

Having moved to New Cross from Carlisle in around 1881, census and electoral roll data suggests that Wannop was a carpenter by trade, born John Wannop in 1855. He was muscular, with a fighting weight moving from 11.5 to 13 stone over the years, and by all-accounts, a humble and generous man. A single Old Bailey transcript from 1884 indicates that he had just one brush with the law, but was proven to be an innocent bystander to a fight between one of his brothers and another man. Jack was vindicated and praised for his character, as he was throughout later newspaper reports on his activities as a fighter, trainer and businessman.

His family life was tragic: I understand that his wife Miriam gave birth to 10 children, with two dying in infancy. By the time of Jack's death in 1923 at the age of 67 all but three of their children were gone, including Sidney, whose body was never recovered after his death on the Somme. Sidney's name is listed on two WWI memorials in Lewisham, among them St James Hatcham Church on Goldsmiths' campus.

By the time of his death, Jack too appears to have been forgotten. He did not retire from active competition as a wrestler until well into his 40s, and he appears to have had great success as a businessman and trainer, initially at the New Cross House where he managed the pub's boxing and wrestling club, before later opening one gym above a pub in New Cross, and another in Forest Hill. In the early 1890s he founds what I believe to be a social club for amateur sportsmen and publicans 'done good'. Known as the High Hat Brigade, they organised picnics and good-natured cricket games with east London rivals, and had bizarrely strict rules about what sort of ties to be worn at meetings.

But by 1914, the young men of South East London had a bigger fight to win, and it seems that Jack's gyms failed as wrestling and boxing temporarily fell out of favour. After 1907 his name stops appearing regularly in local and sporting newspapers, although Jack Jnr. pops up occasionally in local amateur boxing competitions.

In 1923 a national sports columnist noted very briefly that he had heard of Wannop's death. His last memory was seeing the old fighter hobbling along the road using a stick. Hospital records indicate that he died of 'senility' at Greenwich Infirmary on 11 February.

Through research using Find My Past, Deceased Online, and with the help of the Friends of Brockley and Ladywell Cemeteries, I located a Wannop grave to the south of the Brockley site. Above and below Jack lie Miriam (who lived long enough to see the bombs fall on New Cross and died in 1948) and two of the Wannop children, Mary (1918) and Thomas (1928). The plot is virtually unmarked. There is no headstone, just the remains of grey stone edging and a broken stone vase in the centre of the plot.

Three years before Jack's death, William George Matthews – later known as the wrestler Mick McManus – was born on the Old Kent Road, close to Jack's New Cross gym. He began training as a wrestler in the 1940s, and went on to become a major name in the 1960s and '70s. Quoted in Simon Garfield's 'The Wrestling' (1996) McManus noted that wrestling was popular in the US in the mid 1860s and after the Civil War, but the sport's golden age in the UK was 1899-1914, when it "dwarfed" boxing. He does not acknowledge, because he possibly just did not know about, the sport's popularity in his own back yard two decades earlier.

Garfield wrote that even around 1904 "myth was everything" and my research to date backs this up: certainly wrestling during the late 1800s and early 1900s was a sport (to which many no doubt lost huge sums of money betting), rather than the sports-entertainment we know today, but the theatrics of modern wrestling is clearly visible in the sporting newspapers' coverage of events and their depictions of the sport's characters. I want to bring those forgotten characters back to life.

Some historians like to argue that a historian who becomes too attached to their subject loses the capacity to write objectively and their writing becomes inherently flawed. To love (or indeed, to hate) your main character too much damages your ability to analyze the evidence and present the truth. Well, if that's the case then I'm happy to be a bad historian. I've spent longer with Jack in the past year than any living man and I'm open to declaring an obsession far beyond the borderline.

Jack's also awakened a love for wrestling that disappeared almost half my lifetime ago. If I'm not chasing him in the archives, I'm watching pro-wrestling on YouTube. If I'm not watching on YouTube I'm at a show in Bethnal Green, Sydenham, Camden. If I'm not at a show I'm training multiple times a week with my latter-day Wannops, Greg Burridge and Garry Vanderhorne at the London School of Lucha Libre. I'm not very good, and not sure I ever will be, but it has been a hell of an experience to try.

Whenever I am passing through Brockley, I stop by and see Jack. When my MA dissertation is finished I'll let him know and have a sherry with him - his favorite tipple. There are grand plans for a book, but it may take a couple of years. In the meantime he'll lie there forgotten until I've raised the money for a marker: to Jack Wannop (1855-1923). Champion Wrestler. Boxer. Teacher. The Most Popular Man in New Cross.

Sketch of Jack Wannop published in a 1901 issue of Famous Fights magazine

Evan 'The Strangler' Lewis, 1888

In 1889 Jack Wannop and his pupil Tom Thomson modelled for the photographs illustrating Walter 'The Cross-Buttocker' Armstrong's book, Wrestling

The Brockley grave (central plot) of Jack and Miriam Wannop, and two of their children, does not have a headstone

282

Gemma Coombs - Why Wrestling Crowds can be Intimidating for Women

Little blonde thing, fairly new to the crazy world of wrestling. Usually at a show cheering as loudly as she can., Her Twitter is https://twitter.com/gemzcoombs.

Telling someone you are a wrestling fan can be difficult at the best of times. People who do not understand it often try to dismiss you and it can be met with snide comments and derision.

"Why would you want to watch that?", "You do know its fake don't you?"

Add being a woman in to the mix.

Not only is your loyalty and interest as a wrestling fan questioned by people who do not even understand the sport, but also by other wrestling fans. As though being a woman somehow invalidates your interest in a sport.

In the last few years, wrestling has seen a resurgence in popularity, and with the rise of female talent and the women's revolution this has bought a long more female fans who maybe would not have associated with the sport in the past. I myself, became a fan to wrestling quite late in life. My husband would always watch shows and I just didn't fully understand the appeal until I saw The New Day. The fun they bought to the stage was infectious and at that moment I was hooked. I was fortunate enough to be able to go to WrestleMania 2017 in Orlando when they hosted. Since then I have found a love of British Wrestling, trying to go to as many shows as possible and cheer on the veteran talent as well as the up and coming stars of tomorrow. However our presence at shows and on social media is not always met with welcome.

In mid-2019, on social media especially, our way of dressing and looks have been called into question. Some male fans believe they have the right to tell us how to dress and how to look, but trust me this is not confined just to a wrestling crowd. Wear something slightly showing a bit of flesh, be that leg or cleavage, or do your make-up a bit and all of a sudden you are questioned with 'whose attention are you trying to get?' or 'which wrestler are you trying to sleep with?' as though this is our whole reason for going to a show. I'm lucky enough that I have never been subjected to this sort of behavior but we cannot pretend that it doesn't happen. I've met people through shows and know that a show night is their "night out on the town", a chance to see friends who they haven't in a while, have a bit of fun and a few drinks, sometimes making the wrestling a secondary part to it all. In the same way that people dress-up and go out drinking and see their friends on a weekend, this is our equivalent and yet we are demonized for wanting to look nice and feel good about ourselves. So let me say, nobody should ever be made to feel bad about what they wear or what they look like.

Wrestling crowds are very male heavy dominated and for someone just over 5ft this can be the worst of it all. In everyday life my height doesn't make me feel anxious at all however when at a show and being towered over and pushed by people trying to cram in to the space in order to see the show, doesn't make for a pleasant viewing experience. Men by in large are taller than women, so to have people stand in front of you all because they want "the best view" is something that I will never get my head around, especially if you are over 6ft and can get "the best view" from anywhere. Luckily, whenever I have asked people if they didn't mind moving or letting me stand in front of them, they have always been more than understanding and usually apologetic for standing in front of me. Though this is an issue mostly associated with the independent shows were there is little to no seating so you do have to stand, at larger shows or shows with tiered seating this isn't an issue. I know this may sound trivial but I really hate being crowded and the feeling of someone towering over me is not a feeling I welcome with open arms, trust me. It does not take much to think about the people standing around you. I am not saying 'let everyone under 5ft stand in front of you' just have a little compassion for those around you and if someone looks like they are not able to see properly, just ask them if there view is ok or if there is anything you can do to help them. A little bit of consideration for people goes a long way.

Like life, for all its bad parts, the good always out weigh it. Due to going to shows I have found a new passion. I have found a new hobby to share with my husband and many new friends.

When you are in that venue, be it a warehouse, theatre or a club, for a few hours you are exported in to another world. You can cheer, you can boo, go get a drink and have a great time surrounded by your friends and like-minded people who share the exact same passion as you.

However, remember, sometimes your words and your actions can have an impact on someone and their enjoyment of this crazy world that is wrestling.

At the end of the day we all just want to have fun and watch some graps!

Chloe Warner-Harris: Improvements in Gender Equality in WWE

21-year-old wrestling fan that shamelessly wears wrestling shirts to work. Patiently waiting for AJ Lee's return. Becky Lynch is her spirit animal and she is on Twitter at https://twitter.com/ChloeOTC.

By now a few of you may be wondering, 'how could a woman like WWE so much, considering how atrociously they've treated women in the past?'. You would have a very valid point. From 1983, when female competitors first graced the WWE ring, all the way up until the present day, they have been treated as second-class citizens compared to the male roster. It fills me with shame sometimes, I can't lie, at the state of women's wrestling in the WWE. But as wrestling fans, we've learned to take the rough with the smooth, to turn a blind eye to some of WWE's worst practices over the years, all because when wrestling is good, it's GREAT. However, I've always had hope that one day WWE would catch up with the rest of the world in terms of gender equality. It's been difficult sometimes, but I've had reason to believe, and nowadays, I can see with certainty that WWE is improving. As a fan of the WWE for the past seven years, and having watched a lot of the back catalogue, I have seen the progression of the women's division - known as the divas division until WrestleMania 32 in 2016 - first hand. Through the next few paragraphs, I'm going to outline the women's division, the inequalities it has faced, and the signs of improvement we've been seeing to prove that nowadays there's nothing wrong with being a female wrestling fan.

The best place for us to start is the spark that set everything in motion for gender equality in the WWE - the Divas Revolution or, as it's now known, Women's Evolution. On the February 23 2015 episode of Raw, female superstars The Bella Twins fought Paige and Emma in a match that only lasted 30 seconds. After the match, the hashtag #GiveDivasAChance trended worldwide on Twitter, with fans protesting the little airtime the WWE divas received on WWE TV. This soon caught the attention of many media outlets and even the CEO of the company himself, Vince McMahon, who responded in a tweet, "We hear you. Keep watching". What became known as the 'Divas Revolution' started on the July 13 2015 edition of Raw as female competitors - Charlotte, Becky Lynch and Sasha Banks, known as "legitimate athletes" - moved up from the developmental territory and were given the spotlight on Raw. The developmental territory in question is called NXT, and the reason why fans were so excited about the #GiveDivasAChance main show call-up was that it was bringing into the spotlight wrestlers that had made a name for themselves on NXT shows that some fans were watching on the WWE Network. Namely, Becky Lynch, Sasha Banks and Charlotte Flair, all legitimate athletes with professional wrestling backgrounds to their name instead of reality show or modelling careers (WWE's previous hiring pool). NXT, at the time, was arguably producing some of the finest women's wrestling in the world, and a 'Divas Revolution' had already happened for this brand; the aforementioned Sasha Banks had just main evented a live special in a thirty minute ironman match, and regular shows featured actual matches, not 30 second cameos. NXT was a much smaller brand, its target audience more hardcore wrestling fans instead of the casual audience Raw and SmackDown receive. They were the perfect test audience for this 'Divas Revolution' and after the overwhelming success of the women's division in NXT and the fan backlash for the women's treatment on the main roster, a Divas Revolution was long overdue and well deserved.

Before this, the women were usually part of a male wrestler's storyline, serving as his valet, or fighting with other female wrestlers over a man's affection. These stories were always in relation to men, never in isolation. In movie terms WWE was failing The Bechdel Test, an experiment where a film is watched to see how women are portrayed in it, and asks whether a work features at least two women who talk to each other about something other than a man. While the WWE back catalogue is too vast to accurately put it to the Bechdel Test, taking an average episode of Raw in the height of the 'Divas Era' would likely have WWE fail such a test. It is no exaggeration to say that in the darker eras of women's wrestling, female superstars were used for solely sexual titillation and voyeurism. This was proven by the influx of models who had no wrestling experience - such as Layla and Eve Torres - being imported into the WWE in the early to mid 2000s, cheapening the product. The sexual appeal and viewing of women as commercial objects on which the franchise capitalizes is evident from the costumes, body language and script of the matches. These matches would act as a bridge between two more important matches in a card structuring technique that allowed fans to recharge or use the facilities, hence why women's matches were given the term, 'the toilet break match'. It was an era of "brazen sexuality" by the women's performers, as demonstrated in bikini contests, bra and panties matches, and pillow fight matches, all with little to no class, taste or tact.

That's not to say that there weren't brief pockets of progression before the Divas Revolution; Chyna, a female wrestler with a masculine physique, won the Intercontinental Championship in 1999, a title that is generally accepted as being male-only and has never been held by a female wrestler since. Alongside this, Trish Stratus and Lita main evented Raw in 2004. However, these victories were quite hollow; Chyna's title match was in a 'Good Housekeeping match' - a match where the ring is surrounded by misogynistic household objects which the wrestlers can use against each other, and Trish Stratus stated that any time she performed legitimate wrestling moves or spots that were somewhat hardcore, management told her, "that's not how the women fight".

Therefore, when looking at the road to equality, what female wrestling fans look for is way the women's division is treated equally to the men's. With that in mind, a textbook case to show how far women have progressed in the WWE is when highlighting their participation in the

Royal Rumble match. First starting in 1988, the Royal Rumble match is part of a signature pay-per-view held in January, and is one of the four biggest shows of the year. The Rumble is a 30-person match, starting with 2 in the ring and another entering a set intervals (usually 90 seconds). You are eliminated by being thrown over the top rope, and the last man in the ring after all have entered is the winner, going on to challenge for the world title at the biggest show of the year, WrestleMania. The Rumble itself is the main attraction, and was a male roster only match until 2018, almost 30 years after it debuted. On the 18 December 2017 episode of Raw, it was announced that the women would "make history once again" by partaking in a Rumble of their own for the first time, and that the rules for the women's Rumble would be the same as the men's, emphasized by Kurt Angle - Raw General Manager - stating that "what's good for the men is good for the women, so the same rules apply". Beforehand, in battle royale matches (these are similar to the Rumble, only every competitor starts in the ring at the same time) women could be eliminated by going through or under the ropes, not just over them. Many saw this as a way of 'dumbing down' the concept, making it slightly easier for the competitors just because they were women.

Though the Rumble has been generally accepted as a male-only match, a few instances have occurred where women have partaken in the match. All instances, unfortunately, were short and did not give the women involved much legitimacy or credibility. For example, in the 2010 Rumble, Beth Phoenix entered and only eliminated one superstar by distracting him with a kiss. Using sexuality as a weapon or a distraction technique was common place in the women's division of old as they're were basically lingerie-wearing eye candy who defend, cheer, or distract the real male wrestlers in the ring. To have female wrestlers participate in a Rumble themselves was a huge step in the right direction as it moved away from the ridiculous notion WWE once held that women were too 'fragile' and 'passive' to compete in such stipulations. I'll give you a moment to let that idiotical statement sink in, but know this was indeed the view held for too long by the WWE.

Therefore, one factor that highlights the differences in women's wrestling across the years is the use of hardcore items. These items are a term used for the weapons sometimes utilized during a match. For men, these weapons are ring bells, steel chairs and sledgehammers, to name a few. In comparison, women used to use ironing boards, broom sticks and hair dryers, items that strengthen and propagate already existing stereotypes and biases about gender roles. They symbolize domestic femininity and separate them from the violent and more 'legitimate' means of hardcore fighting that the men engage in. At Extreme Rules 2010 - a hardcore-based pay-per-view - Michelle McCool fought Beth Phoenix in an Extreme Makeover Match where hair spray, a bucket and ironing boards were used offensively, while a fully decorated makeup table stood at ringside. This match lasted six minutes and thirty-two seconds. On the same show, male wrestlers John Cena and Batista fought in a near twenty-five minute Last Man Standing match where tables, steel chairs and steel steps were used as weapons. Seven years later, however, change was evident and the divide between male and female hardcore matches had lessened. At the 2017 edition of Extreme Rules, female competitors Alexa Bliss and Bayley fought for the Raw Women's Championship in a brutal match that feature dozens of vicious kendo stick shots, leaving Bayley "beaten to a bruised pulp by Alexa Bliss". A hardcore bout in the women's division such as this would be unheard of years ago.

As a part of the progression seen in the women's division, a lot of 'firsts' have occurred. Alongside the Royal Rumble in 2018, recent years have seen the first ever women's Money in the Bank match on June 17, 2018 and a Hell in a Cell match in October 30, 2016, the latter being most noteworthy as it ran for over twenty minutes and was the first ever women's match to main event a pay-per-view for the company. WWE

Evolution on October 28, 2018 was also the first ever women's-only pay-per-view, and the Mae Young Classic was a tournament solely dedicated to women's wrestling. Each of these could be an essay onto themselves, but the last issue I want to round out this excerpt is to do with the pay gap between male and female wrestlers. Unfortunately, unequal pay is a grave issue in every industry out there with women roughly earning 78% of what men earn. The professional wrestling industry is not exempt from the unfair gender pay gap. Former female wrestler AJ Lee once tweeted to Stephanie McMahon - the Chief Brand Officer of the WWE and daughter of the owner Vince McMahon - in regards to the issue, "your female wrestlers have record selling merchandise & have starred in the highest rated segment of the show several times, and yet they receive a fraction of the wages & screen time of the majority of the male roster". A prevailing statistical fact that proves women's wrestling has not reached the credibility and legitimacy of men's is the difference in pay between the wrestlers. To take two of the 2018 champions from one of the company's main shows - SmackDown Live - then female champion Charlotte Flair earned an a reported $550,000 a year, while then male champion AJ Styles earned 3.5 million, so stated 'The Ring Report' in an article in March of 2019. This is arguably to do with the drawing power of AJ Styles being higher than that of Charlotte, but the immense difference of pay damages the idea that female wrestlers could ever be equal to men. Charlotte is one of - if not the - biggest female wrestler in the company. She is the champions equivalent of AJ Styles, yet why is she not treated the same when it comes to salary? This is not to say that things have not improved in the WWE for female talent; in a period between 2004 and 2006, prominent female wrestler Mickie James only earned an estimated $72,000 despite having been working in wrestling since 1999 and having one of the most memorable female feuds of the era. After a leave of absence from the WWE in 2010, she returned to the company in 2016 and now earns an estimated $350,000. In 2019 Becky Lynch has been the biggest sellers of merchandise while main evening shows, which should see her among the top earners and make her well above the reported $250,000 downside in her contract, the minimal amount WWE would pay her before such bonuses.

In conclusion, the women's division has progressed greatly in the last couple of years. The eras of old presented women as a "sideshow", and their inclusion was nothing short of "exploitative". Nowadays, the women's division consists of legitimate athletes that are slowly lessening the divide between the male and female rosters. While pay gaps and an ingrained perception in many fans' minds on the women's division are difficult hurdles to overcome, there is reason to be optimistic for the female competitors of the WWE, and that optimism helps me keep coming back to the product.

Acknowledgements

The editor would like to thank all of the contributors in this book for their time and effort. It has been a lot of work pulling this together and I hope I have done you all proud with the standard of production achieved. Special thanks to Heather Bandenburg and Jacqui Pratt for their time, as it lead to this idea really growing, and to Kristen Ashly for helping to recruit several of the writers that contributed.

Thanks are also due to my wife Naomi for putting up with me spending so much time talking to her about the book and all the other women I met on the internet.

Thank you to the friends I have made while co-running the Watch Wrestling London Meet Up group for the past several years, you allowed me to really share my passion for wrestling and not be afraid to tell people I am a wrestling fan. Without such a lovely group of fans I would have never started going to indy wrestling events, ticked WrestleMania off my bucket list or worked on the podcast that in turn lead to this book. Dave, I guess this all stems from you!

Lastly, thank you to you dear reader. I hope you enjoyed this book and it helped grow your understanding of professional wrestling. If you really enjoyed any chapters please tweet at the authors, I am sure they will appreciate hearing from you.

Made in the USA
Middletown, DE
13 October 2023